Travellers' Tales of Old Hong Kong
and the South China Coast

TRAVELLERS' TALES
OF
OLD HONG KONG
AND THE
SOUTH CHINA COAST

compiled by
Michael Wise
with
Mun Him Wise

In Print

In Print Publishing is registered with the Publishers Licensing Society in the UK and the Copyright Clearance Center in the USA.

British Library Cataloguing in Publication Data: a catalogue record for this book is available from the British Library.

ISBN 1 873047 86 X

Cover print of Hong Kong and the harbour by a Chinese artist c.1865 courtesy of Martyn Gregory Gallery, London.

Cover design by Russell Townsend
Additional pages for this edition typeset by MC Typeset Ltd
Printed by Utopia Press, Singapore

Originally published in Singapore by Times Books International
First published in this edition in 1996 by
In Print Publishing Ltd, 9 Beaufort Terrace, Brighton BN2 2SU, UK.
Tel: +44 (1273) 682836. Fax: +44 (1273) 620958.

Preface

". . . tea and rhubarb are necessaries of life to every foreigner . . ."
Chinese Imperial Edict, 1838

From mandarin to merchant, shopkeeper to coolie, the Chinese simply could not comprehend the western world which seemed to be ever at their gates demanding trade.

Equally, western minds failed to come to grips with the Chinese puzzle. An English writer in the 1840s seriously proclaimed that most Chinese women were bald by the age of thirty-five; another condemned China as a land "where roses have no fragrance, the women no petticoats, and the magistrates no honour".

It was at Canton – the Great Mart of the East – that these two worlds came face to face in mutual incomprehension, and over succeeding years conflict and commerce were inseparable. Gradually Hong Kong grew up to rival Canton, while Macao continued its stately decline. In the foetid lanes of these southern cities it was not easy for visitors to recognise the graceful land they had glimpsed on their willow-pattern plates.

This book contains the personal reminiscences and adventures of travellers on the South China Coast between the years 1816 and 1942. Whether they came to trade, to convert, to fight, or just to see, China was an experience they were not likely to forget.

M.W.

Michael Wise was born in London in 1937 and is a graduate of Oxford University where he obtained an MA in Philosophy, Politics and Economics. His subsequent business career took him overseas, particularly to the East, where he lived and worked for several years.

His historical and literary interests led him to pursue the travel literature of the countries he came to know best, and in the 1980s he had three collections published covering Singapore, Hong Kong and Japan. His most recent work, *True Tales of British India*, was published in 1993. Michael Wise now lives in England with his Cantonese wife.

Contents

Preface		5
1816	**The Ship's Pigeon**, Capt. Basil Hall	15
1828	**The Crime**, Francisco Mangiapan	20
c.1829	**At the City Gates**, W.C. Hunter	23
1830	**'All Samee Boy'**, Harriet Low	27
1835	**Through the Streets**, Anon	31
1839	**The Schoolmaster**, G. Tradescant Lay	34
	Carry on Housekeeping, Robert B. Forbes	37
1841	**Merchant Princes**, A Field Officer	40
1844	**A Barren Rock**, R.M. Martin	42
	Wicked Men, Rev. George Smith	44
1847	**Chinese Fellow-Travellers**, Ida Pfeiffer	46
	Barbarians, Thomas Taylor Meadows	51
1848	**Hong Kong Fever**, A Resident	53
1854	**'Fanny! Fanny!'**, Fanny Loviot	55
	The Ancient Families, Dr. Yvan	62
1856	**Turbid Waters**, Henry T. Ellis	65
1858	**Dreadful Dens**, George Wingrove Cooke	66

1859	**Flesh and Blood**, Maj. W.H. Poyntz	69
	Paper Horses, Peter George Laurie	72
	True Feelings, A.F. Lindley	75
1864–65	**Cruel Climate**, Thomas Lyster	78
c.1868	**The Stripling Missionary**, Thomas G. Selby	81
1869	**Luxurious Quarters**, J. Thomson	87
1870	**A Lucky Grave**, Margaretha Weppner	92
1873	**'Gem of the Orient'**, E.K. Laird	94
1874	**The Only European**, Walter William Mundy	97
	Buried Alive, Rev. C. Piton	100
1876	**The Hall of Justice**, Henry M. Field	102
1877	**Unexpected Meal**, Mrs. Gray	106
	Ah Kum, James Hingston	109
	Baby-Talk, Mrs. Brassey	113
1878	**Dogs, Rats, and Mice**, Andrew Carnegie	116
1879	**Agreeable Hours**, Capt. S.H. Jones-Parry	119
	In the Zenana, C.F. Gordon Cumming	121
c.1880	**Chinese Devils**, Edward S. Morse	125
c.1882	**The Hour of Death**, A.L.	129
1886	**The First Day**, Thomas Stevens	131
	Strange Guest, B.C. Henry	134
1889	**Chinese Ponies**, Lt. C. Cradock	137
c.1890	**The Funny Man**, Walter H. Young	139
1890–91	**Beetle on a Pin**, E.T.C. Werner	143
1893	**Only a Girl**, Rev. A.B. Simpson	145
	John Chinaman, Thomas R. Dewar	148

8

1894	**Sudden Death**, Charles J.H. Halcombe	150
	Ghosts with Pigtails, Capt. G.J. Younghusband	154
1900	**The Man of Science**, E. Burton Holmes	157
	Bound Feet, Mrs. Archibald Little	159
1901	**A Pile of Dollars**, C.D. MacKellar	163
1903	**'Can Do'**, Oliver G. Ready	167
1905	**The Hong Kong Season**, Rev. E.J. Hardy	171
c.1906	**Such a Reputation**, F. Dumont Smith	174
1908	**Chinese New Year**, Count Fritz von Hochberg	177
	The Spell of Hypnotism, John Stuart Thomson	181
1911	**Pirates at Last**, Sybil Ready	185
1915	**Secret Communication**, C. Winifred Lechmere Clift	189
1923	**Government House**, Commander C.H. Drage	192
	Fragile Guide, Grace Thompson Seton	195
1924	**The House of Lin**, Nora Waln	197
1924–25	**Timid Tourists**, Harry A. Franck	200
c.1925	**'Pleasant Surplise'**, Clifford W. Collinson	203
1930	**Night Life**, James Lafayette Hutchison	208
1932	**Conspiracy of Silence**, Ramnath Biswas	210
c.1933	**What a Racket!**, William Martin	214
c.1936	**On the Water-Front**, C.S. See	218
	A Wonderful Dragon, Francis de Croisset	221
1937	**Nobodies**, Charles Richard Thomas	226
1939	**'Tipperary'**, Carveth Wells	228

1941	**In the War**, B.C. Redwood	232
	Surrender, R.S.M. Charles Ford	234

| 1942 | **Bid for Freedom**, E.D. Crossley | 236 |

Glossary	240

| Background Events | 246 |

| Acknowledgements | 250 |

| Index | 252 |

Illustrations

	Page
Chinese Merchants	24
A Schoolboy	35
Hong Kong in 1844	43
On Board the Junk	58
Macao Harbour	63
Execution at Canton	70
Cantonese Boat-Woman	76
In the Countryside	85
Plan of Canton about 1865	90
Coolies' Barracoons, Macao	95
The Foreign Settlement, Canton	104
Uncut Finger-Nails	111
A Canton Lady	123
A Waterway near Canton	127

	Page
Hong Kong Harbour	138
Coming on Board	149
Plan of Victoria, Hong Kong, in 1890	152
Li Hung Chang about 1900	160
In a Macao Gambling House	165
A Coolie	175
A Toy Seller	179
An Old Pagoda	187
At a Chinese Theatre	206
A Chinese Temple	222

THE INHABITANTS OF this country, whom we call *Chinese*, are quite white, excepting those who are tanned by the sun. Most of them look alike; they have short noses, small eyes, short black eye-brows, a broad face, great ears, and black hair, which the men always shave off, having a tuft at the top of the head, which grows as long as it will, and is made up into a broad stiff plait. . . . The men let their beards grow, and divide them into several locks. The *Chinese* are some of them greater and others smaller in size than we are. In conversation they are civil: in their demeanor gentle; in social life diligent, having genius for trade in particular: but they are likewise talkative, inquisitive, loving to take presents; are obstinate, proud and suspicious. They sit upon their feet, for want of chairs. When they meet one another, they lift up their hands; but touch neither hat nor cap, and do not move their feet, but bow a little, saying, *Hoaw, Hoaw,* which is a friendly salute, with which they wish all manner of good to each other.

Peter Osbeck
Canton, 1751
A Voyage to China and the East Indies

13

1816

The Ship's Pigeon

Although the English had traded at Canton for over a hundred years they were still subject to rules and restrictions which they found irksome. In an attempt to improve the situation a diplomatic mission led by Lord Amherst was sent from England to see the Emperor in Peking, travelling out in Royal Navy ships commanded by Captains Maxwell and Hall.

While the diplomats were engaged on their business Captain Maxwell made for Canton to await their return. Captain Basil Hall was about to follow when he received a visit from the Chinese commodore of the war junks guarding the entrance to the Pearl River.

. . . As soon as the sails were furled, the commodore manned his barge, and came himself to pay the *Lyra* a visit. I should have been very glad to have received him, but Captain Maxwell's orders against any intercourse being explicit, I could do nothing but decline his civility, and keep him off. In spite of all I could do, however, he rowed alongside, and sent an officer up with his card. This personage who forced his way on board addressed me in these words, "I come to see about your pigeon." – "My pigeon," said I; "I have no pigeons on board, and you must go away – I cannot receive you – go down the side, if you please." "No! no," exclaimed he, by way of clearing up the mystery, "my master, this great Mandarin," pointing to his chief, "has come to see about the ship's pigeon." While I was puzzling over this speech, I observed the commodore and two or three of his attendants climbing on board the brig, and therefore called out to some of the sailors, "Here, my lads, put this gentleman into his boat again." In an instant a couple of strapping fellows, who liked no better sport, leaped up, and would have tumbled the poor Chinese over the gangway in a trice, had I not caught their arms. The interpreter, seeing what was going to happen, made a wise and precipitate retreat, dragging the commander-in-chief along with him by the tail, and screaming to the boatmen to shove off.

I was really extremely sorry to be guilty of such rudeness; but my orders being imperative, I had no other way of resisting such determined intrusion, but that of threatening to throw the foremost of my visitors overboard. . . .

I afterwards learned that the word "pigeon," in the strange jargon which is spoken at Canton by way of English, means business, so that what the linguist meant to say was, "I am come to see about your business." It is, perhaps, not generally known that all transactions between foreigners, of whatever nation, are carried on here in a singular dialect, called English, but which is scarcely intelligible at first, even to an Englishman, and must be totally unintelligible to every other foreigner. It is made up of English, Portuguese, and Chinese, and although barbarous in the highest degree, must be studied by every trader at the port. Until very lately, all business was transacted by the British Factory in this most absurd language. Of late years, however, the Company's servants at Canton have made themselves acquainted both with the written and spoken Chinese, and everything material now passes in the language of the country. The natives themselves, whose principle it is to discourage all assimilation, sometimes lament this newly acquired power of communicating, and look back with regret to the times when the supercargoes drank a great deal of wine, and spoke not a word of their language. "Now," as I heard one of the Hong merchants say, with a sigh and a shake of the head, "the English speak Chinese as well as I do, and drink nothing but water." . . .

On reaching the *Alceste*, I found orders lying for me to proceed to Canton; and as a captain of one of the tea ships was just setting off in a large and commodious barge, I preferred accompanying him to rowing up alone. Probably, had I gone in a man-of-war's boat, the Chinese, who had treated Captain Maxwell with great politeness wherever he passed, might have been equally civil to his brother officer. But they observed no such delicacy in the case of the East India captain; for wherever we passed, they climbed to the most conspicuous parts of their boats, and saluted us in a style the very furthest removed from good manners; suiting the rudest actions to words probably not more courteous. The eloquence was quite thrown away upon us, but there was no mistaking the purport of the gesture. For some time this was amusing, rather than otherwise; and to me at least the whole scene, from beginning to end, was subject of unmixed entertainment. But my companion, though one of the best men alive, was not the most patient person in the fleet, and replied at first to these insults by a few emphatic oaths in broad Scotch. Presently he stood up, and shook his fist in a very angry manner, which produced nothing but a loud and scornful laugh; this instantly drove my friend into a towering passion; and before I could stop him, he caught up a fowling-piece, lying on the stern sheets, and discharged it directly at a thick cluster of Chinese, not one of whose faces could be seen, but who nevertheless offered a most conspicuous front to his aim. Fortunately the piece was loaded with snipe-shot, and the distance being considerable, the dose, thus promptly administered, acted merely as a sedative, not only upon the crew of the nearest vessel, but upon that of every other in sight. . . . for many weeks afterwards, when I passed in the same boat with the same person, the natives recognised the hand that had peppered them, and were extremely civil as we rowed along.

We had thus to fight our way, step by step, into the good graces of the Chinese. The last conflict which we had with them took place about an hour after I had reached Canton, at Captain Maxwell's lodgings. We heard a great noise at the top of the stairs, and on going out to see what was the matter, found my coxswain and boat's crew in high altercation with a Chinaman, who was endeavoring to deprive them of a trunk which they carried on their shoulders. . . .

As it was an established practice at Canton for no Chinese authority to enter the house of a European resident without first obtaining permission, this proceeding was quite contrary to usage. At all events, Captain Maxwell, who had commenced by assuming a high tone in great matters, was resolved to carry it through even in trifles, and turning to the Chinese, asked him by what right he had dared to violate the quarters assigned to his Britannic Majesty's officers, without first appealing to him. The Mandarin looked a little surprised; but a reply being insisted upon, he said it was quite a mistake – that he had imagined the trunks had belonged to some merchant ship, and not to a king's ship. "Well, then," said Captain Maxwell, "you must learn better in future." And turning to the sailors, ordered them to put the officer out of the house . . .

So much has been written respecting China, and especially about Canton, that I shall be excused for not entering on so threadbare a subject. We were allowed to walk about the streets to a great distance from the Factory, without meeting any kind of obstruction or insult; and when we happened to come near the gates of the Citadel or inner town, were warned off by sentinels with long poles, but no impediments were ever thrown in the way of our examining the shops, or the different manufactories, with which the other parts of this immense city abound; and as the sight of Europeans was familiar to the people, no notice was taken of us, and every one continued at his business as if no stranger was looking on. . . .

The only evil likely to attend these perambulations through the streets, was the loss of a handkerchief or two. A Chinese thief picked my pocket one day, so dexterously, that I did not perceive the loss: but my companion, the same gentleman who had silenced the significant salutation of the Chinese boatmen, and who was better acquainted with the people, detected the rogue, and caught him by the end of his long tail, as it was whisking round the corner of the street. He began instantly to belabour the thief with his cane, and what seemed odd enough, to the entire satisfaction of the multitude, who, so far from attempting a rescue, encouraged the due infliction of this discipline. After a certain number of blows had been given, however, there was a cry of "enough," and I was informed that if the punishment had not been discontinued at once, the extra allowance bestowed on the culprit, would have been paid back to the donor with a certain per-centage of interest. It seems every conceivable offence in China has its numerical value expressed in terms of the bamboo, by which alone it can be expiated; and as this scale is well known to every man in the streets, a stranger is safe in administering the law himself, since he may be quite sure of having a limit set to his proceedings when, according to the refined calculus alluded to, justice has been satisfied. I was never very desirous of putting this to the test of actual experiment, but some days afterwards when the same fellow again picked my pocket, I seized him by the collar and was carrying him to the Police Office close at hand, when he fell on his knees and supplicated me to beat him, knowing perhaps that the sitting Mandarin would not let him off so cheaply as I should. The oddity of the request disarmed me entirely, and I gave him a small copper coin, bidding him not rob me any more – and he adhered faithfully to his promise, although I passed him frequently every day. This man was as well known to the police, as our professional rogues in London are said to be to the officers of Bow-Street, and as far as I could learn, made his bread by the same laudable calling. The convention between him and me did not extend to my countrymen, however, and in the course of ten days, one of the midshipmen of my ship, a careless, gaping mortal, whose insatiable curiosity led him to wander in a sort of ecstacy through the streets, lost no less than twelve pocket-handkerchiefs; so that he became a sort of little fortune to my friend the pickpocket, who looked very ill pleased one day when I passed in company with the youngster, and by keeping between them convoyed him in safety for once. This persevering rogue never shifted his station, but sat curled up like a spider in his hole, at the end of one of the numerous little bridges which cross the streets of Canton.

CAPTAIN BASIL HALL
Voyage to Loo-Choo and other places in the Eastern Seas in the year 1816
(1826)

1828

The Crime

With their ship wrecked on the coast of the South China Sea the crew of the Navigateur *hired a Chinese junk to take them and their cargo of silks, wines and other valuables on to Macao. Of the fourteen Europeans who boarded the junk, only Francisco Mangiapan, an Italian, lived to tell the tale.*

. . . We sailed from Turon on the 15th, and a few days after, we began to experience all manner of vexations, which increased as we approached our destination; but the hope of soon parting with our disagreeable companions, made us bear them with patience. On the 30th or 31st July, an old Chinese who appeared to be the pilot of the junk, tried by every possible means to make captain Romain understand that he ought to be on his guard, being apprehensive that we should be maltreated. The same day another Chinese who paid us some attention, also tried to convey the same impression to us, and even that our destruction was contemplated. But having much difficulty in understanding what was meant, and the conduct of the Chinese crew being always nearly the same, we were in hopes that these suspicions were ill-founded, or that the fear of the crime being discovered would prevent its commission. On the 3rd of August, being eight or nine leagues from Macao, in sight of the Ladrone islands, when twelve Chinese passengers landed about 1 P.M., captain Romain wished to send on shore at the same time four sailors who were ill of a fever when they embarked, and whom the fatigue of the voyage had rendered extremely unwell, and also some more of the crew. The Chinese captain, however, dissuaded him from this, giving him to understand that he would get near Macao during the night, and anchor near the town, and that it would be very easy for him to procure what boats he might require to land his crew, as well as any part he might wish of the goods that were at hand. Captain Romain, however, confiding little in this proposal, persisted in wishing to land a part of his people, and to leave on board only three or four men to take care of the goods; but the notice which we had received respecting the bad intention of the Chinese crew, inspired us with but too just apprehensions, that those who remained on board the junk would lose their lives; we refused to obey the captain's orders, and even to cast lots who should remain behind, wishing that all should land or remain together on board; and unfortunately we took this last resolution. Next day, August 4th, having kept watch till 2 A.M., I went to bed in the cabin upon the poop where were the captain and other passengers. Between 4 and 5, I was awakened by the cries of my comrades, who were attacked by a part of the Chinese crew, who had killed one of our men then upon the deck, and wounded another. In an instant about sixty Chinese were opposed to the few of us who were able to assemble upon the poop, where we could make but a feeble resistance, having few arms, and being surrounded by so great a number of Chinese armed with lances and long bamboos, with which they tried to knock us down, whilst others from below removed the poop deck under our feet, that they might break our legs and kill us the more easily. After firing some pistol shots, the chief mate and two sailors were killed, Mr. C___ was knocked down mortally wounded, and captain Romain, under whose feet they had succeeded in breaking open the poop deck, was seized by the legs, and dragged below; his cries made us suppose that they murdered him in a shocking manner. The few of us who were still capable of resistance, seeing our officers and messmates cruelly massacred, and having no longer any hopes of saving our lives, resolved to rush upon the Chinese, in order to put an end to our sufferings and try to make them pay dear for the existence of which they wished to deprive us. Having executed this project, I succeeded in disengaging myself, and leaped into the sea, and an instant after I saw Etienne do the same. Having approached him, I saw him all covered with blood, being severely wounded in the head and neck; more fortunate than he, I had only received some severe bruises. The junk continuing her course was in an instant far away from us, and being upwards of two leagues from the shore, it is probable that the villains who had just committed so atrocious a crime, believed it impossible for us to escape destruction, and that their crime not being discovered would remain unpunished. Fortunately their boats were too much encumbered to be put into the water, or they might have pursued and drowned us. We were about an hour striving with the waves when a small Chinese vessel passed us, and we succeeded in placing ourselves upon her rudder, but the crew made signs for us to be off, threatening to bamboo us if we did not let go our hold immediately; and absolutely refusing to let us stay or to receive us on board, they threw out a plank at last to assist in keeping us afloat. I laid hold of it immediately, and my comrade did the same, but he was not able to hold out long, his strength being exhausted by the enormous loss of blood which continued to flow from his wounds. Wearied with the motion of the plank he soon let go his hold, and bidding me adieu he disappeared. After being in the water about two hours, a second vessel passed and I succeeded in getting to her, and after some entreaty, was received on board. They were humane enough to throw me a rope, and haul me out of the sea. When I had recovered a little, I gave them five dollars which I had preserved in a handkerchief round my neck; and tried to make them understand that I belonged to Macao, from whence I set out in the morning with three friends, to amuse ourselves in fishing, and that unfortunately the boat capsizing my companions were drowned. Having given me some clothes and a little food, they called a fisherman, to whom after some discussion they gave four dollars for conveying me to Macao, and gave me back the remaining dollar. About midnight of the 4th I was put on shore, and the boat went off immediately. Having proceeded along the Praya Grande, I came to the guard-house, and after putting a few questions to the sentinel, I laid down close by, and fell asleep. At day light, not knowing where to go, I proceeded towards the Senate square, and meeting a Portuguese, requested him to direct me to the house of the French missionaries. My strange language and Chinese dress induced him to put some questions to me, and acquainting him with what had happened, I was conducted by him to the house of the dezembargador, where I made my deposition.

FRANCISCO MANGIAPAN
"Deposition to the Macao Authorities"
The Chinese Repository, Vol. IV, 1835-36

c. 1829

At the City Gates

When he was twenty-three William Hunter joined the American trading house of Russell & Co. at Canton. Hunter spoke Chinese and was soon involved in the seemingly endless battle of wits between the foreign residents and the Chinese authorities.

Under certain circumstances foreign residents could "offer up" petitions at the city gates! It was a privilege that had its origin a long while ago. At the same time it was discouraged by the authorities, while strict orders were given to the guards at the gates to keep a sharp lookout and close them if any number of barbarians were known to be approaching. . . .

Great precautions were taken to keep the intention as quiet as possible, consequently all who were disposed to join a party in presenting a petition were advised in time. None were more anxious to accompany it than the younger members of the community, who considered it great fun! To refer to a particular case, directly in front of the American Factory, at the river side, there existed a huge mound of earth and rubbish that had its origin with the great fire of 1822. While the new Factories were going up and the damaged ones being repaired the workmen and coolies threw all sorts of rubbish on the spot. Subsequently it became a depository of refuse of all sorts, and finally a resort of loathsome beggars, of whom many died on it; but beyond obtaining the carrying away of the dead bodies, all efforts by the foreigners to get the whole thing removed had proved ineffectual.

The Hong merchants now and then sent a number of coolies, but they made small impression upon it; and at length, mostly at their suggestion that it was "Mandarin pigeon," it was resolved to present a petition at the city gates, which they themselves prepared and we copied.

CHINESE MERCHANTS

On the day agreed upon, therefore, the party going were quietly advised and informed at which gate to meet. Taking different streets in small numbers of three or four, all drew towards the "petition gate," as we called it, and suddenly with a rush entered it. The surprise of the guards was complete. They hastily closed the ponderous outer gate to prevent the Chinese entering and possibly creating a row. Seeing the petition on red paper held up above our heads, they knew from experience the object of our visit, and forthwith despatched a messenger to the Hoppo's "Ya-Mun." . . . It happened that on a previous occasion of petitioning an unpleasant incident occurred, which arose from a fancied insult; blows had been exchanged, and certain words used by an excited member of the foreign party in reference to the soldiers became a tradition, "Knock them down, friend Olyphant, they are only tea and rice," and the best of the joke was that the speaker was a Quaker and Mr. Olyphant one of the quietest men in the world, and the last person to strike any one.

Such exhibitions were much to be deplored as encouraging the belief that foreigners were indeed "unruly devils" – a pugnacious, wild, boisterous people. Presently we heard the sound of the gong and the loud cries of lictors preceding the Mandarin calling out his rank and office as well as keeping the street clear. . . . The Ta-Yin (great man) having entered with other Mandarins and attendants, after salutations and surprise at seeing so many foreigners, they seated themselves on chairs brought by their followers. He then commenced by telling us of the extreme impropriety of entering the gates in opposition to the will of the "Son of Heaven," cautioned us to be wary how we did the like again, lest we might check the flow of Imperial benevolence towards all coming from a distance, &c. &c., which was the usual opening formula, when a Linguist being found cut and dried on the spot (sent privately by the Hong merchants), stepped forward, knelt on both knees, and "handed up" the petition. In the meantime it was a strange sight to see the houses, shop doors, and windows inside the city full to overflow of Chinese, intently looking on in profound stillness and curiosity.

His Excellency, having read the paper, said in placing it in the hands of an officer that a communication would be sent to the Hong merchants . . .

Business being thus ended, a disposition was shown for a little conversation. Acting as interpreter, I was invited to speak of the distance of our countries from the "Celestial Flowery Land," how many moons it took to come and to return; all which was done in laying great stress upon the clear light of day into which we emerged as we left our own gloomy shores and approached the "Middle Kingdom"! Questions were asked as to our respective nationalities, our names also; and in their attempts to repeat such as Zacharia, Krieroffski, Burr, and Brown, they turned to one another and laughed heartily at their unsuccessful efforts. The teapot and servants to prepare the infusion being indispensable in the suite of Mandarins (as well as pipe-bearers), tea was presently offered to us; we in exchange "offered up" Manila cheroots. No one exhibited the slightest impatience, no matter how many hundreds of Chinese were obliged, outside or inside, to make great détours to reach other gates.

The Mandarins being provided with two watches each, next began a comparison of time; they asked our ages, how long we had lived within the benign sway of that "Almighty Ruler" under whose protecting wings we found ourselves; and being assured, in reply to other enquiries, that in our distant countries now and then a sun, very occasionally two or

three moons, with a rare glimmer of a star, might be seen, they rose
from their seats, took leave, and were soon out of sight. The great gate
was then opened after a violent effort, with a loud grating of its
enormous hinges, and the "foreign devils" returned to the Factories,
after an hour or two agreeably passed. The petition in question resulted
in the Hong merchants receiving orders for the immediate removal of
the unsightly mound, of course at their expense. They were effectually
carried out and the ground was levelled off. It then became the favourite
resort of the Indian servants of Parsee and Moormen residents.

W.C. HUNTER
The "Fan Kwae" at Canton before
Treaty Days 1825–1844
(1882)

1830

"All Samee Boy"

The Chinese had a detailed set of rules governing the lives of foreign residents in Canton, Regulation 2 of which stated: "Neither women, guns, spears, nor arms of any kind can be brought to the Factory" – so families had to live at Macao. When some English traders' wives defied the ban, two American ladies – Harriet Low, aged twenty-one, and her aunt – followed their example.

Canton, November 6. – Here we are in the Celestial city, in a fine house, with every comfort around us, but the Hong merchants are making a row, and it is doubtful whether we remain long. But I will go back to Macao, and begin my adventures from there, giving you the particulars of our passage up, the difficulties and troubles we had to reach the Celestial city, etc. It is a long story, so be patient.

Well, Uncle arrived in Macao on Wednesday, November 3, in the little brig "Terrier," belonging to Mr. Cushing, and which he had kindly offered for our accommodation, and on Friday morning we . . . went on board the "Terrier," the Chinamen all refusing to give us the least assistance, except one boat-girl, more courageous than the rest, who lent us a board to step on as we got into the boat, for which she was liberally rewarded with a dollar. There is no doubt the mandarins got half, as the system of "squeezing" is carried on through all ranks. We got under way at seven, the wind cold and piercing, and blowing strong from the north (which was dead ahead), and it was not long before both Aunt and myself began to droop, and were pronounced to be quite "under the weather." It would never do to say we were sea-sick. That would be too vulgar. We went below into a neat little cabin, finished off in fine style, where a nice breakfast had been prepared for us, but eating was quite out of the question, and we were very glad to find ourselves on deck again. We beat up to Lintin, arriving there about two. . . . Lintin is a small island with a very high peak, and a fine anchorage for ships, where

27

all the outlaws (alias smugglers) lie, with their opium. l counted about fifteen. . . . There we lay until ten, – a lovely evening, but rather cold. When night approached, it was very natural to think about turning in, but when we asked "were there cockroaches on board," the answer was fatal to our hopes of a night's rest. While on deck, I said I should not mind them, I could sleep anywhere, and at nine I went very courageously below; but when I looked into my berth, nicely fitted up with red silk curtains, a tremendous one appeared at first view, and, while endeavoring to kill him, half a dozen more appeared, which quite cooled my courage, and in despair I took my pillow, and, with my cloak around me, threw my weary limbs upon the transom, hoping to forget the cruel tormentors. But fancy was wide awake, and the moment I shut my eyes she was bringing clouds of them before me. Aunt L. at last composed herself on the floor, with mosquito curtains around her, but there was no room there for two. About ten the tide was again in our favor, and we made sail, and commenced beating up the river. So you may judge that hard was my lot that night. You may suppose we did not feel much the better for it in the morning. About daylight we again anchored, a few miles below the Boca Tigre, or the Tiger's Mouth, as the Portuguese call it, where we found the "Sylph," a schooner of about thirty tons, ready to take us the rest of the way. On each point of land here there is a Chinese fort, and, while we were waiting for the tide again, we might easily have been sent back from here, had the mandarin suspected our presence. So we both wore velvet caps and cloaks, to prevent their recognising us as women. At noon we went on board the "Sylph," and passed the Boca in safety, passed a man-of-war, too, but they did not molest us. We were well armed. Had a delightful head wind till we reached Whampoa, too late to see the beautiful scenery and the fleet of ships now there. At eleven the moon rose in splendor, so that we had a fine view of the pagodas as we neared Canton, and the endless variety of boats. I forgot all my fatigue, and we stayed on deck, admiring everything. Everything was still and quiet, thousands and thousands at rest in a small space. It was more Chinese than anything we had seen before. The tea-boats are immense, and ranged along in such order that they form complete streets upon the water. There are also houses built upon boats, and forming streets. I have enjoyed it all very much, and have not yet repented that I came. We anchored about half-past twelve Saturday night, and came ashore without the least difficulty. Indeed, no one would have known that we were not "all samee boy" in our cloaks and caps, as we jumped out of the boat without waiting for arms. I said to Captain R., "Now I will walk directly to the factory"; and I did go straight to the door, I knew it so well by description. The porter opened the door, and for the first time we entered a Hong in the Celestial city of Canton. And now you will perhaps wish to know what a Hong, or factory, is. Perhaps you will fancy looms about; but it is nothing more nor less than a range of houses built one back of the other, and entered by arches, with a passage under the houses to get to each. We have the advantage of being in front, where we can see everything that goes on. The rear houses are like prisons, as there is nothing to be seen from them but the walls of the houses in front. There are four houses in this Hong. . . .

November 15. – These despicable Chinese, who are not worth our notice, have the power to disturb us all. They yesterday issued a chop saying that trade would be stopped "if one Low did not immediately remove his family to Macao." Now it is so provoking that the [East India] Company ladies, because they are a body and can bully them, are permitted to stay, and we, poor creatures, must go. . . .

We do not feel convinced that this chop is from the Viceroy, but suspect it is a forgery of the Hong merchants, and we shall have to go back to Macao, while the English ladies stay here and enjoy themselves. Mr. L. says it will be attended with great *éclat* if the trade of an empire is stopped on our account; but the upshot of the matter is, if the trade is stopped, we shall have to budge.

November 17. – We are still here, and all they wish us to do now is to say when we will go. They say if we tell them three or four weeks hence, and then are not ready, "putty off a little, that have mandarin fashion," – good-for-nothing creatures that they are!

November 27. – About dark it grew rather cool, and a fire was proposed; and you have no idea how cosey we looked, with our carpets down and a blazing coal fire. . . . a walk was proposed, as it was a delightful moonshiny night. We walked in front of the factories without exciting much observation. We then went up Old China Street, through Bouquiqua Street, and down New China Street. We were discovered to be Fanquis there; and lights were called for, that the Chinamen might look at us. They kindled up fires in an instant to behold our fair faces, and we had quite a rabble round us before we reached the front of the factories again, though they were all perfectly civil, and made no noise, but only showed a little curiosity, of which they have a share in common with their fellow-creatures of more enlightened parts. But, when we reached the open square, the "gallant tars" that were

29

promenading there espoused our cause, and scattered the mob in quick time. After they had dispersed, we sallied forth again, and went to Mr. L.'s house. You have no idea how elegantly these bachelors live here. I don't wonder they like it.

It is now decided that we are to leave Canton on Tuesday or Wednesday next. They grant us a chop-boat to go down in ... We should have been very happy here for three months if they would have let us stay, but they will not.

HARRIET LOW
"A Letter"
My Mother's Journal (1900)
Ed. Katharine Hillard

Through the Streets

These observations of everyday life in Canton were featured in The Chinese Repository, a monthly journal published locally.

Rats. . . . I saw an old man approaching me in the street, carrying on his shoulder a long pole or bamboo, loaded with rats. My attention was attracted to him by the tinkling of little bells which he carried in his hand fastened to the end of a short stick. . . . On inquiry, I ascertained that the rats were not for sale; this indeed I suspected when the man passed me, for the animals seemed to be nothing more than rats' skins stuffed: and such I understand is the fact. The man was by profession . . . a rat-catcher; and those which he carried on his shoulder were designed to point out his occupation. He and his fraternity have various methods of destroying rats, but the most usual is by poison. *May 2nd, 1835.*

Circulating libraries. I have often heard of "circulating libraries;" but before I reached this country I never saw them carried through the streets so as to accommodate every man at his own door. As in the countries of the west, some of the circulating libraries here are stationary, and every customer must go or send to the depository for the books which he wishes to obtain. Often, however, he is saved this trouble. The librarian, with an assortment of books in two boxes, suspended from a bamboo laid across his shoulder, and with a little rattle in his hand to advertise his friends of his approach, sets off on his circuit, going from street to street, and from door to door. In this way he passes his whole time, and gains his livelihood. He loans his books, usually for a very short time and for a very small compensation; they being generally small volumes and only a few in a set. The books thus circulated are chiefly novels, and sometimes those of a very bad character. The system, however, is a good one, and worthy the attention of the friends of useful knowledge. The librarian, whom I met at the door of the hong this afternoon, loaning books to the servants and coolies of the factories, said that his whole stock amounted to more than 2000 volumes. He had with him, however, not more than 300 volumes; the others being in the hands of his numerous customers. *June 19th.*

Flogging with the rattan is the most common punishment in China. It is adjudged and inflicted by the lowest officers or servants of the police, with the utmost dispatch, and without the least regard to any formalities of time or place. A poor ignorant person led on by his vices becomes a bankrupt; then driven by hunger he has recourse to theft or robbery to obtain food; the officers of the police seize him, and perhaps while his booty is still with him, pinion him, strip off his jacket, if he chance to be so clad; then with a chain or cord about his neck or his arms, and a soldier before him beating a gong, and another one behind him with a rattan beating his bare back, he is marched through the streets and market-places to be a terror to evil-doers. Within the last few days I have seen several persons flogged in this way. One I saw to-day so beaten that the blood run down to his heels. *June 29th.*

Gambling is known to prevail extensively among the Chinese; but never, before to-day, have I seen women engaged in it. Walking through the streets in the western part of the suburbs, I came across two old dames quietly seated by the wayside, gambling for a pair of cloth shoes. A few words to them attracted a crowd; and a few words more made them objects of derision, but did not deter them from their game. *Wednesday, [September] 2nd.*

A lost child. Children are often stolen in the streets of Canton, and carried off and sold. To-day I met two criers in pursuit of a lost child, – a little girl eleven years old. The men carried a heavy gong and a flag: the first to attract attention, and the latter to announce their object, which was done by broad characters written on the flag. Sometimes rewards are offered for the lost children; but nothing was offered in the present instance. *Tuesday, [September] 15th.*

Horseflesh must be poor food, if what I saw this afternoon was a fair specimen of it. A man passed me in a crowd, carrying on his shoulder something like a slab of oak, and I was surprised to notice, by the hoof which formed a part of it, that it was the hind quarter of a horse. The people who can relish such food must be "hardy" indeed. *Thursday, [September] 17th.*

Dried Tongues

The tongues of ducks, I learned to-day, are among the dainties of Chinese epicures. In one of the lanes running westward from Levenhing keae, there is a shop containing a great variety of live fowls, besides several species of dried ones, for sale. One article puzzled me much; and by inquiry I found it to be nothing more nor less than a string of dried tongues, obtained from ducks. They were stretched out to their utmost length, resembling awls in shape, and hardened almost to the firmness of iron. *Thursday, November 12th.*

ANON
"Walks about Canton: Extracts from a Private Journal"
The Chinese Repository, Vol. IV, 1835–36

1839

The Schoolmaster

As a naturalist George Tradescant Lay had accompanied the Beechey Expedition to the Pacific in 1825–28; now living at Canton he acted as agent for the British and Foreign Bible Society. His visit to Hong Kong was made two years before the British took over the island.

In the spring of 1839, I visited the harbour of Hong-kong, for the sake of enjoying those fresh breezes that were said to blow there, and that exhilaration which change seldom fails to produce in those whose minds and bodies have been enfeebled by anxiety and disease. . . .

Among the friendly people of the villages near the harbour, I often sought for opportunities to distribute the Scriptures, but was not always successful, since only a few could read well enough to covet them. They would sometimes turn over their pages very carefully, as if in search of interesting matter, and appear so much engaged in the pursuit, that I began to promise myself the pleasure of bestowing these sacred memorials where they would be read and valued; but, alas! after some time had been spent in expectation, a lack of scholarship, or a disinclination to meddle with any subject which use had not rendered familiar, would lead them to return me my volumes in a sombre silence . . . In one of my rambles, the inhabitants of a group of dwellings advised me to take my books to a school which they represented as in their immediate neighbourhood. Glad to hear of such an establishment so near, I started in the direction pointed out to me, and at every house made fresh inquiries, and gained fresh instructions, which disagreed so much with each other, that at last I had . . . fully satisfied myself that I was seeking for what had no existence in the place. When I had given up the search in despair, I learned from a peasant, that the school alluded to by my informants was situated in a little hamlet on the other side of the hill. . . . I found the master and a friend in conversation,

34

while half-a-score little boys were poring over as many well-worn books. . . . After the exchange of courteous greetings, and being pressed to take my seat in a great chair . . . I seized the first opportunity of displaying the eight cumbrous volumes which I had got under my arm. "Here," said I, "are a few books which I am going to present to you for the use of yourself and your scholars." This announcement was received with a courteous expression of thanks, and the master and his literary friend began forthwith to examine the pages with much apparent attention, and I to congratulate myself upon so fair a chance of doing good . . . After one of the twain had ended his perusal, he took a pencil and wrote, with the light and graceful air of a ready penman, a sentence upon a piece of paper. There is something serious in the atmosphere of a Chinese school, because the discipline is strict and the basis of instruction is laid in morals: surrounding circumstances, therefore, as well as the literary character of the individuals who presided in it, authorized me in thinking that he was writing a note in reference to the books, and that this note would be a record of the value he had set upon my present. This pleasing dream was soon interrupted, for upon

A SCHOOLBOY

reading the scroll which was politely handed to me, I found a sentence to the following effect:- *"Will you buy an ox, for I have an ox to sell?"* The feelings of disappointment at once wrought a change in my countenance, which the writer of the scroll and his friend ascribed to my dullness, and fancied I did not comprehend his meaning. In this I endeavoured to undeceive them, by saying I was not the captain of a ship, but a poor traveller, and that I spent my time in distributing good books and in studying and collecting the objects of nature. A Chinaman has always an eye that is fully awake to the concernments of self-interest, and so the schoolmaster felt that he could read the books at any time, but should not always have a chance of selling me his ox.

G. TRADESCANT LAY
The Chinese As They Are (1841)

1839

Carry on Housekeeping

Robert Forbes, an American merchant in Canton, found himself under house arrest along with others of the foreign community when the Chinese government decided to clamp down on the opium trade and sent Commissioner Lin to implement the policy.

. . . Without any warning, Lin made his appearance at Canton on the 10th of March, and on the 19th he issued a proclamation demanding of the foreign community the instant delivery of every chest of opium within the waters of China! The Hong merchants, through whom all legitimate foreign trade was conducted, were threatened with death if the imperial mandate was not immediately obeyed.

In order to show that he was in earnest, Lin threw a cordon of boats filled with soldiers around the river-front of the residences of the merchants; all the servants, compradores, and cooks were ordered off; in one word, we were prisoners in our own factories or houses; all trade ceased, and we were thrown on our own resources. . . . It was arranged that Mr. Johnson, second superintendent of British trade, should proceed to the Bocca Tigris, the fortified entrance of the river, and deliver to Lin's officers 20,283 chests of opium of the then *nominal* value of ten millions of dollars. During the progress of delivery, the foreign community was kept under strict guard. Not desiring to starve them, the officers of government, or the Hong merchants, sent in supplies of food in the shape of pigs, fowls, and sheep on the hoof. Fortunately several boats' crews were in Canton at the time of closing the doors, and they were utilized as far as possible as servants, cooks, &c; but the supply, not being equal to the demand, other means had to be resorted to in order to carry on housekeeping.

In the American hong . . . lots were drawn to settle who should cook, and who play the part of waiters, chambermen, &c. It fell to me to be chief cook. The first thing to be done was to clean out the kitchen, into which no white man had before entered; all hands went at it, and soon made things fit for my new work. My first effort was fried ham and eggs; when the dish came to table, it was difficult to distinguish between eggs and ham: all bore the color and partook of the consistency of dirty sole-leather. It was immediately voted to depose me, and to put Warren Delano in my place, and I assumed his duties, which were to look after the glass and silver; to this end I put upon the side-board a piece of sheeting, and when I required towels I had only to tear off a strip, wipe my utensils, and throw the strip into a corner. W.C. Hunter was lamp-trimmer, and all had something to do. The live-stock was driven into the rear, and barricaded, – pigs, sheep, and fowls all mixed up together, and making day and night hideous with their smell and noises. . . . Bathing being important, and no coolies at hand to carry water to the upper rooms, we rigged whips, and attempted to hoist up the big pails into the verandas; but this proved a failure, the ropes twisted up, and the pails remained suspended in mid air. The venerable consul mourned much over this state of durance vile, and lamented his hard fate. One morning I met him on the stairs, intent on some household errand, when he opened his heart to me in this wise:-

"Is this not too bad, Mr. Forbes, that a public official at my time of life, not owning a pound of opium, should be imprisoned, and compelled to do chamber-maid's work?"

Many ludicrous scenes occurred during the five or six weeks of our imprisonment. Terrier dogs being abundant as well as rats, the younger members of the community got up regular hunts, and killed many fine specimens. The Chinese guards outside filled the square, and they imagined we lived principally on rats and beer. Foot-races were organized, cricket and ball matches, and some of the sailors competed for prizes in climbing flag-staffs. Every one tried to be jolly. Some wore very long faces, thinking something would surely happen to endanger our lives. Before the arrangements were completed to deliver the goods, at a meeting of the chamber of commerce Houqua and one or two other principal Hong merchants appeared, with very lugubrious faces and with chains round their necks; but the chains were so very light, that I could not help thinking this was a farce got up to frighten their friends into compliance with Lin's demands. The city authorities through the Hong merchants endeavored to induce Mr. Dent, one of the principal holders of drug, to go into the city; but the community with one voice opposed this, – some believing that he was wanted as a hostage for the delivery of the opium, and some went so far as to fear that if he went in he would be executed. . . .

Early in May, the last chest having been delivered, and the whole 20,283 destroyed by dumping into trenches and admitting the river water, the treble cordon of guard-boats was removed, and trade was opened; servants came back, and all breathed freely again.

ROBERT B. FORBES
Personal Reminiscences (1876)

1841

Merchant Princes

With the outbreak of war against China the foreign trading community had to fall back on Macao, thus giving the old Portuguese colony a brief revival of fortune. This period was described by "A Field Officer" – a member of the British Forces – in private letters which were later published.

The English merchants only rent houses here: but since they have been forced to retire from Canton and to reside in this place, Macao has risen from an almost ruined to a very flourishing condition. The Portuguese as well as Chinese thrive on British wealth and industry; and both will suffer when Macao is abandoned for Hongkong.

The English merchants in China are very hospitable, and keep up the character of merchant princes: the houses they rent here are very large, and elegantly furnished, at least those in which married ladies are found. There are no very fine buildings, architecturally speaking, except the ruins of the ancient San Paulo church; of which, however, the front alone is standing. It was once the finest Christian church in the East. . . .

Of the fine arts, painting is enthroned at Macao: our countryman Chinnery is supposed to be the greatest of Eastern painters. . . . He certainly paints and draws beautifully; but I cannot say whether he takes good likenesses. I read in a certain Indian journal the description of some scenery which was said to be "worthy of the pen of a Byron and the pencil of a Chinnery," a juxta-position of names which rather astonishes an Englishman.

Chinese artists abound. Some – the pupils of Chinnery – are very respectable performers. Lunquah is the first; but he is gone to Canton. They take accurate likenesses, and will make copies of paintings to resemble the originals to such a degree that none but an artist can tell the difference. They don't know how to flatter yet; but English dollars will one day teach them that profitable art.

A lady at Macao was having her portrait drawn. As the work proceeded, she expressed her strong dissatisfaction at the performance. . . . the indignation of the fair one was so great and so disagreeably expressed, that the irritated artist naïvely exclaimed, "If handsome face no got, how handsome face can make?" English artists could teach him. . . .

Shopping at Macao is a laborious operation. Curiosities are easily procured; not so European or Eastern articles of clothing and comfort. The Chinese almost invariably take less than they ask of a foreigner, but always more than is fair. If you are polite, they are insolent; if you are cold and contemptuous, they are civil and obliging. Those, however, who know Englishmen, will generally behave respectfully, and may be civilly treated. . . .

One of the greatest annoyance in dealing with the Chinese is the coin. Some dollars they object to take, apparently because they have a new appearance, and others because they are too old. The fact is, they are great rogues in Macao; and, as they often try to pass off bad money, they suspect foreigners of a similar intention towards them. . . .

There are no carriages in Macao. Ladies and even gentlemen going to their houses of business, ride in sedan chairs. Horses by no means abound. . . .

The Government of Macao is below all criticism. It is said that some of the senate cannot write their own names, but they *can* thwart the Governor, who is a very respectable officer.

Lucky it is for them that European politics will always prevent our attacking what is called the brightest jewel in the Portuguese crown. I would not give much for the other jewels if that is true. But should it ever be necessary, a subaltern and sixty men will be all the force required to accomplish the conquest.

Barracks are going to be erected to the south of Hongkong, to contain 200 Europeans as an experiment of the salubrity of the place. These wooden tenements are already made, and only require to be transported. I expect to form part of the first garrison, and should be glad to be on shore.

A FIELD OFFICER
The Last Year in China to the
Peace of Nanking (1843)

1844

A Barren Rock

---

*Would the new colony of Hong Kong succeed? The Colonial
Treasurer, Robert Montgomery Martin, had some rather decided
views on this question.*

It is, indeed, a delusion or a deception to talk of Hong Kong becoming
a commercial emporium, and to liken it to Singapore. The circumstances
and position of Hong Kong and Singapore present no resemblance
whatever. Hong Kong is a barren rock, producing nothing – not leading
to any place – surrounded by no trading or populous communities, with
various commodities for barter – and disadvantageously situated at the
most impoverished part of a coast-line of 2000 miles, and which, for half
the year, is only readily accessible in one direction. . . .

. . . There is no apparent prospect of Hong Kong ever yielding any
revenue adequate to more than a very small civil government. The
limited size and rocky nature of the island, – the absence of agriculture,
manufactures, or commerce, – and the fluctuating and predatory
character of the population, forbid the hope of an income being raised
to sustain a regular Government Establishment on the scale now
adopted, and which, indeed, is far beyond the present or prospective
wants of the island community. . . .

As a general principle, colonies that will not pay at least the expense
of their civil government are not worth maintaining. There does not
appear any reason why Hong Kong should be an exception to this rule.
There is not, as has been fancifully supposed, any analogy whatever
between Hong Kong and Gibraltar. Hong Kong commands nothing: a
glance at the chart will show that the navigation of the China seas is
perfectly independent of Hong Kong; even the entrance of the Canton
river is not controuled by Hong Kong. It is not possible by any outlay of
money to make the island a fortress . . . But supposing several millions
sterling were spent in fortifying Hong Kong, and half a million annually

42

HONG KONG IN 1844

expended for its garrison, the *cui bono* would constantly recur: from a Chinese enemy the island has nothing to apprehend even at present; no European or American state would think of capturing Hong Kong, for it would be valueless to them; and if mere glory were sought by the acquisition, they must be aware the fame would be of short continuance . . .

Numerous as are the colonies of the British empire, they are each of some utility to England: for their territorial extent as emigration fields to provide employment for a surplus population; for their production of sugar, coffee, corn, cotton, silk, indigo, timber, oil, wool, &c.; as maritime positions or military posts; as trading emporiums or fishing stations.

I have in vain sought for one valuable quality in Hong Kong. There are other good harbours around, and for 200 years we have not found the want of such. I can see no justification for the British Government spending one shilling on Hong Kong.

R.M. MARTIN
"Report on the island of Hong Kong"
Reports, Minutes and Despatches on the
British position and prospects in China
(1844)

Wicked Men

With peace restored, the Reverend George Smith was sent out from England by the Church Missionary Society "to explore the ground, and to prepare the way for other Missionaries". In Canton he met Leang Afa, the first Native Evangelist, and his son.

Oct. 29th – Leang Afa called to introduce to us his son, A-tuh. The latter is a smart, intelligent, and well-educated young man. He has, for some time, been under the instruction and care of the Rev. Dr. Bridgman, of the American Board of Missions. Under his roof he received advantages which place him, intellectually, far above any other individual among his countrymen. . . . Having recently abandoned the Missionaries at Hong Kong, and connected himself with the mercantile establishment of Powtinqua, the principal native merchant and gentleman at Canton, he is naturally regarded by the Missionaries with some suspicion; and it is to be feared that he has been tempted by the superior gains and secular advantages which he receives as interpreter, to desert the quiet life and less alluring prospects of the Missionary body. He professes a temporary absence, and states his intention soon to return to Hong Kong. . . .

He speaks English fluently, and interpreted between us and his father. . . . Both of them spoke unfavourably of Hong Kong, as the resort of the worst classes, driven thither by destitution or crime. A-tuh especially spoke of the insolent treatment to which the Chinese residents were exposed from the police and the Europeans generally; and became much excited when he spoke of a recent indignity of treatment, which his father had suffered. He said the English had always been overbearing towards his countrymen, and until they showed a kinder spirit towards them, Christianity would never be respected. Especially, continued he, since the war the Chinese generally hated the English to a much greater degree than ever before, as they had done so much greater mischief. On this account they were more disinclined than formerly to listen to Christian doctrines; thinking that if Englishmen were Christians, it could not be a good religion which permitted them to be so insolent and mischievous.

. . . Afa said, with evident feeling, "If foreign Christians have such love for souls as to come to preach the Gospel to the Chinese, who hate them, how much more ought I, a Chinaman, to exert myself for the conversion of my countrymen." On my asking him what were the principal obstacles to Missionary success, he replied, "The Chinaman's heart is very hard: they will listen to European Missionaries, and not bring objections till they have departed. But to me they will address remarks of this kind: 'Perhaps this English doctrine may be very good; but we wish that you would first try it on the English themselves, for they are wicked men. When this doctrine has made them better, then come and speak to us.'"

REV. GEORGE SMITH
*A Narrative of an Exploratory Visit to each
of the Consular Cities of China* (1847)

1847

Chinese Fellow-Travellers

When Austrian widow Ida Pfeiffer, aged fifty-four, arrived on the
China coast she was – like many a later visitor – rather short of
funds, having already been fourteen months on her journey.

I resolved to stop only a few days in Victoria, as it was my wish to
arrive at Canton as soon as possible.

In addition to the great politeness he had previously shown me,
Captain Jurianse conferred another favour, by allowing me, during my
stay here, to live and lodge on board his ship, thereby saving me an
expense of 16s. or 24s. a day ...

Victoria is not very pleasantly situated, being surrounded by barren
rocks. The town itself has a European stamp upon it, so that were it not
for the Chinese porters, labourers, and pedlars, a person would hardly
believe he was in China. I was much struck at seeing no native women
in the streets, from which it might be concluded that it was dangerous
for a European female to walk about as freely as I did; but I never
experienced the least insult or heard the slightest word of abuse from the
Chinese; even their curiosity was here by no means annoying. . . .

I had not been above a few days in Victoria before I had an
opportunity of proceeding to Canton on board a small Chinese junk. A
gentleman of the name of Pustan, who is settled as a merchant here, and
whom I found excessively kind, endeavoured very earnestly to dissuade
me from trusting myself among the Chinese without any protector, and
advised me either to take a boat for myself or a place in the steamer; but
both these means were too dear for my small finances, since either
would have cost twelve dollars, whereas a passage in the junk was only
three. I must also add, that the appearance and behaviour of the
Chinese did not inspire me with the slightest apprehension. I looked to
the priming of my pistols, and embarked very tranquilly on the evening
of the 12th July.

A heavy fall of rain, and the approach of night, soon obliged me to seek the interior of the vessel, where I passed my time in observing my Chinese fellow-travellers.

The company were, it is true, not very select, but behaved with great propriety, so that there was nothing which could prevent my remaining among them. Some were playing at dominoes, while others were extracting most horrible sounds from a sort of mandolin with three strings; all, however, were smoking, chatting, and drinking tea, without sugar, from little saucers. I, too, had this celestial drink offered to me on all sides. Every Chinese, rich or poor, drinks neither pure water nor spirituous liquors, but invariably indulges in weak tea with no sugar.

At a late hour in the evening I retired to my cabin, the roof of which, not being completely waterproof, let in certain very unwelcome proofs that it was raining outside. The captain no sooner remarked this than he assigned me another place, where I found myself in the company of two Chinese women, busily engaged in smoking out of pipes with bowls no bigger than thimbles, and in consequence they could not take more than four or five puffs without being obliged to fill their pipes afresh.

They soon remarked that I had no stool for my head. They offered me one of theirs, and would not be satisfied until I accepted it. It is a Chinese custom to use, instead of pillows, little stools of bamboo or strong pasteboard. They are not stuffed, but are rounded at the top, and are about eight inches high, and from one to three feet long. They are far more comfortable than would at first be imagined. . . .

It is only during the last few years that we European women have been allowed to visit or remain in the factories at Canton. I left the vessel without any apprehension; but first I had to consider how I should find my way to the house of a gentleman named Agassiz, for whom I had brought letters of recommendation. I explained to the captain, by signs, that I had no money with me, and that he must act as my guide to the factory, where I would pay him. He soon understood me, and conducted me to the place, and the Europeans there showed me the particular house I wanted.

On seeing me arrive, and hearing the manner in which I had travelled, and the way that I had walked from the vessel to his house, Mr. Agassiz was extremely surprised, and would hardly credit that I had met with no difficulties or injury. From him I learned what risks I, as a woman, had run in traversing the streets of Canton, with no escort but a Chinese guide. Such a thing had never occurred before, and Mr. Agassiz assured me that I might esteem myself as exceedingly fortunate in not having been insulted by the people in the grossest manner, or even stoned. Had this been the case, he told me that my guide would have immediately taken to flight, and abandoned me to my fate.

I had certainly remarked, on my way from the vessel to the factory, that both old and young turned back to look after me, and that they hooted and pointed at me with their fingers; the people ran out of the booths, and gradually formed a crowd at my heels. I had, however, no alternative but to preserve my countenance; I walked, therefore, calmly on, and perhaps it is to the very fact of my manifesting no fear that I escaped unmolested.

. . . I have to thank Mr. Agassiz that the time did not hang heavily upon my hands; I was most kindly and hospitably entertained, and enjoyed the opportunity of noting the mode of life of those Europeans who have settled in the country.

Very few take their families with them to China, and least of all to Canton, where both women and children are closely imprisoned in their houses, which they can only leave in a well-closed litter. Besides this, everything is so dear, that living in London is cheap in comparison. . . .

A family of only four persons requires at least eleven or twelve domestics, if not more. In the first place, every member of the family must have an attendant, especially for his or her use; then there is a man-cook, a number of nursery-maids, and several coolies for the more menial duties, such as cleaning the rooms, carrying the wood and water, and so forth. In spite of this number of servants, the attendance is frequently very bad; for, if one or other of them happens to be out, and his services are required, his master must wait until he returns, as no servant could ever be prevailed upon to do another's duty. . . .

The following is a tolerably correct account of the mode of life pursued by the Europeans settled here. As soon as they are up, and have drunk a cup of tea in their bed-room, they take a cold bath. A little after 9 o'clock they breakfast upon fried fish or cutlets, cold roast meat, boiled eggs, tea, and bread and butter. Every one then proceeds to his business till dinner-time, which is generally 4 o'clock. The dinner is composed of turtle-soup, curry, roast meat, hashes, and pastry. All the dishes, with the exception of the curry, are prepared after the English fashion, although the cooks are Chinese. For dessert there is cheese, with fruit; such as pine-apples, long-yen, mangoes, and lytchi. The Chinese affirm that the latter is the finest fruit in the whole world. . . . I do not think the pine-apples are so sweet, or possessed of that aromatic fragrance which distinguishes those raised in our European greenhouses, although they are much larger.

Portuguese wines and English beer are the usual drinks – ice, broken into small pieces, and covered up with a cloth, is offered with each. The ice is rather a costly article, as it has to be brought from North America. In the evening tea is served up. . . .

As may be seen from what I have said, the living here is very dear for Europeans. The expense of keeping a house may be reckoned at 30,000 francs (6,000 dollars – £1,200) at the lowest; a very considerable sum, when we reflect how little it procures, neither including a carriage nor horses. There is nothing in the way of amusement, or places of public recreation; the only pleasure many gentlemen indulge in, is keeping a boat, for which they pay 28s. a month, or they walk in the evenings in a small garden which the European inhabitants have laid out at their own cost. This garden faces the factory, surrounded on three sides by a wall, and on the fourth washed by the Pearl stream. . . .

On the 8th of August, Mr. Agassiz set out with a friend, intending to return the same evening. I was left at home alone with the Chinese servants. Mr. Agassiz did not return at the appointed time. At last, about 1 o'clock the next morning, I suddenly heard voices in loud conversation, and a violent knocking at the street door. I at first supposed it to be Mr. Agassiz, and felt much surprise at the late hour of his arrival, but I soon perceived that the disturbance was not in our house, but in that on the opposite side of the way. It is easy to fall into an error of this description, as the houses are situated quite close to each other, and windows are left open day and night. I heard voices exclaim, "Get up, – dress!" and then, "It is horrible – shocking – good heavens! – where did it happen?" I sprang quickly out of bed and huddled on my gown, thinking either that a fire had broken out in some house or other, or that the people had risen in insurrection.

Seeing a gentleman at one of the windows, I called and inquired of him what was the matter. He told me hurriedly that intelligence had just arrived that two of his friends who were proceeding to Hong-Kong . . . had been attacked by pirates, and that one was killed and the other wounded. He then immediately retired, so that I was unable to learn the name of the unfortunate victim, and was left all night a prey to the greatest anxiety, lest it should be Mr. Agassiz.

Fortunately, this at least was not the case, as Mr. Agassiz returned at 5 o'clock in the morning. I then learned that this misfortune had happened to Monsieur Vauchée, a Swiss gentleman, who had passed many an evening in our house. On the very day of his departure I met him at a neighbour's, where we had all been in the highest spirits, singing songs and quartettes. At 9 o'clock he went on board the boat, set off at 10, and a quarter of an hour afterwards, in the midst of thousands of schampans and other craft, met his tragical end.

Monsieur Vauchée had intended to proceed to Hong-Kong, and there embark on board a larger vessel for Shanghai; he took with him Swiss watches to the value of 40,000 francs (£1,600), and, in speaking to a friend, congratulated himself on the cautious manner he had packed them up, without letting his servants know anything about it. This, however, could not have been the case; and, as the pirates have spies among the servants in every house, they were unfortunately but too well acquainted with the circumstance.

IDA PFEIFFER
A Woman's Journey Round the World
(1850)

Barbarians

Because he could understand the local language, Thomas Meadows, an interpreter at the British Consulate in Canton, found the workings of the Chinese mind more accessible to him than to most of his compatriots.

It is well known that the Chinese, who are not forced to it, are by no means fond of bodily exertion; and that the long nails worn by all who can, are longed for and cultivated, chiefly because they are a proof that the possessor is not obliged to perform any hard manual labour. . . . In England, where peers of the realm, and commoners with large hereditary properties, not only hunt, fish, and shoot, but also take long walks, row, fell trees, &c. &c., for amusement and exercise; these employments are, under certain circumstances, indicative of a person belonging to the higher classes, and are never considered necessarily vulgar. The Chinese, however, not only consider it very extraordinary that rich Europeans should walk and row, but look on the latter employment – the only safe exercise the antipathy of the people permits us beyond the factory squares – as exceedingly vulgar; and with them it is a strong proof of the naturally coarse inclinations of the barbarians. It seems as if many of them – believing, as they do, that England is so small, that if all of us who are abroad and in ships were to return thither, it would scarcely contain us, and that, consequently, a large number of us are born and bred on the water – think we should not be happy unless we got out occasionally on our native element. At all events, far from admiring the manliness of the exercise, they consider the pulling as very vulgar. I, who for obvious reasons am looked upon as civilized to a certain degree, have frequently been remonstrated with, in a delicate manner, on the impropriety of going out in the evening to pull in a gig, when if I *must* go I can engage boatmen to row. And it is to little purpose that I can explain the necessity of taking some exercise, and that pulling on the river is somewhat less monotonous than walking up and down a hong; or in one of the factory squares; to them it appears, that, although reclaimed in some measure, still the force of early habits is too strong, and the barbarian rushes, with ill-concealed delight, to indulge for an hour or two in the propensities of his nature.

The walking puzzles them not a little. Every one who has been at Canton knows, that they will stand for a whole hour, looking at a foreigner walking backwards and forwards, in one of the squares before the factories, their staring eyes following him slowly and regularly, as he passes and repasses them. They cannot consider it a vulgar employment, for the lowest Chinese coolie was never seen walking up and down, without an apparent object; they have, in consequence, got several odd notions on the subject; as, that the foreigner, in his inability to use a swan pan or abacus, reckons up his accounts in this way; that it is a religious observance, &c.; and the common answer to an enquiry made after one thus engaged is, that he is walking his "thousand steps."

THOMAS TAYLOR MEADOWS
Desultory Notes on the Government and People of China (1847)

1848

Hong Kong Fever

*In the early years Hong Kong was not a healthy place. People thought
that a deadly miasma was being released from the ground by the
continual excavations and building works; but in fact the open drains
were probably more to blame for the sickness. A resident – identity
unknown – wrote this letter of warning.*

Hong-Kong, Sept. 28, 1848

The winter from November 1847 to April 1848 was a very mild one.
The south-west monsoon set in early; the periodical rains fell late. June
came, and with it fever; but by the men who possessed houses, by the
Government who had drained Victoria, and erected costly buildings, by
the merchants who were sharply turning bales of opium into solid bars
of silver, – by *these* men it was said that a little sickness must be
expected. Nevertheless, June went on, and brought with it the end of
July, without any improvement; and it was found that H.M. 95th
Regiment had buried 47 men, and had as many as 299 sick out of 450.
Then came August, and death was still walking about; and men began
to conjecture where it was to end. August, however, came to its close,
and the 95th Regiment buried 47 more men, and the corps was put into
hired vessels anchored in the harbour of Victoria, to save those who
remained. September set in, and brought hope with it; but hope came,
though it was false, for death had not been satisfied, and they continued
to fall victims. And now that the month draws to its end, the living hug
the idea that the winter is coming on, and that it will set up their
constitutions. Time will prove how far they will have reason to
congratulate themselves.

For men here are friendless, being brought to this desolate spot only
by the love of gain, or the predisposition to smuggle, or by the
obligations of duty. England, mistress of the world and of the sea, as she
is, may have lots of men and of life to throw away, but, looking to the

schedule of her finances in 1848, she can but ill spare her wealth ...
The expenditure of men is looked upon in England as a dry matter of
numbers, and the actual cost is overlooked ... Without calculating that
every soldier as he stands on this accursed soil costs the country about
130*l.*, and that, therefore, the 95th Regiment alone have laid under its
fruitless and cheerless earth – to say nothing on the score of humanity –
about 14,000*l. worth of men in three months.* The strong man and the
weak, the sober man and the drunkard, the man who never exposed
himself to the sun, he who defied it – all died alike: the healthy man,
the woman, and the infant withered under the poison of Hong-Kong
fever with equal rapidity. If any man, therefore, have a mind to visit
China, from curiosity, let him turn his time and his money to better
account. If any man be allured to it by the love of gain, let him think
that health is better than wealth; and if any unfortunate individual in
either of her Majesty's services be compelled to come, by duty, just let
him have a stout heart and "a lively faith in God's mercy," which latter
may spare him to curse the place, as it has done the writer of these few
lines; and if, after his term of service here, he leaves it for a more
hospitable shore, after having escaped fevers and typhoons, he may say
and think to himself, "that verily Providence has watched over him."

A RESIDENT
China and the Chinese (1849)
Henry Charles Sirr

1854

"Fanny! Fanny!"

Fanny Loviot, a Frenchwoman, was sailing away from Canton after a short visit when, near Macao, the ship was attacked by Chinese pirates. Fanny and another passenger Than-Sing, a middle-aged Chinese merchant, were taken prisoner and held to ransom aboard the pirate junk.

The pirates who had us in charge then lifted a kind of trap, about two feet square, and pushed us down into a narrow dark hole below deck, where we had no room to stand upright and could with difficulty lie at full length. When we sat, our heads touched the flooring above. The trap being left open, we could at least breathe the fresh air, and look up to the sky; but, once shut in, our only light proceeded from a tiny port-hole of some eight inches square, which looked out beside the moving helm, and was not made to open. . . .

Towards evening they brought us a small bucketful of water, with which we washed our hands and faces; also some dried fish, some rice, and a little tea. So weak was I, that my head seemed too heavy for my body, and I now loathed the very sight of food. But Than-Sing ate eagerly, and implored me to partake of some little nourishment. Above all, he counselled me not to seem mistrustful of our foes, or of the food they gave us. Thus urged, I contrived to eat half a saucer of rice, and drink a little tea . . .

One of the pirates now brought us a light, which consisted of a little wick in a saucer of oil. Feeble as it was, it yet sufficed to light up the walls of our narrow dungeon. Scarcely had I looked round, when I uttered a cry of horror. Ceiling, walls, and floor were peopled by a multitude of huge velvety spiders, enormous beetles, and monstrous wood-lice, horned and shiny. In another instant, three or four great rats rushed out of a corner, and ran between my feet. Seeing my disgust, Than-Sing offered to put out the light; but I preferred the sight of these reptiles to the torture of hearing and feeling them in the darkness of night. Fortunately, I still had a pocket-handkerchief remaining. With this I covered my head and face and, hiding my hands under my clothes, crouched motionless in the middle of the floor throughout the remainder of the night. Towards morning the vermin disappeared.

Not long after daybreak, we were again supplied with provisions, and with a bucket of water, in which we washed our hands and faces. Than-Sing then informed me that the Chinese never eat till they have performed their morning's ablution. As before, our food consisted of rice, fish, and tea. With these they sent us two pairs of tiny chop-sticks, each about a foot in length, and as thick as an ordinary pencil. The Chinese hold them as we do a pen, and handle them with the utmost dexterity. Notwithstanding all the patience and skill with which Than-Sing endeavoured to teach me the use of these little sticks, I found them so impracticable as to be obliged at last to give up the attempt, and eat with my fingers.

To-day, again, the pirates came to watch and mock at us. One of them, more insulting than the rest, pointed first at me and then at the Chinese merchant, and represented the action of two persons embracing. This cowardly insult pained me more than all their previous cruelties. I felt myself become scarlet with shame and anger, and gave way to a passion of tears. In the midst of my distress the pirate-captain happened to pass by, and as if moved by my affliction, ordered the trap to be closed above our heads. . . .

The following day went by without any event of interest. I only remember that the pirates questioned Than-Sing about my name and country; and, having learned these facts by heart, amused themselves by perpetually shouting "Fanny! Fanny!" which often startled me. . . .

That night I strove in vain to sleep. The insects which infested our dungeon tormented me incessantly, and my feet were blistered all over from their bites. The rats, also, which at first had fled before the sound of our voices, were now grown but too friendly, and ran over us in broad daylight, as we were lying on the floor.

It was now the thirteenth day of the month. The junk still coasted along close in shore, and our position was as yet in nowise altered. In the evening we heard a great commotion upon deck, and found that one of the pirates had fallen overboard. Not having perceived this accident until too late, the man was quite dead by the time they succeeded in picking him up. They laid the corpse so close beside the opening to our cell, that the water came streaming from it full upon our heads. After a quarter of an hour of confusion, they gave up all hope of bringing him back to life, and, with sullen imprecations, flung the body back into the sea.

On the morning of the 15th, we came up with several other pirate-junks, and joined them in giving chase to a merchant-junk, plying between Hong-Kong and Canton with goods and passengers. All was now excitement on board. . . . When the evening came, we were fastened down in our dungeon more closely than ever. . . .

We had hoped that the day would, as usual, bring us some little liberty and fresh air; but the pirates were too busy to heed us. Absorbed in the pursuit of gain, they were all day occupied in negotiating the sale of their plunder, and for that purpose received on board those traders whose special line it is to buy up stolen goods. Bathed in perspiration, racked with acute cramps, and half stifled by the long-confined air, I suffered horribly. My skin, too, was covered with a painful eruption, and I had become so weak that, although my companion strove to amuse and cheer me, I was no longer able to reply. By and bye, we heard the pirates counting their gold, and then the splashing oars that bore the purchasers away. This done, our jailors at length remembered our captivity, and opened the trap. It was time they did so; for we had lain there upwards of four-and-twenty hours! The delight which it was once more to breathe that fresh night-air, I shall remember to my dying day.

The next day was the 17th, and a glorious morning dawned. To our surprise, the pirates came at sunrise, and quite removed the trap. They seemed almost pleasant, and, when the hour of breakfast came, brought us not only an abundance of food, but even some wine. This liquor, which is extracted from rice, is as transparent as water, and by no means unpalatable. The flavour of it, indeed, is not unlike that of new Bordeaux.

The junk was now coasting beside an uninhabited shore, and the pirates, assured that we could not here be observed, left our cell uncovered throughout the day. They even suffered Than-Sing to remain some time on deck, and behaved towards us with an amazing degree of good humour. The weather was so fine that I almost envied my companion, and longed to follow him in his walk. Not daring, however, to get out without permission, I ventured to stand up in my place, and look round at the land and the sea. Oh, how delicious seemed that sight! After having lived for seven long days in a dark and filthy den, I now beheld the broad bright ocean, the golden sunlight, the blue sky, and the verdant shore! Here and there, in the midst of trees and

pastures, lay tiny white villages, dotting the coastline far away, like white flowers in the grass. The sight of this landscape intoxicated me. I fancied myself once more in sight of my own dear France, and wept as I have seldom wept before or since. . . .

The cook to-day was fully employed with his stewpans and braziers, and appeared to be giving himself airs of no little importance. A feast was evidently in course of preparation, and he well knew that on his skill depended the success or failure of the entertainment. First of all, he opened and shelled the oysters, and put them over the fire in a huge sauce pan. He then fried a quantity of delicious little fishes, besides attending, every now and then, to a quarter of pork, which was browning before a fire close by. The sight of all these things sharpened our appetites, and we asked each other if we had any chance of sharing the feast. When the hour of repast came round, Than-Sing and I went back to our dungeon, scarcely hoping to be remembered till the best of the dishes were eaten. How much, then, were we surprised, on finding

ON BOARD THE JUNK

the pirates assemble and seat themselves all round about our cell, while the cook, ladle in hand, went round, and helped the company to saucerfuls of smoking oysters. Of these, Than-Sing and I received as large a share as the rest, and although I was at first somewhat doubtful of the sauce in which they were floating, I soon came to the conclusion that I had seldom tasted anything more savoury. After the oysters came the pork, and after the pork, wine, tea, and fish fried in rice. We were liberally helped to all these dishes. Indeed, it seemed as if the pirates wished to show us how sociable they could be, and for this day, at least, we were treated less as prisoners than guests. They enjoyed the dinner immensely themselves, and more than once asked Than-Sing how I liked their cookery.

Towards the close of the feast, just as I was anticipating the comfort of a few hours' rest, a large merchant-junk came in sight to the leeward. Every man was on his feet in an instant, the remains of the dinner were cleared hastily away, the flags were hoisted to the mast-head, and the pirates, running eagerly hither and thither, prepared for fighting. Plunder was once again the order of the day, and we, crouching silently in our little den, awaited whatever might take place. The merchantman, however, made too much way for us, and the pursuit was presently relinquished. I was inexpressibly thankful that this comparatively happy day was not destined to end in bloodshed and pillage. . . .

The next day was Wednesday, October 18th, 1854 – a heaven-sent day, never to be named unless with prayer and thankfulness! It might have been about four o'clock in the morning, when we were awakened from our sleep by the sound of hurrying feet and eager voices. After having sailed fast all the night, the junk was now riding at anchor, and the trap was closely fastened above our heads. I could not conceive what our captors were about, or why they should be thus active at so early an hour. . . . I turned to Than-Sing, who was awake and listening also, and asked him what he thought could be doing overhead? He laid his finger on his lip, and, bending breathlessly forward, paused for some moments before replying. . . .

. . . "It is a steamer! The pirates have seen a steamer, and they are escaping to the mountains." . . .

"You are wrong," I said. "Would they lie at anchor if they were pursued?" . . .

"I tell you that I am not mistaken. Steamer or no steamer, the pirates are fled! Listen how their voices die away."

I listened. A profound silence reigned around us, and I only heard a sound of murmuring voices, which became, every moment, more and more distant. . . . At that instant, a heavy footstep echoed overhead, and the trap was lifted from without. It was the ship's cook, who, with startled face and hurried gestures, looked in upon us.

"Fear nothing," said he. "It is a steamer! You are saved! It is a steamer!"

And with these words he also fled, and we were left alone. Quick as thought, I jumped up and sprang upon deck. . . . We were alone, utterly alone, on board the junk, which, having anchored somewhat too close in shore, was left half stranded by the ebbing tide, and could not be pushed off. They had ventured here in search of fresh water, and it was not till daybreak that they found themselves in such close neighbourhood with the steamer. This latter, it seemed, was also lying at anchor, and had been partly hidden by a jutting tongue of land. Terrified, then, by the imminence of the danger, and finding it impossible to put off to sea, the pirates had preferred flight to fighting. . . .

... I felt myself grasped by the arm, and found that Than-Sing had followed me to the after-deck.

"Look! look!" said he. "Do you see the three boats yonder?" I looked, and there indeed were three boats rounding a point of land, and making directly toward us. . . . Dreading lest his Chinese dress should mislead our friends, I entreated him to keep out of sight; which he did, willingly.

. . . I rushed to the prow . . . I pulled off my cap – I waved it wildly to and fro – I tried to shout aloud, and immediately a prolonged "Hurrah!" broke from every lip, and told me that a crew of English sailors were our deliverers! They waved their hats in reply to my signal; then bent to their oars again, and cleft the waters as an arrow cleaves the air.

They had recognized me now, and we were saved at last!

FANNY LOVIOT
A Lady's Captivity among Chinese Pirates in the Chinese Seas (1858)
Trans. Amelia B. Edwards

c. 1854

The Ancient Families

The people of Macao interested Dr. Melchior Yvan and he spent some time visiting a Portuguese family there. Dr. Yvan was the physician with a French Scientific Expedition to China.

Macao may be described as a combination of two towns, the one Chinese, the other Portuguese; the latter ... has been named by its founders, *Cidade do Santo-Nome-de-Deos de Macao*, and when one becomes acquainted with the spot on which it stands, one cannot but wonder by what miracle of labour a city was ever erected on such a barren, rocky place, the streets, houses, and quays being all built amongst huge blocks of detached granite, deep ravines and hills; the patient industry of the Chinese has overcome all these obstacles, and notwithstanding the enormous sums amassed by the English at Hong-Kong, Macao is in the present day the most *European* of all the cities in this part of the world; it cannot be denied that the streets are narrow and crooked, but they are, at the same time, very clean and airy, their deficiency in width sheltering them from the burning heat of the sun, and their numerous windings favouring the free circulation of air; in short, the Portuguese have certainly made the most of the spot conceded to them by the parsimonious Chinese.

Most of the houses have but two stories, the facade and interior walls being built of brick, while the stairs and roof are of wood; the rooms are ventilated by large windows, and protected from the glare of the sun by long blinds, similar to those used in Spain and Portugal. Although the European Macaists have been connected for more than three centuries with the Chinese, they do not seem to have borrowed anything from them – in architecture they have not adopted a single ornament or arrangement which recalls the taste or customs of the latter nation, whilst, in their mode of furnishing, they appear to have scrupulously avoided all resemblance to them; this is particularly manifested in the luxurious air of their apartments, the passages and the white walls of their saloons being covered with frightful pictures, French and English curiosities of doubtful taste, all of which seem to be preferred by them to any of the beautiful articles manufactured at Sou-Tchou-Fou, Canton, or Ning-Po.

There is something curious in the appearance of the Portuguese streets here, for the European buildings seem exclusively tenanted by Chinese merchants and workmen: one might almost fancy that the original inhabitants had departed and had been replaced by Asiatics; wherever any kind of merchandize is to be seen, or the sound of an anvil or saw is to be heard – wherever the shop of a tailor, shoe-maker, painter, or smith is visible, the industrious son of the celestial empire is sure to be recognised. As to the Portuguese Macaists, they remain quietly in their houses, employing themselves in various in-door occupations, men and women alike awaiting the approach of evening to issue forth from their habitations. These poor people have an idea that it is derogatory to their dignity to learn any useful trade, and being the descendants of sailors and illustrious adventurers, would willingly assume the importance of their ancestors; but, unfortunately, their once-prosperous condition has shared the same fate as their political position in Europe; their merchants carry on but very little commerce, the navigation of their sailors is confined to coast-trade, and the ardent spirits, who desire

MACAO HARBOUR

nothing better than to engage in exciting adventures, are reduced to the smuggling of opium on the coasts of Fo-Kien and Shang-Hai: there is, however, one profession, viz. – that of printing, which forms an exception to their general ideas of usefulness; but the misfortune is, that at Macao but few persons can be employed in it; the Chino-Portuguese town is as celebrated for this art, as Paris once was for its noble manufacture of glass.

Almost all the Portuguese inhabitants of Macao were born in the city itself, and as most of the ancient families intermarried with the Asiatics and Africans, the origin of their descendants is of a very mixed nature . . . one remarkable circumstance with regard to this heterogeneous mass of population is, that the members of one family rarely bear the slightest resemblance to each other, and now and then there reappears amongst them a striking likeness to some one long since dead and forgotten.

I used often to go and visit a Portuguese family residing at Macao, near Praia-Manduco; they were the undoubted descendants of the ancient conquerors, and their European origin was universally acknowledged; these good people lived in a little cottage of one story, and the family consisted of six persons, the mother, two sons, and three daughters; the latter, who bore the names of Mariana, Maria, and Monica, were all as opposite in appearance as possible; Mariana was a white negress, with rather woolly hair, thick lips, coarse features, high cheek bones, and a pale face: Monica, on the contrary, had the dark rich tint of the Andalusian, the upper lip covered with a light down, and remarkably beautiful hair; as to the third, she was as yellow as amber, more resembling the women seen on the shores of the Ganges than her sisters; the two sons were thoroughly Chinese. . . .

As may readily be imagined, the education of both sexes is very much neglected here, and the means of obtaining instruction extremely limited . . .

I need scarcely say, that with such a neglected state of education, the amusements and conversation of the natives are not very interesting; in his own house the Portuguese reads little, yawns a great deal, and fans himself the whole of the day, while his wife in a light style of *déshabillé* seats herself behind the blind, and with her fan in her hand, and a cigarette or a morsel of *arec-nut* in her mouth, gazes listlessly at the passers-by, who are not very numerous in the quiet streets.

DR. YVAN
Six Months among the Malays and a Year in China (1855)

1856

Turbid Waters

After four years' service in the colony, naval officer Henry Ellis had come to dislike Hong Kong society.

The English residents at Hong Kong, like many other small communities, were divided by exclusive feelings, which rendered society far less agreeable than it might have been had a better understanding existed among them. As each little coterie was headed by its own peculiar lady patroness, it was a difficult matter to find any half-dozen who would meet any other half-dozen, without their evincing mutual marks of contempt or dislike. Naval officers, as a rule, mixed but little with them, and caring as little who sank or who swam in these turbid waters, had the best opportunity of judging of the game, which was often more amusing than edifying. The most absurd part of this purse-proud stuck-up-ism, was that with the exception of a few Government *employés*, they were all more or less rowing in the same boat, *i.e.*, striving to amass as many dollars as opportunity would admit of; and though some were called merchants, and others storekeepers, such was the undercurrent of retail speculation, that it was hard to define where one batch ended and the other began. Nay, even for those who were not supposed to be personally engaged in commercial pursuits, the chance of a little *private pidgin* (as we used to call it) possessed irresistible charms, and the grandeur of their position was not sufficient to deter them from competing secretly with their fellow colonists who were openly in business, and consequently beyond the pale of "good society."

HENRY T. ELLIS
Hong Kong to Manilla (1859)

65

1858

Dreadful Dens

George Wingrove Cooke was Special Correspondent for The Times in China when, at the end of the Second Opium War, Canton fell to British and French troops. In company with an Allied search party Cooke set out to rescue any Europeans being held in Canton's gaols.

It was not until our second day's search that we were able to discover the prison in which Europeans had been confined. Threats, and a night in the guard-house, at last forced the discovery from the mandarin or gaol inspector in our custody. It is called the Koon Khan, is in the eastern part of the city, and is distinguishable from the others only in that it is surrounded by a high brick wall. Nearly the whole of our second day was passed in this place. It has only one yard, and into this the prisoners are not allowed to come. . . . Opening from this yard are four rooms, each containing four dens. The hardest and most malignant face I ever saw is that of the chief gaoler of this prison. The prisoners could not be brought to look upon him, and when he was present could not be induced to say that he was a gaoler at all, or that they had ever seen him before. But when he was removed they always reiterated their first story, "The other gaolers only starve and ill-treat us, but that man eats our flesh."

How, step by step, we followed up our inquiries, and how we cast about hither and thither for a clue, and at last found one, which was often lost and refound, would be too long to tell. Mr. Parkes conducted this business with a vigour and intelligence that cannot be over-estimated. At first they had never heard of a foreigner; then a heavy box on the ears administered by one of the orderlies, in punishment for a threat to a prisoner, produced a recollection of *one* European prisoner. Then the gaolers were roughly handled in sight of the prisoners, and, together with the mandarin, were taken out in custody of the soldiers.

Gradually the prisoners began to give credence to what we said – that we were now the mandarins of Canton, and could protect them if they spoke out. One produced a monkey-jacket from his sleeping-place at the back of the den; another had an old jersey; all of them soon had stories to tell. Many of the prisoners had been inmates of the place for many years, and upon reference to the books we found that they were all originally placed here for very trifling crimes. Old stories get mixed up with new; the difficulties of Chinese dialects come into play, and we often fancied we were unravelling some sanguinary iniquity of yesteryear, when we found at last that it was two or three, or even ten, years old. It is only by small degrees that the collated evidence of these vermin-bitten witnesses is made to assume some form and consistency. It appears at last almost certain that six Chinese were beheaded last night, their fate being, in all probability, precipitated by our visit to the other prisons. It also appears quite certain that, within a period dating from the commencement of the present troubles, six Europeans, two Frenchmen, and four Englishmen, have found their death in these dreadful dens. Many different prisoners, examined separately, deposed to this fact, and almost to the same details. The European victims were kept here for several months, herding with the Chinese, eating of that same black mess of rice which looks and smells like a bucket of grains cast forth from a brewery. When their time came – probably the time necessary for a reply from Pekin – the gaoler held their heads back while poison was poured down their throats. The prisoners recollected two who threw up the poison – and they were strangled. We asked how they knew it was poison. There was no doubt on this score. It is a curious circumstance, illustrative of the prostrate state of terror that exists here, that the gaoler's fowls scratch about, untouched, among all the famishing men within the Canton prison, and feed upon the vermin. It was remarked that the fowls fed upon the vomit of these two Europeans, and died.

Only two of these prisoners had excited much sympathy among the Chinese. One of them was a sailor, who spoke the language, adapted himself to their habits, and told them stories. He was cheerful, or pretended to be cheerful, at first; but in a short time he grew sick, and cried, and spoke of his friends far away. Even the Chinese were sorry when his time came, and when the gaolers poisoned him. There was another, an old white bearded man, who was there some months. He spoke only a few words of Chinese, but the Chinese veneration for age came to his aid, and they pitied him also.

Some of us thought that this must have been poor Cooper, the owner of the docks at Whampoa, who, probably mistaken for his son, was kidnapped from his chop boat, lying within a hundred yards of the *Sybille*. His wife and daughter were on board with him. A sanpan came alongside with a letter. While he leaned forward to take it he was drawn into the sanpan, and he was away up a creek before the alarm could be given and a boat lowered from the man-of-war.

The others, we were told, were not favourites. They could not speak, they held themselves aloof. If two of them happened to be in prison at the same time they conversed together. If there was only one, he either fought with the gaolers or sat alone covering his face with his hands.

It is, I suppose, contrary to our principle and our policy, and the custom of civilized nations when a city has been taken by assault, to punish these acts; but we stretched a point. We carried away the principal gaoler and the secretary – two terrible ruffians, the head and the hand of this iniquity; and we also carried away the prisoners who had given us trustworthy information, but we only took them as witnesses, and lodged them in our guard-house.

GEORGE WINGROVE COOKE
China: being "The Times" Special Correspondence from China in the Years 1857–58
(1858)

1859

Flesh and Blood

William Poyntz was a twenty-one-year-old officer with the British troops stationed at Canton. By his account the arrival of British justice did nothing to reduce the level of violence usual in Cantonese administration.

In the course of duty as adjutant I have had to be present at severe floggings of both soldiers and sailors, but never did I see such punishment as was meted out to a wretched Chinaman, who had been found selling "samshu" (a most vile spirit, made from rice) to our men. The strictest orders had been issued against it, and this fellow well deserved what he got, as he was one of several who had a special permit and pass to enter our lines to sell anything but liquor. The provost-marshall, Captain Usher, of my battalion, just the man for the billet, ordered him fifty lashes. His flogging staff consisted of two very fine young men, boatswain's mates, belonging to H.M.S. "Hornet," attached to the army for castigatory purposes. One of them, Angel (what a misnomer under the circumstances), was left-handed, the other right-handed, so that each dozen was inflicted crosswise. The effect was terrible. Some of the culprit's countrymen were present, and I don't think any of them afterwards similarly risked their backs. When the ordeal was over, the poor Celestial's tail was cut off, the worst punishment, in a social point of view, that can be, as it is what happens in the case of men convicted as "laliloons" or robbers.

A still more dreadful scene I witnessed at another time, but one, indeed, thoroughly deserved also and ordered by the Emperor himself, with the sanction of the Allied Commissioners. . . . the population living alongside the rivers are almost one and all pirates, noted for cruel atrocities. In this case the nineteen Chinamen who were executed had, in collusion with the captain and crew of a Portuguese merchant ship (many of which dealt largely in a slave trade as bad as ever was practised in Africa), invited some of the inhabitants of a village to come on board and take a look round the vessel. Having enticed them below, the hatches were immediately battened down, the anchor got up at once, and off to sea they went with their live cargo; all will allow a most abominable and cold-blooded proceeding. On the morning of the execution, just after our old Plymouth friends, the 67th Regiment, had landed at Canton, in October, 1859, we asked them to breakfast with us, several of their officers, as well as our own and others, went down to the execution ground to see the sentence carried out. Certainly our hearts were hardened by the rascality the wretches had been guilty of to their own flesh and blood. The first to arrive there were the two executioners, tall, strong, young men, about three or four and twenty. Their swords were long, clumsy, heavy, and sharp; they let us take them in our hands and inspect them; evidently the fellows were nervous. In a few minutes the head of the procession entered the yard, which had a very high wall all round it. First came a few soldiers with all sorts of weapons, then the prisoners and various officers with flags, followed by mandarins of different grades and buttons in sedan chairs, with two bearers each. Lastly, the chief magistrate, a high native official, with four

EXECUTION AT CANTON

bearers. In front of him were carried placards, on which was published the crime for which the prisoners were to suffer, and the Emperor's order and sentence; a few more soldiers brought up the rear. There was no confusion whatever, and all quietly took their allotted positions. I ought to have mentioned that the nineteen culprits were each seated in a sort of round basket, suspended from a pole, and carried in the usual way between the shoulders of two coolies, their wrists alone being fastened with a cord behind their backs. An official, probably clerk to the justices, read out the sentence. The poor wretches on arrival had been tilted out of the baskets, and were set up in a kneeling position in two ranks, ten in the first, and nine in the second, at a half face to the left. An executioner stood at the head of each line, and at a given signal both commenced. Not a single flinch was visible, though the feelings of each man at seeing the head immediately in front of him coming off, and his own fate so close, without hope of reprieve, must have been terrible. Certainly nothing could have been easier than their decapitation . . . for each head went off like a tulip. When the execution was over, the procession moved away in as systematic and orderly a manner as on its arrival. It is a universal feature among Orientals how callous they seem to death, and yet in some ways what cowards they are. I was informed that it is customary on such occasions to drug the prisoners with opium and samshu; but certainly in this instance there was no appearance of insensibility to what was taking place, though I have no doubt some must have been administered.

MAJOR W.H. POYNTZ
Per Mare Per Terram (1892)

1859

Paper Horses

Peter George Laurie and a friend went to pay their respects to the late Governor of Canton, Pei-quei, who was lying in state at the palace.

As we entered the outer wall of the Yamun a huge gong sounded in our ears, reverberating throughout the entire palace, and my companion being a visitor of some distinction we soon heard a shuffling of feet, and observed numerous half naked figures hastily thrusting themselves into their jackets. In the midst of the confusion the aide-de-camp to the late Governor sallied forth, stationed himself at the head of the steps, and awaited our approach. He was without doubt the most filthy, dirty, villainous looking creature I thought I had ever set eyes on. His clothes were filthy, and so was himself, and the hair upon his head, which could not have been shaved for many months, was bristling up like quills upon the fretful porcupine. "You would not have thought," said my companion, "that only a short time since that man was a most pleasant and gentlemanly looking personage." "No," I said, scarcely able to repress a smile, "I certainly should not. He looks to me more like a long-haired Nanking rebel than an aide-de-camp to a Governor." "He cannot shave his head," said my friend, "he is in mourning." "And he cannot change his clothes?" "No, he is in mourning." "And can he not wash himself?" "No! certainly not, he is in mourning." Thus a man who is in mourning cannot change his clothing, shave or even wash himself, sometimes for months together, and this in a climate where it is absolutely necessary for decency and saintliness, to say nothing of comfort, to change one's raiment at least two or three times a day. A man may not perform these very necessary operations, but he may eat and drink and be merry; he may talk, and laugh, and gamble, and smoke opium as much as ever he likes. These observances are ordained in the Book of Rites . . . After having duly saluted us, the aide-de-camp escorted us into a small chamber, in which were about twenty human beings, all very dirty, but not half as dirty as the aide-de-camp. In his case excess of dirt showed excess of grief. In an inner chamber were two or three beings smoking opium, whom our presence and the terrific sound of the gong had not even had the effect of arousing. Tea was brought as usual in the little tiny cups, and it was fearfully hot and full of tea-leaves and some preserves, the like of which I had never tasted before. We were at a loss here to possess ourselves of these preserves, there being no implements of any description supplied to us for that purpose. The aide-de-camp observed our discomfiture, and intimated to us that he could not accommodate us with knives and forks, as all the late governor's plate was packed up; but he procured some little bits of sticks, which we thrust into the preserves and so hoisted them into our mouths. When he mentioned the knives and forks, we could not help smiling and looking at one another. The aide-de-camp observed this, and immediately assured us that such was indeed the case, that they actually were possessed of knives and forks ... My face had become fearfully red, from walking and exposure to the sun: the Chinese are under the impression that we consider it very handsome to be red (they call us "red devils") and the aide-de-camp, therefore, conveyed to me through the interpreter, that he considered me excessively handsome, my face being so beautifully red.

We now formed in grand procession, and traversing long corridors and halls were escorted solemnly to the spot where lay the last remains of the great Pei-quei. In these halls were a great number of white paper horses waiting to convey his spirit aloft. By the time we approached the sanctuary, a large number of priests had hastily donned their long white garments and stood in their places; some mournful squeaky music also struck up, with which the priests mingled their voices. These priests, according to the great Book of Rites, should never leave the body, either morning or night, but they are in reality only in attendance when strangers arrive; the moment the strangers disappear, the priests disappear too. The coffin in which Pei-quei's remains repose, although singularly plain and simple in appearance, cost two thousand dollars or nearly five hundred pounds. The little sanctuary in which it reposes is most profusely decorated with flowers and scrolls and long streamers, all telling of the many virtues, the high qualities and attainments of the late Governor. Before the coffin, was spread out upon a profusely decorated table, a series of comestibles of the most costly and dainty description. The table was laid out for him just as though he were still alive and able

73

to partake of these luxuries: even the chop-sticks which he had been wont to use were not wanting. It was to show the real appreciation in which they held him, that even in death no selfish notion entered their breasts. . . . We returned in the same solemn procession, the aide-de-camp leading the way. Ere we had reached one-half the length of the corridor, the music suddenly ceased, and the priests might have been seen all shuffling away from the spot. Two minutes later, and they might have been seen half naked and lying about the floor, just like ordinary Chinamen, and with nothing but their shaven heads to show their holy calling. As we were leaving a little boy almost in rags, and shockingly dirty, came up and shook hands with us. He was a nephew of Pei-quei's, and had a very pleasing smiling face – the dirt and the rags were only mourning.

P.G.L. (PETER GEORGE LAURIE)
A Reminiscence of Canton (1866)

1859

True Feelings

Although Augustus F. Lindley was later to join the Taiping rebels in their fight against the Manchus, his adventures really began when he first arrived on the China coast as a ship's officer. Here he met the beautiful Marie, who was only sixteen.

After some voyages upon the coast, my vessel was ordered to Whampoa, to be dry-docked and her bottom overhauled. Before entering the dock, and while lying at anchor on the river, I was one evening surprised to see a san-pan . . . containing two Chinese girls, and a third, neither Chinese nor European, hanging about the ship; its occupants evidently desirous to communicate something, yet half fearful to venture. The lady of the unknown nationality seemed endeavouring to attract my attention. I was alone on the quarter-deck, with the exception of an old weather-beaten quartermaster. I beckoned her to come alongside, and descended the gangway ladder. As I was going over the side, the old quartermaster came up to me and exclaimed –

"Keep your weather eye lifting, sir; she's a pi-ar Portuguee."

"Well," I replied; "what if she is?"

"Well, d'ye see, sir, them Portuguee's is awful wild . . . "

"You're out of your reckoning for once, quartermaster; call Mr.____, if I am not on board by eight bells;" and with this I disappeared over the side.

Directly I jumped into the boat, it was shoved off, and dropped astern with the tide.

My attention was, of course, directed to the lady designated a "pi-ar Portuguee" by the quartermaster; I at once discovered that she was a Macao Portuguese, very handsome; and, to all appearances, in great affliction. For some time she made no reply to my inquiries as to what was the matter, but commenced sobbing, and crying as if her heart would break. At last she ceased, and related the cause of her trouble to

75

the following effect:- She was the daughter of a rich Macanese, who was principal owner of one of the Whampoa docks, and was also Portuguese consul at that port. Her mother was dead, and her father had determined to compel her to marry a wealthy Chilianian half-caste; in fact, everything was arranged for the marriage to take place in ten days' time. She hated the fellow, in spite of his dollars, which, it appeared, was her father's idol, and was re-solved to suffer anything rather than submit. She came off to my ship to try and obtain a passage down to Hong-Kong, where she had friends who would take care of her. . . .

The longer I listened the more interested and determined to help her I became. She was very young, and it seemed irresistible to sympathize with and pity her. At last, in the midst of a protestation of assistance on my part, and of fervent thanks on hers, we were interrupted by one of the China girls thrusting her head under the mat cover of the boat, and exclaiming –

CANTONESE BOAT-WOMAN

"Hi ya! missee! more bettah go shore, – belong shih tim cheong" (ten o'clock).

The poor girl seemed quite alarmed to find it so late, and told the boatwomen to pull ashore as fast as possible.

We soon reached the bank, but my interesting friend would not allow me to land with her, stating she lived close by; however, she promised to meet me at the spot we then occupied, the next evening. The China girls quickly pulled me off to my ship, and then I was alone to think over the singularity and probable issue of the adventure.

. . . True to her promise, she saw me the following evening; then the next; and so for several consecutive days. It happened that, fortunately for the fulfilment of our appointments, Marie's father never returned from the docks, at the opposite side of the river, till late in the evening. We were thus constantly thrown together, and who can wonder that we insensibly allowed ourselves to become deeply attached?

Upon the ninth day after our first meeting, my ship was undocked, and prepared to sail for Hong-Kong in the morning; the morning, too, that, as Marie told me with tears in her eyes, would usher in her bridal day. Although Marie and I had never till then spoken of love, we both knew that it was mutual, and at this moment of peril and uncertainty we threw off all disguise and expressed our true feelings for each other. She felt no regret at sacrificing all other ties for my sake – I was but too anxious to risk anything to save her. On the evening of this, the last day that was to separate us, Marie entered her cruel father's dwelling for the last time; and, having quickly made some slight preparations, rejoined me in the boat with which I awaited her.

This boat was the same in which I had first seen her, and the poor girls who worked it being slaves of one of the old Whampoa laundresses, I determined to rescue them from their doubtful future, and prevent them making any disclosure as to Marie's escape, by carrying them down to Hong-Kong with her, and there giving them liberty.

I had already made every preparation on board, and had taken the gunner and carpenter into my confidence, as I had decided to stow them away in the sail-room; and to do this rendered it necessary for them to pass the berths of those officers. About midnight, sending the quarter-master of the watch off the deck upon an errand to get him out of the way, I smuggled the girls aboard and secreted them at the back of the sail-room well hidden by spare topsails, &c., piled up before them.

Early in the morning we lighted fires, and soon after daybreak, with steam up, commenced to get under weigh. Just then, as I fully expected, off came Marie's father and the old laundress . . . with warrants from the British consul for the delivery of the three girls if found on board. I was in charge of the deck, and took care to receive the bereaved parties at the gangway. After hearing their complaints, I reported the case to the captain, and received his orders to have the ship searched. This duty I took upon myself, rousing all hands out, and searching every part of the ship except the sail-room, which I took care to allow no one to approach. By the time the unsuccessful search was concluded, the anchor had been weighed, and we immediately commenced to drop down the river.

When we reach Hong-Kong, Marie landed and went to reside with her friends. She had become my betrothed, and seemed truly happy in the thought that nothing now could cause our separation.

LIN-LE (A.F. LINDLEY)
Ti-ping Tien-kwoh (1866)

1864–65

Cruel Climate

Service in northern China and Japan had undermined the health of
Lieutenant Thomas Lyster, Royal Engineers. He was invalided to
Hong Kong and when partially recovered was sent across to Kowloon
to take charge of government building works there. These letters were
to his sister in Ireland, the second letter being written just two months
before he died, aged twenty-five, on the troopship returning to Britain.

[Hong Kong]
December 28th, 1864

. . . I will soon, please God, be with you all again; the time is rapidly
approaching when I shall say farewell to China. All my friends are going
one by one . . . The 9th Regiment will soon be here. I suppose your
friend Mrs. C. will be with it. There are lots of ladies here. It is not a
bad place for them for a short time, but very bad for a continuance. The
children here look awfully pale and delicate. Many of the soldiers are
sending home their children by a government ship which is going next
month. There has been any amount of house-breaking and robberies
going on here lately. The Chinese are the most audacious robbers; they
will steal your teeth almost. What do you think of their getting into a
barrack-room and stealing the men's arms while they were asleep, some
time ago? I was at Whampoa, a place on the Canton river, about forty
miles from here, shooting, a few days ago. We (a party of four)
breakfasted with an Englishman who is in charge of the docks there, and
we were admiring his house, which was nearly new and very nicely
furnished, one of the prettiest houses I have seen for some time. I heard
yesterday that the preceding night the house had been broken into by
an armed gang, who got hold of the Chinese nurse and child (the
gentleman and his wife were here at the time). The ruffians drew a knife
across the child's throat so as to cut the skin, to try to frighten the old

woman into telling where the dollars were – which she could not do, as the gentleman had taken all his treasure to Hong-Kong the day before. They then broke everything in the house. It is satisfactory to know that one of them was killed and several wounded by the watchman. When I go out far into the country I shall certainly take a revolver with me for safety, as this time of year it is even dangerous on the island. (Did you know that Hong-Kong is an island? Some people don't.) When you write again, tell me what you think of China – what your ideas are of the people, and what you would like from China. Choose from these – Peach-stone bracelets carved; ditto brooches; carved ivories, such as bracelets, brooches, chess-men, &c.; sandalwood boxes, fans: I have been out so long that my taste has become quite vitiated, and I can't tell what things are most appreciated by ladies. The paternal Government has required me to repay £53 too much received. I am sure I don't know how – but must obey. However, it is of little consequence, although it is the price of a good horse or gun at home. . . .

[Kowloon]
June 27, 1865

You see I am still in my blissful abode! It is a shame if they keep me four years in this cruel climate. Nell talks of my being *baked!* That is not the word to describe one's sensations here; *boiled* or *stewed* is more like it. No matter how hot it is, you have the feeling of being in a vapour bath, and everything around you is damp and mildewed. The salt on the table every morning is saturated. All those nice gloves you sent me are spoiled, although they were put away in the recesses of my drawers. This is splendid weather for bathing – but alas, what was once my delight I cannot now venture on!

The Chinese sing most wonderful songs, and play some really pretty tunes on an instrument like a guitar. I wish I was musical enough to keep them in my head and write them for you. I am sure you would imitate them capitally. Their minstrels are generally blind. Opposite to where I lived in Hong-Kong a woman used to sing for hours at a time in a loud, melancholy voice: all her tunes ended in a plaintive quavering ā, ā, āā. One can purchase musical boxes here which play the Chinese tunes. I will try to get one, or get the music of their tunes written by some one, if it can be done. I expect they will be written backwards, or upside down if that is possible. Shuttlecock is a favourite game here; but the Chinese play with their feet. . . .

A case of forcible abduction occurred last night in the Chinese village under my quarters, or rather in the bay opposite the village. Some Chinamen in a boat attacked another boat, knocked the proprietor on the head, shied him overboard, and took away the boat with his wife and sister-in-law in it. However, they were pursued by the other boats and the ladies recovered. This occurred close to the police boat, which did not move for half an hour afterwards.

The thieves came a few nights ago, and stole my groom's clothes out of his room, although there was a European sentry, ten yards off, on my quarters. They have also been tampering with the locks of the treasury. The Cantonese are certainly the princes of thieves. I sent some of my valuable things to an Artillery fellow to keep for me, as I had no locks on my drawers, the thieves having stolen them. He actually left the box open! and a gold chain and three gold rings which I got at Tientsin were stolen.

The country must look beautiful now. How I wish I could see it – and those violets and primroses! I don't know when I saw a cowslip last! What would I not give for one week of the weather you are having now? If I were only two months at home, I am sure I should be quite well again.

THOMAS LYSTER
With Gordon in China (1891)
Ed. E.A. Lyster

c. 1868

The Stripling Missionary

The city of Fatshan, a dozen miles from Canton, had a population of half a million people. It was "real" China, where no foreigner had ever lived until Thomas Selby arrived to establish a Mission.

To gain a footing in this burly, bustling place was a task of uncommon difficulty. It is outside the boundaries within which Europeans have treaty rights of residence. Neither trader nor missionary has any legal foothold there. The Consular officials at that time were opposed to our settlement, and never lifted a finger to help us. Local opposition was virulent, and the place had a bad name for its treatment of foreigners. . . .

Most travellers who had passed through Fatshan came home with thrilling stories of hair-breadth escapes from the exasperated mob. Many a worthy Englishman has passed a bad half hour in getting through this narrow neck of water-way out on to the larger rivers to which it leads. . . . The older missionaries were sympathetic, though sceptical, about the feasibility of residing in this notorious place. An old tobacco warehouse, the back entrance of which was approached by water, was to be my dwelling-house. At the back door an old boat-woman had put up a wooden pigsty, which was reconstructed about twenty times after my orders for its removal had been twenty times obeyed, for two or three days. With the thermometer often steady at ninety in the shade the smell was sickening. Two doors away there was a starch factory, where tubs of sour, soaking grain were put out upon the roof day and night. We did need a sanitary inspector there to right things and make life worth living; but it had to be borne for six long years, till the improved tone of Chinese feeling made it possible to build a pleasant little bungalow on the outskirts of the town. The ceilings were low, the air stifling, and the warehouse so void of windows or inlets for the breeze that in the summer months it was necessary to erect a mat wind-sail over a tiny skylight to allure a whiff of fresh air down into this rambling dungeon of heat and suffocation. One room had to serve as study, refectory, bed-chamber; and for years I slept on a camp-bed, which was taken down every morning and put up, with the necessary mosquito-nets, every night. That was no great hardship. For a time I chafed under some of the disabilities of my lot, but they were trifling and a light price to pay for the sake of securing a foothold for our mission in this difficult centre. The only real pain I endured was that of solitude, and the weekly visits of pleasant missionary colleagues from Canton only made the pain the sharper when I was left alone again.

The main question was, Would the people tolerate my stay in their midst? Upon the evening of the day of my arrival the faithful native catechist, who had been stationed there four or five years, came to take me a short walk, for in tropical climates, if health is to be maintained, exercise is a religious duty. The most serious disadvantage of my position was that I had a mile and a half to walk through streets, hot in a double sense, before I could get sight of a green leaf or a blade of grass or paddy. At the close of my first walk I plumed myself on the fact that the people were making an early discovery of my virtue and trustworthiness, and said to the catechist, "The people receive me more quietly than I should have thought"; and he replied, with a peculiar nasal grunt by which he was accustomed to hyphen his words, "Their mouths are not angry, but their hearts are." It was not long before I found out that mouths, hearts, and hands rivalled each other in spitefulness and rage. Untranslatable epithets were hurled at me as I passed through the streets, and the epithets were sometimes followed by other things. "Beat," "Kill," "Knife" were everyday cries, and I felt I was getting on wonderfully well when I was called nothing worse than "foreign devil." Sometimes shopkeepers would set their dogs at me as I walked, and I had to keep a pack of five or six at bay with a stout Penang lawyer. If Chinese dogs had possessed as much spirit as English dogs the situation might have been serious. The crowd would sometimes follow the stripling missionary from the preaching-room to his house, and continue pounding and hammering on his outer door for half an hour together. Now and again it seemed as though they would break through, and there would be nothing for it but to get out by the back door, which opened on to the creek, and take a boat to Canton.

The irritation and annoyance endured at the hands of the street-mob often outweighed the gain to health from the evening walk. The student-missionary would then have to take his regulation exercise on a platform, eight or ten feet square, put up on the roof for drying clothes. . . .

After this exhilarating recreation on the house-top the student-missionary would go down to mosquitoes, suffocation, and a three hours' Turkish-bath study of the Chinese language by lamplight. Bed-time would bring no reprieve from torment and nervous depression, for the nights were broken and sleepless. It was necessary to have every door and window open, and the thud of the watchman's stroke as he sounded the divisions of time at frequent intervals till daylight, the shrieky music of a singing girl at some neighbouring place of dissipation, the shouts of a gambling party on an adjoining verandah, the stamp of the rice-hulling, the clamour of boatmen coming down with the tide, the cry of canoe-paddling hawkers taking round samshoo, bean-curd, sugar-cane, oranges to the flower-boats, would all get on to the callow missionary's nerves and breed nightmares of riot, violence, and disastrous failure. . . .

For two years there was very little to encourage, and we had to be content with rejoicing in the success of our London Mission neighbours, two or three miles away, where work was carried on by two native evangelists. But in a year of great trouble the first beginnings of prosperity appeared. The Tientsin massacre had just occurred, and a London Mission chapel in Fatshan, built entirely by native contributions, had been burned to the ground. All work was suspended, preaching halls closed, country journeys indefinitely postponed . . . After a temporary retirement to Canton, during which time the native preacher had nobly continued at his post, I ventured back again, and my English colleague, whose missionary service and experience was greater than mine, resumed his weekly visit. Our first convert, a fan artist and ornamental penman, was baptized on Chinese New Year's Day. . . . From that time, small, though none the less welcome increases attended the labours of each succeeding year, and before I left that sphere for another a little church of thirty communicants had been gathered together. . . .

Work in Fatshan was varied by occasional visits to two or three out-lying districts, from which the tide of emigration had set to Australia and to the Pacific coast of America, and to which in due time the tide returned in diminished volume. . . .

In the villages dotting these two or three districts, returned emigrants are as thick as blackberries, and every third man on the road makes free to accost the missionary as "John." The most common of all English oaths has become acclimatized in many of the villages, the "G" being modified into a "K" and the "d" into a "t" in accommodation to the limits of a Chinaman's enunciation. I have heard boys who had never seen a foreigner use these two profane monosyllables in their play; and once as I was passing a Chinaman's door, when his dog came yelping at my heels, the owner proved his politeness by hurling the oath at the dog. The dog was evidently as well indoctrinated in the profane watch-word as the boys, for it covered up its teeth and retired without a sign. Some traces of the emigrant life in these villages are pathetic and heart-stirring. The Chinese cabbage-growers and laundrymen in Australia often marry English and Irish wives. When they come back to China for good, they leave their wives behind, possibly because the European women are unwilling to come to China, or because there are Chinese wives and concubines to whom they would have to submit. But the Chinaman generally brings back his sons, if children of that valued sex have been born to him in the land of his sojourn. I have seen a boy playing in one of these villages who had round blue eyes, flaxen hair plaited into the usual pig-tail, and scarcely a trace of the Mongolian in his features. He had forgotten the little English he knew, went to the village school with other boys, and was being trained an idolater. I remember seeing another boy who had just reached the village home of his Chinese father, and who could scarcely speak a word to his companions and playmates. One night I was staying in a small town, and a Chinaman brought his half-caste boy to see me. A letter had recently come to hand from the boy's mother in Australia, whom he would never see again, and no one in the place could read a word of it. "Would I translate the letter, so that the boy might know what his mother wished to say to him, and be assured of her continued thought and care?" Some years after, when my work was taken up by other missionaries, cases were now and again heard of in which the foreign wife had returned with her Chinese husband, and was trying to fit herself to the climate, the food, the drudgery, the irksomeness and frequent cruelty of a Chinese household. . . .

For some years previous to my first visit, emigrant converts returning from Australia and the Pacific Coast had passed through the city of Canton, presented their credentials of baptism to the missionaries, and had then disappeared into these far-off villages. Once or twice a native catechist had been sent to visit the scattered Christians, and to find out if anything could be done towards gathering them into churches. But

IN THE COUNTRYSIDE

the villages and hamlets in which they lived were miles away from the river, and only three or four men had been seen. My first journey did not promise much. The patois was so peculiar that the Cantonese dialect was imperfectly understood, and for every man upon whom I paid a pastoral call I had to tramp an average of fifteen or twenty miles. The crowds rushing together to see a foreigner, when I had managed to find the spoor of a returned convert, made suitable counsel and encouragement almost impossible. Not infrequently I was baffled in my inquiries. Upon asking if So-and-So lived in the village, I was met with the answer, "No one of that name here." The person giving this disappointing reply was probably uncle or first cousin of the lost sheep I was seeking, and had been in conversation with him ten minutes ago. Perhaps there was a suspicion that the emigrant kinsman had forgotten to pay a bill in the land of his pilgrimage, or had transgressed some eccentric law current across the seas, or had entered into schemes that might implicate his village, and this poky foreigner must be balked and sent back upon his own business. . . . It was no easy task to discover these scattered disciples. At the first visit, three or four only were seen, and at the second visit six or seven, and these in their turn introduced me to others. Most of them had lost ground in the spiritual life, and grown indifferent. One had relapsed into opium-smoking, and another, a partner in a rice shop, had done what is comparatively rare amongst Chinese converts, gone back to the worship of idols. With these few exceptions, the men had kept themselves aloof from the current superstitions; and wayside testimonies from strangers were sometimes given to the fidelity of those we were going to seek.

THOMAS G. SELBY
Chinamen at Home (1900)

1869

Luxurious Quarters

John Thomson, a pioneer photographer from Scotland, was amazed at the standard of living enjoyed by the foreign community in Hong Kong; but he saw, too, just how perilous life here could be.

Europeans in Hongkong live in a very expensive style; much more expensively, one would think, than they need do, when we consider that many of the necessaries of life are to be had at prices very little in advance of our market rates at home.

Beer and wine, however, and the countless other little luxuries which one has to purchase at the European stores, make up a startling monthly bill; and, after all, the dollar which would be four shillings and sixpence in London is equal to little more than a shilling in Hongkong, in exchanging it for such commodities as are brought from home. The newly arrived resident may furnish his dwelling cheaply enough by buying at the constantly recurring auction sales of the householders who are leaving the colony; or else of a Chinese tradesman, who will fit up his house for him throughout at a comparatively moderate charge. But then servants are indispensable, and add greatly to the expense of living. The following is a list of those required for an ordinary family, where there are one or two children to be maintained:–

	Monthly Wages
Cook	10 dollars
Two chair-coolies	14 "
One nurse or amah	10 "
One house-boy	8 "
One house-coolie	7 "
	$49

... Then all the washing is done by a Chinese laundryman, whose charge is the same as we pay in London. As for the doctor, he will make

87

a contract to attend the family for an annual retaining fee, say forty pounds, or thereabouts, and no end of medicine has to be bought . . . The doctor is not supposed to have anything to do with the dispensing chemist; but, nevertheless, the enormous quantity of drugs ordered, and at times tossed out at the window by the patient, leads people to draw conclusions which are not always just. Rent would be about one hundred and forty pounds a year for such a house as may be obtained in London for sixty; and altogether, the expense of living in Hongkong may be fairly set down at something more than double what it is at home. . . .

Nothing surprised me more in Hongkong than the expensive way in which English assistants were housed, and the luxuries with which they were indulged. Indeed few more luxurious quarters were anywhere to be found than the "junior messes" of the wealthy British firms. There the unfledged youth, coming out from the simplicity of some rural home, was apt to develop into a man of epicurean tastes, a connoisseur in wines, and to become lavish in his expenditure; proud of his birthright, as a Briton; honest, hospitable, extravagant; despising meanness, and, alas! even thrift. This sort of education was not calculated to prepare the merchant of the future for the cheese-paring shifts of modern times, when markets are overstocked, when competition runs strong, when Chinese companies and German economy are set in array against us . . .

The climate of this quarter of the globe is for about six months of the year dry, with cool nights, and an almost cloudless sky; but when the hot weather and the rain come round, the sky seems to descend and rest like a sponge on the top of the hill; and this sponge, always full of moisture, is frequently squeezed over the town, and the rain falls in a sheet, and floods the streets and rises in hot vapour with the sun; books and papers become limp and mouldy, and the residents feel as in a vapour-bath . . .

I had for long been anxious to see a typhoon, and I had my wish gratified in Hongkong on more occasions than one. The strength of the wind at such times, is greater than I could ever have thought possible. It whirls ships helplessly adrift from the firmest moorings; and I have seen them emerge from the storm with canvas torn to shreds, spars carried away, and masts broken off nearly flush with the decks. In Hongkong the wind with a sudden blast has riven away the corners of houses, and sent projecting verandahs flying across the streets. During the height of the gale the residents for the most part shut themselves closely in their houses, carefully securing their windows and doors, and so remain with constant apprehension and dread, lest the dwelling should in a moment be swept away, and themselves entombed beneath the ruins. Once, while the storm was at its worst, I ventured down to the Praya . . . to see the crowd of Chinese boats and trading craft that had been blown inshore, and piled up in a mass of wreck just below the city . . . One or two intrepid foreigners had been there, and had rescued a large number of the natives, but many more had gone down with their boats. The sky was of dark leaden colour . . . the heavy stone-faced wall of the Praya had given way, and the great granite blocks of which it was composed had been washed in upon the road. Half blinded by the waves as they leapt over the road and dashed in angry foam against the houses, and leaning forward . . . to make headway against the tempest, I at length reached the east end of the settlement, where a number of foreigners were attempting to rescue two women from a small Chinese boat. These boatwomen were using the most desperate exertions to keep their tiny vessel in position, and to prevent it from being dashed to pieces against the breach in the Praya wall, where jagged blocks of stone were interspersed with the fragments of boats that had already been destroyed. So strong was the wind that . . . the tops of the waves were caught up by the tempest in its fury and hurled in blinding spray into, and even over the houses. We had to cling to the lamposts and stanchions, and to seek shelter against the doorways and walls. Advantage was taken of a slight lull in the storm to fire off rockets, but these were driven back like feathers against the houses. Then long-boats were dragged to the pier, but the first was broken and disabled the moment it touched the water, while the second met a like fate, and its gallant crew were pitched out into the sea. In short, every effort proved abortive, and as darkness set in the boat and the unhappy women were reluctantly abandoned to their fate. Next morning the whole length of the Praya presented a scene of wreckage and desolation. Many of the Chinese, notwithstanding their shrewdness in predicting storms, had been taken quite unawares, and hence the fearful sacrifice of life and the loss of property which had ensued.

J. THOMSON
The Straits of Malacca, Indo China and China (1875)

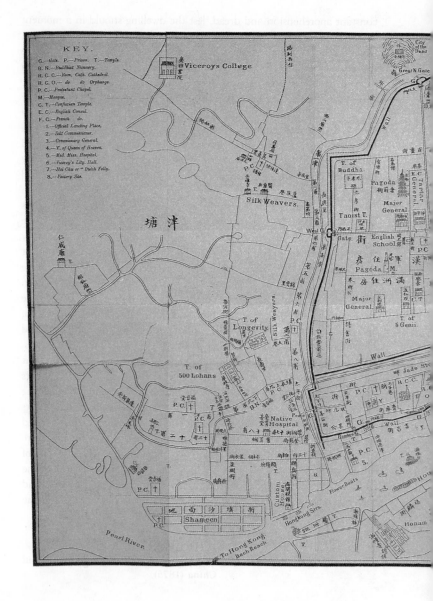

90

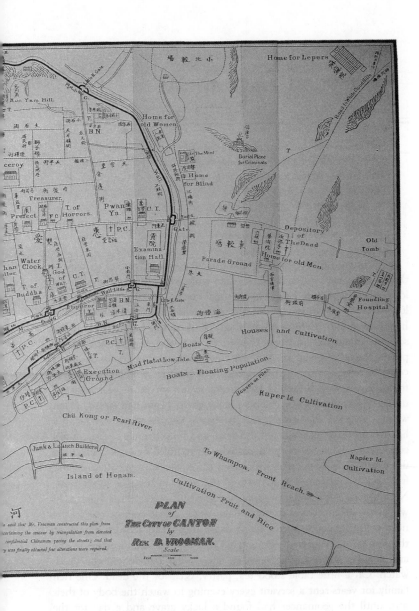

A Lucky Grave

In Canton, German traveller Margaretha Weppner accompanied her
host, Archdeacon Gray, on a full tour of the sights, and it was getting
dark as they approached the city of the dead.

At a distance of one English mile from the Eastern gate of the city is
the so-called city of the dead, a name which well depicts the place. It
looks like a miniature city of many small houses, divided into short and
long streets. The corpses remain in their provisional resting-places until a
happy grave has been found for them. To find this happy grave is the
sole and exclusive business of the geomancers, who, in order to fill their
purses, have recourse to the most exquisite cunning and lies, and
consume several years in the process of finding it. . . . The corpses . . .
frequently remain unburied for fifteen, twenty or more years, that is
until the geomancers have found a lucky grave. Night had already fallen
when I reached this necropolis; the beams of the moon were faintly
lighting up these tenements of the dead, and I must confess I did not feel
comfortable. This city of the departed is surrounded by a lake, which, as
usual in China, is covered with green slime. Sacred storks flew to and
fro, and in and out of the streets of the dead, in the pale moonshine.
Near the lake is a large beautiful garden with several little houses, in
which the relatives and friends of the dead, whose corpses rest in the
necropolis, frequently spend whole days, in order to afford company to
the soul of the departed. We entered one of these dead houses; in the
antechamber sat many servants in effigy, who represented the dead-
watch. On a little table stood tea, pastry, &c., for the dead. One rich
family for years sent a servant every evening to watch the body of their
son, until the geomancer had found a lucky grave and a day for the
funeral. The room next the antechamber was as dark as a cellar, in it lay
the dead man; my companion led me to the coffin, which I looked upon

with a shudder. In another house lay a woman of high rank; two maid-servants in effigy kept watch over her; on the table were tea, pastry, &c. In the third house lay the corpse of the ... Governor of the province of K'wan-tung, who, two years previously, had died suddenly on his return from a feast; the geomancer had not yet found a lucky grave for him. The inhabitants of the necropolis are chiefly dead-watchers, and they seemed to me quite familiar with their wards. My companion informed me that the dead-watchers, before retiring for the night, call the souls of the dead back to their bodies; since they maintain that during the day the souls leave the bodies and get on the roofs, or go into the streets of the necropolis, or into the garden, in the hope of seeing their friends.

The watchman to whom the archdeacon and myself laughingly appealed as to the truth of this, gravely informed us that it was so, and coaxed the souls back to their bodies, much as if he were coaxing pigeons or poultry ... When I saw this superstitious performance, I really seemed to be dreaming. We stepped out into the clear moonlight: the sacred storks flew to and fro over us; each little light in the houses of the watchmen heightened the weird character of the scene.

MARGARETHA WEPPNER
The North Star and the Southern Cross
(1875)

1873

"Gem of the Orient"

From Hong Kong a side-trip to Macao was a "must" for globe-trotting Egerton Laird: he was eager to see the monument commemorating Portugal's most famous poet, Luis de Camoëns. But as Laird's journal shows, not everything in Macao was worthy of a poet's pen.

Tuesday, 24th June. . . . I went straight to the hotel at landing, and then took a chair and proceeded to the Tomb of Camoëns. It certainly seems curious that while he lived this poet was exiled from his own country, and I believe escaped from the ship he was in by swimming ashore; and yet now, a stranger only comes to Macao to visit his tomb – such is the immortality of a poet. The monument is erected in a pretty garden, and there are several sets of verses by different people, cut out on slabs of marble. One set of lines are by Dr. Bowring; I certainly do not agree with him, when he says –

> "Gem of the orient earth and open sea,
> Macao; that in thy lap, and on thy breast,
> Hast gathered beauties, all the loveliest."

Fancy calling Macao a gem, when there is hardly any vegetation; and although there is . . . a certain picturesque appearance from the old forts and churches that crown the summit of the hills – still, even the sea around is muddy, as it is so shallow; however, he is true enough when he says of Camoëns, "That his lyre though known to fame knew misery more." The building in which his bust is placed has a roof in the shape of a dome, and the large plantain leaves and other foliage, form a lovely setting. It is in a private garden, and the paths are so covered with moss and green stuff that it is quite dangerous to walk; evidently there is no care taken of it. I then drove round, or rather was carried to the Praya, which is the fashionable walk; it is sheltered by trees and faces the open sea, from which there was a pleasant breeze – in fact, people come here from Hong Kong to have a breather in hot weather. The Portuguese have been here for upwards of three hundred years. I have never seen so many hideous people in my life – Chinese, Malay, and Portuguese mixed. Brown faces – and oh! so ugly. Sometimes you see a dark olive green complexion; the combination I suppose of the yellow of the Chinese, and the olive of the South; however, whatever they are, they are certainly a very mixed race. There are a few graceful Duennas walking about – *graceful*, because they nearly cover their faces with a black shawl. As is usual in Portuguese Colonies, there are numbers of priests to be seen. There is little or no trade here, unless the traffic in Coolies can be called one. . . . I . . . went to the Barracoons, a place where the Coolies are taken before shipment. There were two groups of about one hundred each, lying on the grass; and inside there were a number being examined by the surgeon. I walked in, but after five minutes a Portuguese came and asked me if I had any business there. I told him "no." "Well," he said, "there is no admittance," so I quietly decamped. I have asked several people since, but they have never been allowed in, so there is nothing like impudence. It certainly does not say much for the Portuguese as Colonists, when one hears that the chief

COOLIES' BARRACOONS, MACAO

revenue is derived from the gambling hells, and the principal trade, if trade it can be called, is the traffic in Coolies. The latter are shipped to the tune of some 13,000 a year to Callao and Havana. One cannot say that they are forced to go into slavery, as when they arrive from the country they are asked if they have any objection to go to Peru or to Cuba, and if they say "Yes," the Chinese Government is obliged to send them back to Canton, or wherever they come from, at the expense of the Mandarin of the district; still I believe that if they do object things are not made as pleasant as might be for them on their return to their native country. So the option is I suppose more nominal than real. The worst part of all is the passage, as they are huddled together 400 or 500 in a barque of 600 tons, and when they are fairly out of sight of land the horrors of the middle passage commence, as I am told the battens are as often as not put down, for there have been cases when the Coolies have risen up and murdered the crew. The Captain receives so much a head, so it is no wonder that he crowds his ship. The Chinese broker who first engages or kidnaps the Coolies, is I think the one most to blame . . .

E.K. LAIRD
The Rambles of a Globe Trotter (1875)

1874

The Only European

When Walter Mundy boarded the Spark *on a business trip to Macao he had no premonition of the horrors that were to follow. The captain, chief mate and purser were all killed in what became known as the* Spark Outrage.

... We left Canton at half-past seven in the morning, and were due at Macao between four and five the same afternoon. The *Spark* ... is a paddle-wheeled steamer somewhat larger than our Thames boats. ... The lower deck was confined exclusively to Chinese passengers, and a winding staircase near the stern led to the quarter-deck, which was for Europeans. ... There were a great many native passengers, but I had the misfortune to be the only European. The crew consisted of about twenty men – Chinese and Portuguese half-castes. The captain, poor Brady, was an American, and although an utter stranger to him previous to our journey, it has seldom been my good fortune to have a nicer or more amiable companion. ... We had a capital run to Whampoa. After leaving here, about nine o'clock, we breakfasted. The Canton steamer to Hongkong, and the return steamer from Hongkong, ought to have passed us soon after leaving Whampoa; but from some reason they were delayed, and did not pass us till after twelve o'clock, which obliged the pirates to put off their attack. The river here, where the outrage was perpetrated, is about one mile across.

So far the trip had been most delightful – nothing had occurred to awaken any suspicion. I was still as wedded to the humdrum existence and safety of English life as if I were but taking a trip in the British Channel, and so little thinking of any peril, that I dozed over my cigar and book under the awning forward. I must have slept here some time, as I certainly awoke with a start; it may have been a noise, it may have been instinct of danger which roused me. Which it really was I am unable to tell; but I immediately perceived a man rushing up the gangway towards me with a knife in his hand, and a gash across his forehead. Surprised and only half awake, my first thought was that he was a madman, and I rushed out to procure help to seize him. In attempting to do so, I was, however, met by two other men, who attacked me with knives. Quickly seeing my mistake, I rushed past them and ran on in search of weapons, endeavouring to find out what it all meant, and to see whether any resistance was being made. I now strove to reach the passengers' gangway to see what the Chinese were doing. In attempting this I had to run the gauntlet of several of the pirates, who wounded me in many places. Two of them here seized me, tearing my watch off, and were going to cut my fingers off for my rings, when, by a desperate effort, I managed to break loose from them. It was then that I saw the Chinese passengers sitting below, looking as unconcerned as possible. I then rushed to the stern, where I saw the poor purser holding on by his hands to the side of the ship, preparing to jump overboard, and a pirate cutting at him. Here also the chief mate was battling most courageously with one arm, while with the other he attempted to loosen a buoy. I tried to join him, but my wounds were beginning to tell on my strength, and numbers easily drove me off. With no hope left I endeavoured to retrace my steps, but was immediately attacked by two or three fresh arrivals. I here managed to get within striking distance of one, whom I succeeded in knocking down; but the success cost me dear, as his companions wounded me at the same moment desperately in the left side. How they let me retire I cannot imagine; how I was able is equally difficult for me to explain! But I was again attacked by two others armed with capstan bars, who successively knocked me down with these weapons. I rolled out of their way, and for a time was left in peace. I staggered to the wheel-house, but had to support myself on an umbrella which I picked up. I was now almost insensible, and leaned against the window . . . On looking down into the captain's cabin, I saw poor Brady lying stretched out on the floor, with his little dog staring mournfully into his face. This sign of fidelity consoled me even then somewhat, and, indeed, my sole wish now was centred in the hope of being able to last long enough to get some chance of revenge by the arrival of assistance. After leaning here for ten or fifteen minutes, I fell on the deck from exhaustion and loss of blood. A few minutes after this the pirates, who had been plundering the ship, returned on deck, battened down the hatchways, and proceeded to count their booty close by me. They continually passed over me, stepping on and kicking me. On receiving my wound in the side, I, luckily for myself, had sufficient presence of mind to shove my handkerchief and fingers into the aperture to staunch the blood. The pirates, either imagining I was trying to conceal something, or in brutal sport, tore my hand several times from the wound. The agony I thus endured I can never forget. How I prayed for unconsciousness! One of them motioned me to throw myself overboard, and even pretended to do it, lifting me up in his arms. Another, whom I judged to be the chief, as he swaggered about in my hat, with a revolver and cutlass at his belt, brandishing his sword, pretended to draw it across my throat several times, to the evident delight of all his comrades. For what reason he did not carry his performance into practice I cannot possibly conceive. I was lying on the deck for six hours with these fellows close to me, but not for one instant did I lose consciousness. A junk then came alongside, when the steamer was stopped for the first time. The plunder was transferred to the junk, and they all hastened on board her, after spiking and breaking the helm.

Immediately on their leaving, the crew came on deck, and, rigging a helm in the stern, commenced working the ship. A Chinese merchant, procuring assistance, carried me to the saloon, placed me on a sofa, and covered me with a tablecloth to keep the cold from my wounds. All on board were so overcome that they had to be kept at their work by a copious supply of brandy. We were delayed some time in Macao harbour before we were permitted to land, a regiment of soldiers being drawn up to receive us on the quay, and no Chinaman was allowed to leave before he was searched and his name and address were taken. When I recall the whole event, it seems like a hideous dream. It is only when I look at the proofs on my body of its horrible reality that I awake to a full sense of all my danger, and a feeling of thankfulness for my miraculous escape drives every other thought away.

WALTER WILLIAM MUNDY
Canton and the Bogue (1875)

1874

Buried Alive

While living among the Chinese the Reverend Piton, a Swiss missionary, unearthed a little known custom, which he described for the readers of The China Review.

During a prolonged stay in the interior of the Canton Province, I was from time to time startled by the report that people had been buried alive by their own relatives. On making farther inquiries into the matter I heard that those who had met with such a horrible fate, had been either lepers or incorrigible thieves. . . .

In the neighbourhood of my residence lived a man, who had formerly been in easy circumstances, but who had, unfortunately become addicted to opium smoking, and in consequence of this sank year by year deeper and deeper into poverty. After having in course of time disposed of his house and fields he proceeded to sell his wife, and finally his three boys one after the other, only that he might be able to satisfy his craving for the pernicious drug. When matters had reached this point, his relatives induced him to stay for a time in my house, that I might try to cure him of his ruinous passion. I used with him the same method which had proved most successful in the case of a great many patients, but he himself lacked that firmness of will which is always necessary to the attainment of the desired end. One morning he was nowhere to be found. The last I heard of the unfortunate man was that, having no other means of getting money to buy his daily dose of opium, he took to pilfering from his relatives. All that he could lay his hands upon, even to the very tiles from the roof of his family's ancestral hall, was sacrificed to his ruling appetite. Hereupon a family council was held, whereat it was resolved to bury him alive. One morning some of his nephews went to dig the grave in a lonely place amongst the mountains, whilst others repaired to the poor man's dwelling and made him acquainted with the decision at which they had arrived. The doomed man did not even object to it, and went willingly to meet his horrible fate. Arrived at the open grave, he unresistingly allowed himself to be put in it, only asking as a favour that his face might be covered with some grass. After this had been done, the bystanders proceeded to cover up the living body with earth, and finally departed to their homes with the gratifying thought that they had put an end for ever to the importunity of their unhappy relative.

REV. C. PITON
"Chinese Charity"
The China Review, Vol. II, No. 6, 1874

1876

The Hall of Justice

*Dr. Henry Field, editor of the New York journal The Evangelist,
was on a world tour when he visited Canton.*

Three spots in Canton had for me the fascination of horror – the
court, the prison, and the execution ground. . . . I wished to see for
myself the administration of justice – to witness a trial in a Chinese
court. A few years ago this would have been impossible; foreigners were
excluded from the courts. But now they are open, and all can see who
have the nerve to look on. Therefore, after we had made a long circuit
through the streets of Canton, I directed the bearers to take us to the
Yamun, the Hall of Justice. Leaving our chairs in the street, we passed
through a large open court into a hall in the rear, where at that very
moment several trials were going on.

The court-room was very plain. A couple of judges sat behind tables,
before whom a number of prisoners were brought in. The mode of
proceeding was very foreign to American or European ideas. There was
neither jury nor witnesses. This simplified matters exceedingly. There is
no trial by jury in China. While we haggle about impanelling juries and
getting testimony, and thus trials drag on for weeks, in China no such
obstacle is allowed to impede the rapid course of justice; and what is
more, there are no lawyers to perplex the case with their arguments, but
the judge has it all his own way. He is simply confronted with the
accused, and they have it all between them.

While we stood here, a number of prisoners were brought in; some
were carried in baskets (as they are borne to execution), and dumped on
the stone pavement like so many bushels of potatoes; others were led in
with chains around their necks. As each one's name was called, he came
forward and fell on his knees before the judge, and lifted up his hands to
beg for mercy. He was then told of the crime of which he was accused,

and given opportunity if he had anything to say in his own defence. There was no apparent harshness or cruelty towards him, except that he was presumed guilty, unless he could prove his innocence; contrary to the English maxim of law, that a man is to be presumed innocent until he is proved guilty. In this, however, the Chinese practice is not very different from that which exists at this day in so enlightened a country as France.

For example, two men were accused of being concerned together in a burglary. As they were from another prefecture, where there is another dialect, they had to be examined through an interpreter. The judge wished to find out who were leagued with them, and therefore questioned them separately. Each was brought in in a basket, chained and doubled up, so that he sat helpless. No witness was examined but the man himself was simply interrogated by the judge.

In another case, two men were accused of robbery with violence – a capital offence, but by the Chinese law no man can be punished with death unless he confesses his crime; hence every means is employed to lead a criminal to acknowledge his guilt. Of course in a case of life and death he will deny it as long as he can. But if he will not confess, the court proceeds to take stringent measures to *make* him confess, for which purpose these two men were now put to the torture. The mode of torture was this: There were two round pillars in the hall. Each man was on his knees, with his feet chained behind him, so that he could not stir. He was then placed with his back to one of these columns, and small cords were fastened around his thumbs and great toes, and drawn back tightly to the pillar behind. This soon produced intense suffering. Their breasts heaved, the veins on their foreheads stood out like whipcords, and every feature betrayed the most excrutiating agony. Every few minutes an officer of the court asked if they were ready to confess, and as often they answered, "No; never would they confess that they had committed such a crime." They were told if they did not confess, they would be subjected to still greater torture. But they held out, though every moment seemed an hour of pain.

While these poor wretches were thus writhing in agony, I turned to the judge to see how he bore the spectacle of such suffering. He sat at his table quite unmoved; yet he did not seem like a brutal man, but like a man of education, such as one might see on the bench in England or America. He seemed to look upon it as in the ordinary course of proceedings, and a necessary step in the conviction of a criminal. He used no bravado, and offered no taunt or insult. But the cries of the

THE FOREIGN SETTLEMENT, CANTON

sufferers did not move him, nor prevent his taking his accustomed ease. He sat fanning himself and smoking his pipe, as if he said he could stand it as long as they could. . . .

But still the men did not give in, and I looked at them with amazement mingled with horror, to see what human nature could endure. The sight was too painful to witness more than a few moments, and I rushed away, leaving the men still hanging to the pillars of torture. I confess I felt a relief when I went back the next day, to hear that they had not yielded, but held out unflinchingly to the last.

Horrible as this seems, I have heard good men – men of humanity argue in favor of torture, at least "when applied in a mild way." They affirm that in China there can be no administration of justice without it. In a country where testimony is absolutely worthless – where as many men can be hired to swear falsely for ten cents apiece as you have money to buy – there is no possible way of arriving at the truth but by *extorting* it. No doubt it is a rough process, but it secures the result. As it happened, the English gentleman who accompanied us was a magistrate in India, and he confirmed the statement as to the difficulty, and in many cases the impossibility, of getting at the truth, because of the unfathomable deceit of the natives. Many cases came before him in which he was sure a witness was lying, but he was helpless to prove it, when a little gentle application of the thumbscrew, or even a good whipping, would have brought out the truth . . .

But there are cases in which a man may be wrongfully accused; an enemy may bribe a witness to make a complaint against him, upon which he is arrested and cast into prison. Then, unless he can bring some powerful influence to rescue him, his case is hopeless. He denies his guilt, and is put on the rack for an offence of which he is wholly innocent. Such cases, no doubt, occur; and yet men who have lived here many years, such as Dr. Happer and Archdeacon Gray, tell me that they do not believe there is a country in the world where, on the whole, justice is more impartially administered than in China.

HENRY M. FIELD
From Egypt to Japan (1877)

1877

Unexpected Meal

As a newcomer and the wife of Archdeacon Gray (a well-known figure in Canton society), Mrs. Gray became a much sought-after guest. At times, though, she found Chinese hospitality rather too much to stomach.

CANTON, August 13th, 1877

MY DEAR MOTHER,

A day or two after I had written my last descriptive letter to you, an invitation came from the Howquas for us. We started from home on Saturday, after having taken luncheon, as we concluded we were only invited to pay a long afternoon call upon our Chinese friends. When we arrived at the Howquas' house the ladies of the family took possession of Minnie and of me, and we scarcely saw Henry all the afternoon, nor anything of the gentlemen of the Howqua family . . . To our surprise we had not sat with the ladies more than half an hour before we were told that luncheon was ready. It was laid out in true Chinese style on a small round table in the atrium outside Mrs. Howqua's bedroom. There was no cloth on the table, nor is it customary for the Chinese repasts to be placed on a covered table; they are laid on the bare board. The usual cakes in great varieties were in the centre of the table, and chop-sticks were placed for each of us. The Chinese ladies stood round the table some short time before they took their seats, as there was a great question as to which of them should take her seat first. This goes on at every meal amongst the ladies; each says the other must take the precedence. My hostess bowed towards her friend, and waved her hand towards the chair, evidently begging her to seat herself; the friend returned the compliment and so the ladies bowed and bowed for some minutes until the friend took her seat. The absurdity of the whole matter is, that etiquette is so strict and defined in China that there was

106

no doubt as to which of the ladies would eventually seat herself first, but it is customary to show this affected humility before accepting the honour. As I could not speak Chinese I thought I had better accept at once, and on Mrs. Howqua requesting me to be seated, I with a smile obeyed, thus of course appearing very discourteous to the Chinese ladies. . . .

The courtesy of Chinese to strangers is very great. You feel on entering one of their houses that their great desire is to please you, and that their whole attention is given to you as a guest. Henry says when he has called at a house of mourning, in which, according to Chinese custom, the seats of the chairs are covered with blue, a servant has been called to bring a red covering to place on the chair intended for him, as a Chinese gentleman considers it is not kind to make his friends mourn for his particular loss. . . . Our small party at table consisted of Mrs. Howqua, her particular friend, a pretty woman, but highly rouged and coquettish, young Howqua, Minnie, and myself. I have never felt more embarrassed than I did at this unexpected meal, for, besides having partaken of luncheon only a couple of hours before, I was feeling ill. How to eat the various dishes placed before me I did not know. I wished my little interpreter to say to my hostess that I was feeling unwell, but she said that this was impossible, as the ladies would be afraid at once that I might be sickening with some contagious illness, or, as they would put it, that I might have brought some evil spirit into the house which would also harm them. So I was forced to hide my feelings and put into my mouth pieces of food which at the best of times would have made me feel very uncomfortable. The ladies often said to Minnie that I was not eating, that I did not like what was provided for me, and Minnie turned to me begging me to make greater efforts. . . . "Pray help yourself," was Mrs. Howqua's frequent remark, "or we shall not think you friendly." All constraint was thrown aside, and I saw the Chinese ladies in their accustomed home life. They and young Howqua helped my little friend and me to many delicacies with their own chopsticks. . . . when I considered my efforts to take the food which was so distasteful to me had been crowned with success, and after I had tasted several sweet cakes, etc., Mrs. Howqua rose from her chair, dipped a piece of duck, at least two inches square, which she held in her chopsticks, into the little basins containing soy and mustard, and put the whole as a *bonne bouche* into my mouth. I rose when I saw the fate coming upon me, smiled I should say a ghastly smile, and was obliged to swallow this large piece of meat. Champagne was supplied; Mr. Howqua came himself and opened the bottle, and you should have seen his struggles to accomplish this. He knelt down, held the bottle at arm's length, the attendants standing at some distance. At last he had in despair to break off the neck of the bottle. He appeared at one time with a bottle of white wine, which by the label I found to be whisky made in Germany. . . .

One dish which was placed before me puzzled me much: it looked like fine grass, and when I asked the name of it, I learned that it was seaweed. It was so entangled that I could not extract a mouthful of it from the basin with my chopsticks. Without speaking to me, my particular attendant took the green tangled contents into her hands from the little bowl, divided it with her fingers, and replaced it in my basin. These amahs are accustomed to help their mistresses in this way. The last dish was rice, and my little bowl was piled up with it, and the ladies tried to teach me to eat it in true Chinese fashion. They place the basin close to the under lip, and then with closed chopsticks push the rice into their mouths with marvellous rapidity. Mrs. Howqua told me not to be shy about it, that it was the custom for all to eat rice in this way. It was not shyness that prevented me from proving an apt pupil, but the desire not to put much of the rice into my mouth, as it was flavoured with something which gave it a pink colour and a most unpleasant taste. I had already done sufficient violence to my feelings in the various dishes of which I had partaken. With the rice a little dish was brought in containing silk-worm chrysalises boiled and served up with chillies. The pretty young lady partook of this dish in great quantities, although it was so hot in flavour that I could scarcely swallow one of the chillies. I could not bring myself to taste one of the fat, soft-looking chrysalises. This dish, so this lady informed me, is a cure for indigestion.

MRS. GRAY
Fourteen Months in Canton (1880)

1877

Ah Kum

Ah Kum *was the most celebrated guide in Canton. Previously he had worked in Archdeacon Gray's household where he had gained both his polish and his ideas of what visitors should do and see. To Australian journalist James Hingston, Ah Kum himself was one of the sights of Canton.*

Canton proved to be a city well worth any trouble taken to see it. The native guide, Ah Kum, who steered me through its network intricacies, was a professional, and none the better guide for that reason.... Ah Kum was a heathen Chinee in every sense – too much so altogether for the good of any one but himself. Canton was to him a certain number of show-places, to be visited and got through with as quickly as possible, and to be done with and paid for. A certain number of shops and stores, at which he had credit, and from which he drew commission, were then to be visited, and purchases there recommended, and there only....

He would not walk, this guide of mine. His ankle was bad ... Palanquins had, perforce, to be taken, and Canton to be viewed over the naked shoulder of a perspiring Chinaman in front, and out of two small window openings at the sides....

The crowds of hurrying human beings, all on industry bent, that are to be seen in Canton give one a good idea of the dense population of this over-populated China.... A dozen people are to be seen in Canton in the same space that only one would be visible in at New York. The struggle for existence seems to be very desperate indeed in these Chinese cities. My thoughts about it were interrupted by a blow on the roof of the palanquin that nearly sent it off the bearers' shoulders, and caused me to clutch at its sides. The palanquin-carriers had jostled a stalwart, blind beggar, who, in a frenzied manner, lashed out right and left with a bamboo staff that he carried. He was evidently a semi-lunatic, who elsewhere would have been in confinement. Looking back towards him out of the rear window of my swinging-cage, I perceived a crowd round him, and the bamboo still at work. . . . Police of any sort do not appear to be about in Canton. The preservation of the peace seems to be left to the co-operation of the public. At one place the street was blocked up for five minutes by a mob that listened to the abuse that a furious coolie was hurling at a shop-keeper. The cause of the trouble was that copper cash, equivalent to a penny, but about a handful, nevertheless, had been paid to him for some small service that he considered worth twice the amount. It was not until his indignation and his lungs became exhausted that the stream of traffic could move on. It was rare strong abuse that he vented forth. His features and the hoarse tone of his deep bass voice told that. I saw no street fights.

While listening to and watching that scene, a skinny arm was thrust within the window of my cage. In place of a hand at the end of it, an earthenware cup was strapped thereon. It was the arm of a leper, whose hand had been eaten off by disease – a horrible sight. These poor creatures are not, as in some places, placed in hospitals, but wander about Canton begging – rubbing shoulders, meanwhile, with the jostling crowds. . . .

Ah Kum's determination to do no walking about Canton was very vexing. I specially thought so when he brought up two palanquins next day, seemingly as a matter of course.

"Is your ankle no better?" I queried.

"No! cannot walk!" He said this with an immediate reference to his gold watch. It was evident that the possession of that article had much to do with his general ideas. He looked at it, not to know the time, but to settle all questions generally. . . . Ah Kum wore his finger-nails very long – over an inch. In China that is done to indicate that the possessor of the fingers does no work with his hands, as the small foot indicates that the owner does no walking. When Ah Kum exhibited his watch, he took care also to show his finger-nails to the best advantage. Of this hideous deformity he was most unwarrantably proud. I doubt if any European could get so elevated in mind on uncut finger-nails. They were always, too, a nuisance to him, interfering with all the movements of his hands. He endured it, however, for fashion's sake, as folks do the modern torture of high boot-heels.

"Very well, then – you will ride and I shall walk. I can see nothing when shut up in those palanquins. Send away the one you mean for my use!"

UNCUT FINGER-NAILS

This satire on his vanity did not seem to suit his feelings, but I was strong on the subject, and the second palanquin was sent away. Being on foot, I was master of the situation for the day, and could stay where I pleased, and for long or short time – using Ah Kum in his cupboard merely for reference now and then. In this style we went to see the great water-clock of Canton. It is not relied upon now, as formerly, for time-telling purposes, but it keeps its count of the minutes and hours as accurately as ever. It differed with my time only two minutes. Ah Kum had his watch out at once, and held it now altogether exposed. Such an opportunity of exhibition was not to be lost. With that watch the clock differed nothing. It was no doubt keeping correct Canton time. . . .

All day has Ah Kum been anxious to take me to the execution ground, which he evidently regards as something good in the way of sights. I have asked him if any one is to be decapitated there, and he has said, "Not till next week – then twenty – you stop." I have explained to him that the attraction is not great enough; also that an empty execution ground is only a vacant piece of ground, and to me nothing to look at. . . . He listens and looks at his watch, he tickles his ear with one finger-claw, and says, –

"Come and see the heap of skulls and bones; all the hair sticking to some of the skulls yet!" . . .

111

We had by this time reached the execution ground, and lo! it was a potter's yard. Space is too valuable to be wasted in China.... The skulls and bones of which Ah Kum had spoken were piled against the side wall. The sight of the hair attachments was wanting. The dogs and rats had no doubt accounted for that. "You can take any of the skulls that you fancy," said Ah Kum ... I wanted to see the headsman's block, but was told that the decapitation was done without it, one cut generally sufficing if the kneeling criminal held his neck steady. "They always do that for their own sake," said Ah Kum.

"Have you seen executions here lately?" I asked.

"No, never come to them now. There were thirty executed here a month ago."

It seemed a great sacrifice until one looked at the super-abundance of humanity that exists in crowded China, and thought of the millions that might be well parted for the benefit of others. Looked at in that cynical light, this clearing away of the people in batches of thirty seemed almost one of the ways of Providence....

A trouble had weighed upon Ah Kum's mind all day since the hour that he had seen me purchase some Chinese books. It was the common leathern purse, of English make, out of which I took the necessary cash, that fixed my Chinaman's fancy. His soul thirsted for that purse. It would match the pencil-case and the watch, and his happiness would be then trebled. He had a small, mean-looking English one that he had thought something of before. It had probably cost 6d. when made, while mine might have cost four times that amount.

"I will change purses with you, Ah Kum" – here his face lighted up – "if you will let me cut your nails down as short as mine are." Here it darkened.

"I am a gentleman," he said, "and must look like one."

"But you look like to a bird of prey, or a madman, with those finger-nails. They don't become a man who carries an English watch like to yours. Besides, I want your nail-tops to take away in a lozenge-box as curios."

I could see the mental struggle that was going on until we reached the dog and rat market; but it finished in favour of the finger-nails. He looked at them several times, and decided to keep them.

JAMES HINGSTON
The Australian Abroad (1879)

1877

Baby-Talk

Arriving at Hong Kong in their yacht Sunbeam *the Brasseys soon felt at ease, finding it very much like Gibraltar – except for the language.*

Monday, February 26th. . . . . Off the town of Victoria the crowd of shipping is immense, and it became a difficult task to thread our way between the fleets of sampans and junks. . . . In these sampans whole families, sometimes five generations, live and move and have their being. I never shall forget my astonishment when, going ashore very early one morning in one of these strange craft, the proprietor lifted up what I had thought was the bottom of the boat, and disclosed three or four children, packed away as tight as herrings, while under the seats were half-a-dozen people of larger growth. The young mother of the small family generally rows with the smallest baby strapped on to her back, and the next-sized one in her arms, whom she is also teaching to row. The children begin to row by themselves when they are about two years old. The boys have a gourd, intended for a life-preserver, tied round their necks as soon as they are born. The girls are left to their fate, a Chinaman thinking it rather an advantage to lose a daughter or two occasionally.

Many of these sampan people have never set foot on shore in their lives, and this water-life of China is one of the most extraordinary features of the country. . . .

After breakfast we landed on the Praya, a fine quay, extending the whole length of the town. On it are situated many of the large stores, offices, and markets of the city. The streets are wide and handsome, and the buildings in European style, with deep verandahs and arcades, all built of stone. . . . Soldiers and sailors abound in the streets; and if it were not for the sedan-chairs and palanquins, in which everybody is carried about by Chinese coolies with enormous hats, one might easily fancy oneself at dear old Gib., so much do these dependencies of the Crown in foreign countries resemble one another, even in such opposite quarters of the globe. . . .

To-day, for the first time, we have heard "pidgin English" seriously spoken. It is very trying to one's composure to hear grave merchants, in their counting-houses, giving important orders to clerks and compradors in what sounds, until one gets accustomed to it, like the silliest of baby-talk. The term really means "business English;" and certain it is that most Chinamen you meet understand it perfectly, though you might just as well talk Greek as ordinary English to them. "Take piecey missisy one piecey bag topside," seems quite as difficult to understand as "Take the lady's bag upstairs" would be; but it is easier to a Chinaman's intellect.

From the Praya we went up the hill to write our names in the Governor's book. It was a beautiful road all the way, running between lovely gardens and beneath shady trees. Government House is a fine building, situated on a high point of land, commanding extensive views in every direction. After a pleasant chat we descended the hill again, and proceeded to the Hongkong hotel for tiffin. It does not seem a very desirable abode, being large, dirty, and ill-kept. At one o'clock a bell rang, and the visitors all rushed in and took their places at various little tables, and were served with a "scrambly" sort of meal by Chinese boys.

After this, a carriage was sent for us, and we drove to the race-course. This is the fourth and last day of the races, and there is to be a ball to-night to wind up with, to which everybody seems to be going. The drive was a very pleasant one, the road presenting a most animated appearance, with crowds of soldiers, sailors, Chinamen, Parsees, Jews, all hurrying along by the side of the numerous sedan-chairs and carriages. We were puzzled to imagine where, on this rocky, hilly island, there could possibly be found a piece of ground flat enough for a race-course. But the mystery was solved when we reached a lovely little valley, about two miles from the town, where we found a very fair course, about the size of that at Chester, but not so dangerous. The grand stand is a picturesque object, with its thatched roof, verandahs, and sun-blinds. The interior, too, looks comfortably arranged, and certainly contains the most luxurious basket-chairs one could possibly desire. There are a lawn and a paddock attached, and very good temporary stables, over many of which are private stands and tiffin-rooms.

Hongkong races are a great event, and people come down from Canton, Shanghai, Macao, and all sorts of places for them. Everybody knows everybody, and it seems to be altogether a most pleasant social meeting. Many ladies were present. Some of the races were capital, the little Chinese ponies scuttling along at a great pace under their big riders, whose feet seemed almost to touch the ground. There was also a race for Australian horses. But the most amusing event of all was the last scramble for Chinese ponies ridden by Chinese boys, in which horses and riders seemed to be exactly suited to one another.

The sun went down, and it grew cold and dark before all was over. The gentlemen walked back to the town, and I went down to the landing-place in solitary state, in a carriage driven by an Indian coach-man, attended by a Chinese footman. I was immediately surrounded by a vociferating crowd, each individual member of which was anxious to extol the merits of his own sampan. The carriage having driven off, I was quite alone, and had some difficulty in dispersing them, and being allowed to enter the sampan I had selected. However, I did succeed at last, and making my boatmen understand that they were to take me to "the white ship," as the yacht is generally called, returned on board to rest.

MRS. BRASSEY
A Voyage in the "Sunbeam" (1878)

1878

Dogs, Rats, and Mice

In Canton and Hong Kong one of America's richest citizens, Andrew Carnegie, rubbed shoulders with some of the world's poorest.

CANTON, *Friday, December 20.* – We have just returned from our first stroll through the narrow, crowded alleys of Canton. Pictures and descriptions had prepared us for what we were to see, but, as is usual in the East, we knew nothing until we had seen for ourselves. . . . We decided to walk instead of following the custom of Europeans, who generally take sedan chairs and dash through, seeing nothing in detail. We cross the river by one of the innumerable boats rowed by women, and are in the city. For five hours we are guided through streets varying from six to ten feet in width through one continuous mass of Chinamen. As for Chinawomen, they are rarely or never seen. A few men are in silks; numbers of coolies, with loads, are almost naked, but more, of a slightly higher order, are in rags; for the Chinese, unlike their scrupulously clean brethren of Japan, appear to pile on one tattered, greasy cloth rag over another until they are a bundle of filth, against which you fear at every step lest you may be pushed. . . . We saw freely exposed for sale dogs, rats, and mice, all nicely dressed and hanging upon spits to tempt the hungry passers-by; while above a large pot from which the steam was issuing was a card, which, being translated by our guide, read, "A big black cat within; ready soon." The dogs which are eaten are fed especially for the purpose, and are hung up in state with labels setting forth their superior merits. As far as I should have known, they might have passed for delicious young roasting pigs, delicate enough in flavor to have satisfied gentle Elia himself.

Our guide, in answer to numerous questions upon the subject, informed us that some of his countrymen had acquired a taste for dogs, while others had succumbed to the sweeter attractions of cats; others again found rats their favorite morsel, but in all cases these penchants are indulged in on the sly. Upon no account would a Chinaman think of taking either of these peculiar delicacies home, for it appears that mesdames, much to their credit, have serious objections to their use. They draw the line here, and the husband must confine the indulgence of his uncanny longings to restaurants, and say nothing about it, or his lady friends might mark him as one of whom "'twas said he ate strange flesh." Contrary to the statement of travelers, I find this food is not confined to the poorer classes. The price of it is about the same as that of pork, and far beyond that of hare or deer. How strange these people are! The price of a black dog or cat is fully double that of a white one, the superstition being that the former makes blood much faster than the other, while rats are supposed to make the hair grow. . . .

Saturday, December 21. – To-day has been devoted, like yesterday, to Canton sights . . .

At almost every corner we pass crowds of poor wretches gambling in various modes, from fantan down to dice and dominoes. Children participate, and stake their "cash" with the elders; indeed, a young Celestial rarely spends his stray coppers in candy without tossing with the stall-keeper, double or quits; the little scamps begin early, and at every corner we noticed the dice lying ready to facilitate the operation. Is it any wonder that the vice of gambling seems inherent in the Chinese character? We saw rather a funny illustration of this practice, at which we couldn't help laughing. A class of venders keep a large pot boiling on the pavement in some partially secluded place, in which is an assortment of odds and ends. Such a mess of tidbits – pieces of liver, chicken, kidneys, beef, almost every conceivable thing! These the owner stirs up, taking care, I thought, to bring the largest bits adroitly to the surface. You should see the longing faces of the hungry beggars around. One risks a cash (one-tenth of a cent), a rattle of the dice – the customer has won. The fork is handed to him, and he has two dabs in the pot. What a prize! Down go the *bonnes bouches* one after the other, and back goes the fork to the pot-boiler, who again uses it to stir up in the pot prizes to tempt the lucky owner of funds sufficient for the indulgence of this piece of extravagance. . . .

HONG KONG, Christmas Eve. . . . The economy practised in China is striking. A sweet potato is sold in halves, or even in quarters, if required; ferriage across the river in a boat – a stream as wide as the Ohio at Pittsburgh – costs one-fifth of a cent, and you can engage an entire boat for yourself for a cent, if you wish to be extravagant; poultry is sold by the piece, as we sell a sheep, the wings, breast, legs, all having their price, and even the very feet of a chicken being sold for soup. Common iron nails are laid out in lots of six each; these have been used and used again, no one knows how often; we see the people at work straightening old nails at every turn. You can buy one-tenth of a cent's worth (1 cash) of either fish, soup, or rice. Verily things are down to a fine point here! . . .

I have not said much about the temples of Canton or of China, as they are poor affairs compared with those of Japan; besides, one becomes sated with temples which are for the most part copies of one another; the pagodas are much more picturesque at a distance than when closely inspected. The Chinese actually prefer all their places to smack of age, and repair them reluctantly, so that all have a dilapidated air, which gives a very unfavorable impression to a stranger. . . .

Christmas Day. – Yesterday's papers announced that the Hallelujah Chorus was to be performed in the English Cathedral this morning at eight o'clock. I had been so long out of the region of music that I rose early and went to church. The Japanese and Chinese music grate so on my ears, I longed to hear an organ once more. I enjoyed the service very much. . . .

Whatever old China may be doing, young China is progressing, for I saw in the park this morning several youthful Celestials, with their pigtails securely tied and out of the way, hard at cricket and baseball. Nor were they "duffers" either . . .

We are all creatures of prejudice, of course, but I could not help being somewhat shocked on Sunday, as I strolled about the Cathedral, to see some thirty odd sedan chairs on one side, and I suppose as many on the other, each with two, three, and some four coolies in gorgeous liveries in attendance, all waiting the closing of prayers . . . It did not seem to me to be quite consistent for some of my Scotch friends who stand so stoutly for Sabbath observance to keep so many human beings on duty, say three for one who worshipped, just to save them from walking a few short squares to and from church, for the town is small and compact. But custom has much to do with one's prejudices, for, after all, how is this worse than to roll in one's carriage to our Fifth Avenue temple? Yet this never struck me so much out of the way before, and I think, unless the future Mrs. C. seriously objects, we shall walk to church as a rule – when we go. Really, three men kept at work that one may pray seems just a shade out of proportion.

ANDREW CARNEGIE
Round the World (1884)

1879

Agreeable Hours

Captain Jones-Parry stopped at Hong Kong to visit friends and do some shopping.

I spent some agreeable hours with my friend of the Peninsular and Oriental. They have a princely office, and the *employes* mess together, living very comfortably; but, alas! here, as everywhere else, trade is so bad that everything has to be cut down, and there is hardly a good opening anywhere for a young fellow in these days. No, dollars counted by hundreds look well on paper at home; but they go by thousands out here, and nothing is left, nothing saved; and this not from extravagance, but simply from necessity, aided by force of example. I had to pay three shillings for having my hair cut; if I had been shampooed or any nonsense of that kind, it would have been six shillings. Living, that is, simply beef, mutton, and fish, is cheap enough; but house-rent, like everything else, is immensely dear; and a climate that necessitates a chair to go barely further than across the street, necessitates also a thousand other costly luxuries. I do not think anyone is too well paid out there, and only the heads of merchant houses and doctors make fortunes. . . .

The races were coming on, and that is the event of the year, but I could not remain for them. I was amused to find how absorbingly interesting they were to those residing out there. . . . Society in Hong-Kong being made up of naval and military officers, civilians, and merchants, runs very much in cliques; the club, however, is neutral ground. But there was the usual amount of envy, hatred, and malice about the exclusiveness of invitations to military and naval entertainments, and especially to Government House. I was surprised to find the Germans generally so unpopular. They seemed to be very clannish, and that may have been the reason; but very probably they were driven to be so by the exclusiveness of the English. The shops at Hong-Kong are particularly good, and indeed the prices are moderate for

119

a place where a dollar and a shilling are equivalent. I subsequently visited Canton, but saw nothing in the bazaars there to equal the carving and curiosities I saw in Hong-Kong. Japanese articles are also very good there. The Chinese are extremely fond of photography, and I got some very superior specimens. I may say that Singapore photographs were infinitely the worst I had met with. I cannot well avoid adding one word on the vexed question of the immense Chinese population in Hong-Kong; there are certainly the elements of great mischief in case of any rising, but danger there is none, compared with that at Singapore, for the men-of-war of all nations . . . would be fully equal to cope with any emergency: they could blow up all Hong-Kong in a few hours. . . .

I was simply astounded one night, on my preparing to depart, at say half-past ten, p.m., from my friend Dr. A____'s, to hear Mrs. A____ ask, "Who will go with Captain Jones-Parry to his hotel?" I said I knew my way, but, although it was not five hundred yards in a direct line through the heart of the town, I was assured that an escort was absolutely necessary, unless I was armed or had a servant with me. And so, on this and every occasion, I had an escort.

Whether it was absolutely necessary or not I cannot say; but all the gentlemen there present (and they were all officers connected with Government) assured me it was, and that several people had been attacked at night within a short time previous to our conversation.

CAPTAIN S.H. JONES-PARRY
My Journey Round the World (1881)

1879

In the Zenana

Constance Gordon Cumming was a travel writer who became personally involved in relief work for the blind in China. However it was not only the less fortunate who interested her: while in Canton she spent an afternoon seeing how the rich Chinese lived.

... We were received by our host and half a dozen gentlemen of the family, and for some time we sat in a fine open reception-hall, drinking pale straw-coloured tea in its simple form, and playing with a nice small son, the hope of the house.

Presently our host (who is very friendly to foreigners, and from intercourse with them, is less punctilious than most Chinamen on the matter of being seen speaking to his women-folk) led us aside, and presented us to his most kindly and courteous old mother, who conducted us to her apartments, her son accompanying us. He then introduced us to his little bride, aged thirteen. His matrimonial ventures have so far been unlucky, two previous wives having died very early. This one seems a nice, bright little lady.

She was very highly rouged, as was also her sister-in-law. Another sister being indisposed, was not rouged, nor was the mother, and, therefore, pleasanter to our eyes; but the Canton ladies love to lay on the colour thick. There is no deception about it! it is good, honest red, laid thick upon the cheek, and carried right round the eyebrows. The latter are shaved to refine their form. They cannot understand why English ladies should abstain from such an embellishment. Only when in mourning do they refrain from its use, and one notable exception is that of a bride, who on her wedding-day may wear no rouge, so that when her red silk veil is removed and the fringe of artificial pearls raised, her husband, looking on her face for the first time, may know for certain what share of beauty unadorned has fallen to his lot! ...

... we find an abundant luncheon awaiting us, but only the

gentlemen shared it with us. Even the fine old mother could not venture so far to depart from the customs of well-bred Chinese ladies as to cross the threshold, though she just glanced in to see that we were happy. Everything was excellent and abundant, and semi-European, some of the party, including our host, using forks, while others preferred chop-sticks. We tasted a spirit called rose wine, and our hosts enjoyed good English sherry. There was much health-drinking, quite in what we should call old English style, which here, however, is genuine old Chinese style. Gentlemen pledge one another in brimming wine-cups of small exquisitely chased metal-work, and having drained the cup, they turn it upside down on the table (which table, of course, has no cloth) – a white tablecloth would be deemed a most unlucky symbol of mourning.

Leaving the gentlemen to finish their wine, we rejoined the ladies, who now, in the absence of any lord of the creation, were much more at their ease. . . . They gathered round us to examine such jewels as we wore, and to show us theirs, and were pleased by our admiration of their quaint and elaborate head-dressing, their glossy hair being ornamented with artificial flowers (one had natural flowers), and valuable hairpins of gold, pearl, or jade-stone. Some wore . . . kingfisher's feather jewellery, but the principal ladies wore necklaces and bracelets of clear, bright-green jade, the Chinese equivalent of diamonds. One lady who wore large pendants of jade as ear-rings, and also attached to the silken cord of her fan, was the proud owner of enormously long third and fourth finger-nails on the left hand. These were shielded by golden nail-protectors (excellent weapons for the infliction of a vicious scratch! They are simply half-thimbles about three inches in length. I have invested in a very pretty silver set of four.)

All these ladies wore the same excess of jewellery covering the back of the head, but a singular prejudice forbids a woman ever to cover the top of her head, even when out of doors; so they think our hats very eccentric indeed, though these town ladies understand that it is not indecorous for foreign women to wear such headgear.

There is just one exception to this otherwise general rule, namely, that if a lady is of sufficiently high rank to attend court, she then appears in a hat precisely similar to that which her husband is entitled to wear, and adorned with the coloured button which denotes his exact rank. The mother of our host being entitled to this honour has had her portrait painted in oils, in full court dress, with beautiful symbolic embroidery of birds, and a handsome rosary of jade-stone, such as is worn by high mandarins.

A CANTON LADY

We also unfeignedly admired these ladies' exquisitely embroidered
silken skirts, all of different colours, and all folded into tiny plaits.
These skirts are worn one above the other. But their chief pride evidently
centred in their poor little "golden lily" feet, reduced to the tiniest hoof
in proof of their exalted station. Of course, the so-called foot is little
more than just the big toe, enclosed in a dainty wee shoe, which peeps
out from beneath the silk-embroidered trousers. Whether to call
attention to these beauties, or as an instinctive effort to relieve pain, I
know not, but we observed that a favourite attitude in the zenana is to
cross one leg over the other, and nurse the poor deformed foot in the
hand.

As they could scarcely toddle without help, their kindly-looking strong large-footed attendants were at hand, ready to act as walking-sticks or ponies, as might be desired. However ungraceful in our eyes is the tottering gait of these ladies when attempting to walk, it is certainly not so inelegant as the mode of transport which here is the very acme of refined fine-ladyism. The lady mounts on the back of her amah, whom she clasps round the neck with both her arms, while the amah holds back her hands, and then grasps the knees of her mistress. Very fatiguing for the poor human pony who sometimes is called upon to carry this awkward burden for a considerable distance, at the end of which, it is the lady, not the amah, who refreshes her exhausted strength with a few whiffs from a long tobacco pipe!

To-day the only work of the attendants was to fan us, and assiduously feed us with luscious preserved fruits and cakes, which it would have been deemed uncourteous to refuse, though it was terrible to have to swallow so many. One or two would really have been enjoyable, but here hospitality involves surfeit. It was a delightful relief when one of the amahs brought in a basket of pumeloes (the huge pink-fleshed citron), whose sweet acid flavour was a blessed change; and then another woman produced some of the nut-like seeds of the lotus plant, which are very nice. Chinese hospitality is only satisfied so long as the mouth of the guest is well filled.

One of the older ladies of the last generation was suffering from headache, and as a cure she wore a circular patch of black plaister on each temple. We very soon felt that the like fate would be ours, were we to stay much longer in the small crowded room, where the atmosphere was most oppressive for lack of ventilation, though it is hard to see why it should be so, as there are no doors in any Chinese house, only open portals embellished with the highest open-work carving, and there is much carved lattice-work all about the place.

As soon as we could venture, we rose to take our leave, which is necessarily a slow process, as in any case Chinese politeness requires the hosts to make every effort for the detention of their guests, and in the case of such *rara avis* as ourselves, I have no doubt the regret at parting was genuine. When at last we had successfully manœuvred our way out, hospitality still followed us in the form of baskets of fruit and of rice-cakes with burnt sugar.

C.F. GORDON CUMMING
Wanderings in China (1886)

c. 1880

Chinese Devils

Edward Morse, who was to become a leading authority on oriental ceramics, went to visit a pottery workshop outside Canton. He had been warned there would be trouble, so he packed a revolver along with his lunch before setting out on the twenty-four-mile river journey with a small boy as guide.

The place where we landed was covered with stacks of jars and pots of various kinds, and I hoped that a pottery was in the immediate vicinity, but, on inquiry, my guide found that the pottery was at the upper end of the town, a place we might easily have reached in the boat. I then discovered that the guide had never been to the town, and really knew nothing about it. However, there was no backing out now. The boat's crew had pulled out into the river, and the guide started ahead, and I after him. I certainly did not relish going through the narrow streets with a hooting mob as an escort, – a mob that had begun to collect the moment I landed. A troop of the dirtiest and raggedest hoodlums one could imagine started after us, and ran ahead yelling "Fanquai" at the top of their lungs. Men joined this mob, some of them insolently thrusting their heads under the broad brim of my sun-hat and grinding their teeth at me; indeed, I believe that the looks of withering scorn and hatred can be better portrayed by a Chinese face than by that of any other race in the world. It was useless to make any friendly advances, and so I did not attempt it, but looked as firm and defiant as possible under the circumstances, and kept one hand in my pocket holding on to a cocked revolver. . . . My little guide was in a complete funk, and I feared he would sneak off into the crowd and leave me alone. The boat's crew had pulled off into the middle of the river, for even they, though Chinese, came in for rough treatment, probably for being in the employ of a foreigner. I went into a shop to buy a piece of pottery, and the man looked deeply insulted by the intrusion. The extravagant sum I offered

125

for a modelled bird, fresh from the oven, could not be resisted, and I brought back with me a single trophy of my adventures. We had gone over a mile and passed large shops of pottery, but no sign of its manufacture. The guide frequently and timidly inquired, and was told to go on. . . . The streets were very narrow and literally stinking; the crowds increased in number and turbulence; boys ran far ahead to tell their people that a foreign devil was coming up the street. It reminded me of the way boys run ahead of a circus, and a circus it was, and I would gladly have been out of it.

Finally, and to my great relief, we turned up a narrow alley, followed by the howling mob of roughs. The alley led direct into a pottery. The potters left their work as they heard the racket, and so when I entered the place work had ceased, and a number of rough and savage-looking potters surrounded me with angry and inquiring looks. I made my way through the crowd, found a potter's wheel, and made gestures to a man, evidently the boss, that I wanted to see how they turned a pot, and the sight of a fee that was probably equal to a month's wages induced him, without an expression of thanks, to shout to a fellow to go to work. I was at last to see the working of a Chinese potter's wheel. I crowded back the mob, stepped on a naked toe now and then, and fairly bluffed myself into a place where I was enabled to make a hasty sketch of a potter at work. . . . In this pottery there was not a sign of a green leaf or flower; it was as barren as a brickyard. What vivid memories came back of the Japanese potter with his charming surroundings, the offering of tea and cake, the children in the neighborhood bowing as one passed . . . In contrast, this Chinese pottery in a desolate yard, the ground strewn with pottery fragments, a number of workmen shouting to each other or at me, a horde of ragged men and boys howling vile names, and I thought of my long walk back through the city, followed by this venomous mob of thoughtless brutes. I no longer wondered that magistrates could order these people to be beheaded by hundreds without a quiver of feeling, and, at the moment, I should have enjoyed the ordering of such a performance, and might have witnessed it with equanimity. By their disputes and gestures it was evident that they could not understand the reason of my visit. That a barbarian and foreign devil should hire a boat's crew of six men and a guide, and come all the way from Canton just to see a pot turned, was simply preposterous, and I must be a spy. A shout of contempt went up when I turned my back on the pottery and started down the narrow lane. The crowd kept up such a yelling that my approach was signalized far ahead, so that I

A Waterway Near Canton

passed through a serried array of frowning and angry faces. It was a relief to find that my boat's crew had not deserted me, but, hearing the uproar, had pulled in to the landing and was ready to row out the moment I got aboard. As we pulled into the stream, a salute of contemptuous shouts and a few stones followed us. Why they had not assailed me and smashed the boat, I could not understand, unless they had noticed that one hand had been in my pocket all the time, through which the outline of a rather heavy revolver might have been detected. We pulled across and down the river some distance, and running the bow ashore I prepared to eat my lunch, feeling a great relief in having left the Chinese devils behind, when a number of shadows fell across me and, looking up, I found the high embankment fringed with a lot of peasants, men and boys, who began jeering at me. These twenty or thirty seemed so harmless compared to the hordes in the city that I felt bold, took out my sketch-book, and began to set them down. This act instantly frightened most of them away, evidently disturbed by some superstition in having their pictures taken. A few men remained and defiantly made up faces at me, and jerked their arms in a peculiar gesture which the guide said meant to choke me.

If one soberly considers the manner in which the Chinese have been treated by Christian nations, he cannot be surprised at the attitude of the Chinese towards him. In the plainest way, it may be stated that the "Foreign Devils," under the guise of a diplomatic phrase known as "spheres of influence," have stolen thousands upon thousands of square miles of territory, have robbed them of nearly every open port, and have extorted untold millions in indemnities.

It was a relief to start for Canton, and leave these justifiable ruffians to their filth and superstitions.

EDWARD S. MORSE
Glimpses of China and Chinese Homes
(1902)

c. 1882

The Hour of Death

Fundamental misunderstanding between Chinese and Europeans was probably the root cause of most of their quarrels over the years. A.L., sometime Coroner of Hong Kong, discovered just how fundamental the problem could be.

It is a striking example of the practical difficulties which beset the task of forensic Interpretation in China that such a simple question as *Was he dead?* should admit of two different answers, *Yes* and *No*, according to whether the European or the Chinese idea as to when death occurs be followed. We believe, and probably with accuracy, that a man is dead when he has ceased to breathe, and when his blood no longer circulates; the Chinese consider him still alive whilst a trace of warmth lingers in the body. Thus the two estimates may differ by several hours.

The writer was for some years Coroner of Hongkong, and was able effectively to follow and check his very competent Interpreter, when the language was Cantonese. The time of death formed a stumbling-block in almost every Chinese case, even when there was no suspicion and the question was immaterial. The medical evidence would shew that the deceased must have been dead some hours when brought to Hospital, the relatives swear he was alive at the gate! One old woman coolly informed the Court that the Doctor did not know what he was talking about, she knew the man was *not* dead ... In other cases the apparent perjury of the witnesses on a point of probably trifling importance rendered it difficult to believe any statement they might make. "Can these people speak the truth about *anything* even if they try," was the feeling which frequently arose in the writer's mind, when the inevitable difference took place between the native witnesses and the Doctor or Inspector as to the hour of death.

Meanwhile it never seemed to occur to anybody in Court that *death* did not mean the same thing in either language, or that the term *hi*, not unnaturally translated *life* or *breath*, really signified neither in a European and scientific sense. It was not until some years after the writer had ceased to be Coroner that he was called to see one of his own servants who had suddenly died. The old dispute, as to whether the man was dead or not, sprang up with the relatives, literally *super visum corporis*. The man was as dead as Julius Caesar, but his relatives persisted he was not, and they appealed to a little lingering warmth about the chest to prove it. Subsequent enquiry shewd that this is the general view amongst Chinese. A person is considered to be dead when he is cold, and not before.

A.L.
"Chinese Notions as to
the Moment of Death"
The China Review,
Vol. X, No. 6, 1882

1886

The First Day

Cycling from Canton to Shanghai on a "penny-farthing" bicycle might seem foolhardy to some people. But to young American Thomas Stevens it was just another leg in a journey which had started two years earlier and had already taken him across the United States, Europe, and much of Asia. His tour through China was to take only five weeks, although he got off to a rather shaky start.

The consuls and others express grave doubts about the wisdom of my undertaking in journeying alone through China, and endeavor to dissuade me from making the attempt. Opinion, too, is freely expressed that the Viceroy will refuse his permission, or, at all events, place obstacles in my way. The passport is forthcoming on October 12th, however, and I lose no time in making a start.

Thirteen miles from Canton I reach the city of Fat-shan. Five minutes after entering the gate I am in the midst of a crowd of struggling, pushing natives, whose aggressive curiosity renders it extremely difficult for me to move either backward or forward, or to do aught but stand and endeavor to protect the bicycle from the crush. They seem a very good-natured crowd, on the whole, and withal inclined to be courteous, but the pressure of numbers, and the utter impossibility of doing anything, or prosecuting my search for the exit on the other side of the city, renders the good intentions of individuals wholly inoperative.

With perseverance I finally succeed in extricating myself and following in the wake of an intelligent-looking young man whom I fondly fancy I have enlightened to the fact that I am searching for the Sam-shue road. The crowd follow at our heels as we tread the labyrinthine alleyways, that seem as interminable as they are narrow and filthy. Every turn we make I am expecting the welcome sight of an open gate and the green rice-fields beyond, when, after dodging about the alleyways of what seems to be the toughest quarter of the city, my guide halts and points to the closed gates of a court.

It now becomes apparent that he has been mistaken from the beginning in regard to my wants: instead of taking me to the Sam-shue gate, he has brought me to some kind of a house. "Sam-shue, Sam-shue," I explain, making gestures of disapproval at the house. The young man regards me with a look of utter bewilderment, and forthwith betakes himself off to the outer edge of the crowd, henceforth contenting himself to join the general mass of open-eyed inquisitives. Another attempt to again enlist his services only results in alienating his sympathies still further: he has been grossly taken in by my assumption of intelligence. Having discovered in me a jackass incapable of the Fat-shan pronunciation of Sam-shue, he retires on his dignity from further interest in my affairs.

Female faces peer curiously through little barred apertures in the gate, and grin amusedly at the sight of a Fankwae, as I stand for a few minutes uncertain of what course to pursue. From sheer inability to conceive of anything else I seize upon a well-dressed youngster among the crowd, tender him a coin, and address him questioningly – "Sam-shue lo? Sam-shue lo?" The youth regards me with monkeyish curiosity for a second, and then looks round at the crowd and giggles. Nothing is plainer than the evidence that nobody present has the slightest conception of what I want to do, or where I wish to go. Not that my pronunciation of Sam-shue is unintelligible (as I afterward discover), but they cannot conceive of a Fankwae in the streets of Fat-shan inquiring for Sam-shue; doubtless many have never heard of that city, and perhaps not one in the crowd has ever been there or knows anything of the road. As a matter of fact, there is no "road," and the best anyone could do would be to point out its direction in a general way. All this, however, comes with after-knowledge.

. . . Finally the people immediately about me motion for me to proceed down the street.

Like a drowning man, I am willing to clutch wildly even at a straw, in the absence of anything more satisfactory, and so follow their directions. Passing through squalid streets occupied by loathsome beggars, naked youngsters, slatternly women, matronly sows with litters of young pigs, and mangy pariahs, we emerge into the more respectable business thoroughfares again, traversing streets that I recognise as having passed through an hour ago. Having brought me here, the leaders in the latest movement seem to think they have accomplished their purpose, leaving me again to my own resource.

Yet again am I in the midst of a tightly wedged crowd, helpless to make myself understood, and equally helpless to find my own way.

132

Three hours after entering the city I am following – the Fates only know whither – the leadership of an individual who fortunately "sabes" a word or so of pidgin English, and who really seems to have discovered my wants. First of all he takes me inside a temple-like building and gives me a drink of tea and a few minutes' respite from the annoying pressure of the crowds; he then conducts me along a street that looks somewhat familiar, leads me to the gate I first entered, and points triumphantly in the direction of Canton!

I now know as much about the road to Sam-shue as I did before reaching Fat-shan, and have learned a brief lesson of Chinese city experience that is anything but encouraging for the future. . . . The lesson of Fat-shan it is proposed to turn to good account by following the country paths in a general course indicated by my map from city to city rather than to rely on the directions given by the people, upon whom my words and gestures seem to be entirely thrown away.

For a couple of miles I retraverse the path by which I reached Fat-shan before encountering a divergent pathway, acceptable as leading distinctly toward the northwest. The inevitable Celestial is right on hand, extracting no end of satisfaction from following, shadow-like, close behind and watching my movements. Pointing along the divergent northwest road, I ask him if this is the *Koon lo* to Sam-shue; for answer he bestows upon me an expansive but wholly expressionless grin, and points silently toward Canton. These repeated failures to awaken the comprehension of intelligent-looking Chinamen, or, at all events, to obtain from them the slightest information in regard to my road, are somewhat bewildering, to say the least. So much of this kind of experience crowded into the first day, however, is very fortunate, as awakening me with healthy rudeness to a realizing sense of what I am to expect; it places me at once on my guard, and enables me to turn on the tap of self-reliance and determination to the proper notch.

Shaking my head at the almond-eyed informant who wants me to return to Canton, I strike off in a northwesterly course. The Chinaman grins and chuckles humorously at my departure, as though his risibilities were probed to their deepest depths at my perverseness in going contrary to his directions. As plainly as though spoken in the purest English, his chuckling laughter echoes the thought: "You'll catch it, Mr. Fankwae, before you have gone very far in that direction; you'll wish you had listened to me and gone back to 'Quang-tung.'"

THOMAS STEVENS
Around the World on a Bicycle **(1888)**

c. 1886

Strange Guest

*While hiking through the countryside outside Canton, American
missionary B.C. Henry had to put up with whatever accommodation
he could find.*

A tramp of four miles up the ascending grade brings us to a mountain
inn, the only one in the pass. . . . Immediately in front of the inn are
two beautiful liquid amber trees, backed by a fine old pine, which gives
an air of grace and refinement to the place. But the inn itself! Perhaps
the less said about it the better. It is a one storeyed structure, about
twelve by eighteen feet in dimension, with no windows, and a single
narrow door. There are two beds, with covers you shrink from touching,
and shudder as you see your own bedding laid upon them, and
hurriedly command it to be removed before anything adheres. Two rude
fireplaces, and before them two great heaps of ashes, kept in the house
lest dampness should destroy their fertilising qualities, a heap of
conglomerate rubbish, and an unspeakable loft, complete the general
view of the interior. In the absence of the regular inn-keeper, a gruff old
party (a stonemason, as we afterwards learned) left in charge growls out
a negative to all questions about beds, provisions, and general
necessaries. Happily provided with all that is needful, our supper is soon
prepared, and with appetite sharpened by a walk of twenty miles, we eat
with stoical indifference to the surroundings. Our attendants also
manage to find the rice jar, and some doubtful-looking wisps of dried
salt greens, which they appropriate.

As soon as darkness falls we spread our beds, some boards from the
loft being made to do duty in the space before the door. We have
scarcely fallen into the first doze, however, when a loud knocking at the
door calls forth emphatic growls from our quasi-host, and we are
entertained by the following dialogue:

Caller. "Open the door."

Host. "I can't."

C. "You must."

H. "There is a bed against it."

C. "Take it away."

H. "The men are asleep."

C. "So early? Wake them up."

H. "What do you want?"

C. "I want to see your strange guest."

H. "How do you know we have a strange guest?"

C. "Some men who were passing told it in the village."

The bed is moved back at last, and the door opened. A man comes in with noisy greeting, which is met with emphatic but suppressed disapprobation. I lie still under the cover, listening to some original remarks upon shoes and various articles of wearing apparel. A light is thrust over my face in spite of the host's remonstrances and sharp rebuke, for such a gross breach of propriety in prying into people's privacy. The intruder having satisfied his curiosity sums up the result of his observations in the remark, "Humph! it is only a foreign devil," and takes his departure.

Sleep comes as sweet and refreshing in the dingiest, dirtiest inn as in the most palatial hotel, as we proved on this occasion; and soon after the first rays of light found their way through the glass tiles in the roof, we arose with a feeling of renewed strength and vigour. I had breakfast served on the lid of a travelling basket under the graceful branches of the liquid-amber trees, and was the object of great curiosity to the dozen or more rustics from the neighbouring villages, who came with the earliest dawn to see the stranger. When breakfast was ready they were quietly reminded that good manners required them to withdraw while the guest was eating. They withdrew as requested, but from around the corners and the doorway kept a close watch upon all the proceedings. After breakfast I invited them near, and had a long and friendly conversation, winning their good-will to such an extent that they pressed me to remain several days with them and explore their mountain possessions. The leading man, a cross-eyed teacher, was especially agreeable, and displayed considerable intelligence on subjects of general interest. I found them to be a colony of Hakkas . . .

. . . I declined the cordial invitation of these mountain people, urging lack of time. The usual examination of my hair, clothes, shoes, etc., was submitted to, one of them naïvely remarking that my shoes were not made of iron as the visitor at the inn the night before had given them to understand, and another asking me to give some proof to them that I could see seven feet down into the earth, saying it was the general belief among them that foreigners could see as far into the solid earth as Chinamen could into clear water. Unable to gratify them on this point I took leave of them. The hotel bill, which included supper and breakfast for my four Chinese attendants, lodging, and the best bed for myself, with lights and other necessaries, reached the surprising sum of twenty-two cents, and a smile of pleasure actually spread over the stonemason's face as the money was placed in his hands.

B.C. HENRY
Ling-Nam or Interior Views of
Southern China (1886)

1889

Chinese Ponies

Lieutenant Cradock (otherwise Sir Christopher Cradock) was a sporting kind of man, and to him Hong Kong meant racing.

Hongkong, amongst its other attractions, enjoys the distinction of being the "Newmarket" of China, racing being indulged in in the East, far greater extent than people at home might imagine: every Coast Port, from "Sporting Shanghai" southwards, having its own little Meeting, regularly every year.

The several events are solely for Chinese ponies; and great is the number of "almighty dollars," that change hands over the efforts of these game little "rats."

These ponies have truly a curious career!

Born and bred in Mongolia, a country many hundreds of miles away from any of the Coast Ports, they probably spend the earliest and best years of their lives as pack animals, or beasts of burden: after which, those for disposal to the "despicable foreigner" are annually collected together in herds, and driven down by easy stages (taking weeks on the journey), to one of the northern Treaty Ports – from whence they are distributed by steamers to other places.

On the arrival of the herd, or mob as it is termed, they are taken to one of the large pony repositories, and there sold off either by private contract or by subscription lottery. . . .

It must be a great change for these beasts, when after living for years in the open, in a most severe climate, feeding on the roughest and coarsest food, they find themselves suddenly plunged into a life of good shelter, good food and grooming; and if they are meant for racing later on, they are never allowed to leave the stable door unless hooded and sheeted from nose to tail, like any English thorough-bred.

The principal features (I was going to say "points") of Chinese ponies

137

HONG KONG HARBOUR

are (with a few exceptions) heavy narrow heads, pig eyes, thick in the neck, and very short in the rein, straight shoulders, fair legs and feet, good ribs, drooping, badly furnished quarters: and the whole "bag of tricks" topped up with a tail set on half way down to their hocks. They are also hard pullers, and are bad tempered in the stable; the latter vice, being no doubt increased and encouraged by the Chinese *mafoos* (horse-boys), who I think, *taking them as a lot*, are without exception the worst, and most cowardly set of grooms in the world.

I am afraid I have not given so very encouraging a description of Chinese ponies; but . . . for all their misshape, the "records" in the table below, will show that *some* of them, when trained, can cover the ground at a very fair pace.

Place	Distance	Date	Name of Race	Name of Pony	Time
					m. sec.
Shanghai	Half mile	1875	–	Ravenscote	0 57
"	One mile	1881	–	First Cornet	2 04¾
Hongkong	One mile and a half	1889	Hongkong Club Cup	Pao-shing	3 11
"	Two miles	1883	Exchange Plate	Driving Cloud	4 22½

LIEUTENANT C. CRADOCK
Sporting Notes in the Far East (1889)

138

c. 1890

The Funny Man

Walter Young was in his early thirties and working for a bank in
Hong Kong. He spent weekends literally on the South China Coast.

. . . When we youngsters could leave the office we would hire a steam-
launch, say, on the Saturday afternoon, take with us our Chinese boys
and Ah Fong, the cook, a few "comestibles," and also a few sticks of
dynamite for fishing purposes . . . When we reached a certain quiet bay
we knew of, some twenty miles from Hong Kong, we would anchor our
launch; put on our bathing suits; drop into the dinghy, have a swim
round and some cherry-brandy; and then go a-fishing with our little bits
of dynamite tied to sticks of firewood, with a foot or two of fuse
attached. Having lighted the fuse, we would chuck it far away from the
boat; then lie on our oars holding ready little rope nets, tacked to the
end of long bamboos. When the explosion occurred, lots of fish came
stunned to the surface, and these we used to rake in for chow-chow.
. . . On one occasion, our dinghy kept drifting nearer and nearer the
dynamite, which smouldered but wouldn't go off. When we were nearly
on top of it expecting at any moment to be frightfully shocked (we were
too paralysed to pull away) one of our pals in the boat – a nervy chap –
dived overboard in a mortal funk. Then the long-waited-for explosion
exploded, and, as usual, the shock struck downwards; so our dear old
pal with the other silly fishes came floating to the surface tummy
topside! We didn't cook or fillet him – just smacked him to life – then
passed the cherry-brandy round! When we had gathered from the Pacific
Ocean sufficient fish . . . we returned to the launch and in due course
had a good fishy blow-out, with Cambridge sausages richly fried a lovely
toasty-brown to follow. You can just fancy us; on a tropical night, our
launch lying idly at anchor in a beautiful bay; the yellow moon as big as
a balloon, the yacht heaving gently with the tide and smacking the little
wavelets as they lapped her sides . . .

No other sound except an occasional snore from the Chinese servants would disturb us. None remained on deck save my dear faithful Ah Fong, cook, butler, boy and general factotum, who was ever at hand to serve us silently on the slightest pretext with iced drinks in nice long-sleeved tumblers. We lay stretched out in pyjamas on long cane chairs, a cheroot in one hand and something else within easy reach of the other. No mosquitoes to bother us – no lovely ladies to talk prettily to – just old pals swopping chestnuts, and sleepily gazing at the misty paddy-fields two hundred yards away, which we were to tramp over on the morrow in search of the zigzagtic snipe!

The next morning we were up bright and early, and after removing the cobwebs from our eyes by an early morning plunge into the cool and sparkling sea we, with amazing appetite, tackled our breakfast and prepared for the business of the day – the slaughter of snipe. Guns on our knees, we then made for the shore in the dinghy, in our big mushroom solar-topees; having previously told the Chinese servants to follow later on with the tiffin-baskets.

Each of us was loaded up with a hundred cartridges, and a flask of noble dimensions to provide against faintness. The usual little crowd of pigtails was waiting on shore to see what we were after; and when we wended our way towards the paddy-fields, one or two Chinese men with little children detached themselves from the crowd and ran off to await us later on. They had a horrible custom of sending their kiddies into the rice-fields with instructions to crouch down, and to bob up serenely as soon as they heard a shot, in the hope of getting a pellet in the eye or elsewhere. If, from the parental view, one of the little nippers had the luck to get one in the eye it was as good as a hundred dollars to the father. A few pellets in the sitting-down place were worth twenty-five dollars. . . .

Towards noon, when the day becomes stiflingly hot, snipe-shooting is not easy, for the heat seems to rise from the earth in quivering steamy columns. The paddy-fields are warm liquid mud in which the young rice is planted. The fields are divided for irrigation purposes by little ridges about eighteen inches high and some six or eight inches in width. On this slight footing the sportsman has to walk, and he, of course, is continually slipping off the ridge up to his knees in the hot mud bath on either side of him. He generally does this at the critical moment when a bird has risen, with a harsh screechy note as if old Harry were after him.

After two or three hours of this sort of work the sweat would pour down our faces and blur our eyesight – the mosquitoes simply awful. . . .

About one o'clock we were quite ready to chuck it and go for the tiffin-baskets. On the particular outing I have in my mind, we had told the servants to set the lunch under a fine big umbrageous tree near the roadside. . . . Under this refuge from the burning sun the boys had spread the table-cloth on the grass. We were delighted to see our noble Shanghai-hump and game-pie ready for an attack in force, also a few tins of *pâté de foie gras* and other little trifles to play with. After taking an appetiser from the quart bottle of ready-made cocktails Ah Fong had thoughtfully provided, we uncorked a few bottles of beer and, in muddied ducks and singlets, we squatted down and did ourselves jolly well!

About eighty couple of snipe lay alongside and we felt absolutely happy. . . .

The funny man of our party – there is always a funny man – was a merry soul with an abnormally long body and abnormally short legs. . . . he was a restless chap, and while we were lazily wishing we could consume more game-pie he fossicked around and eventually spotted, tied to a stake in a grass-field across the road, a wicked-looking water-buffalo. To this animal he gleefully called our attention and promised us some amusement.

. . . Although the water-buffalo, or carabâo, may be led by a little Chinese or Tagalo boy, he is dangerous to white men, for he seems to object to our aroma. It is always a ticklish business to pass through a field where a loose carabâo is grazing.

We sleepily watched little Longbody doing his funny piece by jeering at the beast, and dancing like a marionette in front of him. Longbody's little legs hopped about while he flourished his fingers a few inches from the bull's eye. We became tired of his antics, and were thinking of taking forty winks when we were alarmed by a shout. Much to our horror we saw the silly ass twenty yards away, sprinting in a direct line towards us with the carabâo a short head or two in his rear. After a little partial paralysis we realised the imminent danger of becoming spiked like herrings on a toasting fork, so we jumped to our feet and clambered into those heavenly branches. Just as we Absaloms had all magically disappeared, Longbody flew under us, stupidly putting his foot into and spoiling the remains of the game-pie; he stumbled, and the carabâo was almost on him! The beast just missed our pal with his wicked horns; but his skull caught Longbody exactly in the place where his singlet ended, and with an awful boost, chucked him ten feet away into a dry leafy ditch, where he disappeared.

Luckily for us, the infuriated animal galloped on, bellowing and lashing his tail; while we, after giving him ample law, dropped from the tree like caterpillars. Watching fearfully from the corner of our eye for the return of the native we took a drink. Then we walked to the ditch, raked over the leaves, and found our little pal, jarred and bruised, but more frightened than hurt. . . . We poured neat whisky down his throat till his back teeth were submerged; and when he had recovered asked him what the deuce he meant by trampling on the game-pie and decoying the buffalo to our tiffin table! . . .

This unfortunate incident put an end to our snipe-shooting for that day, so we told the boys to take all the stuff on board the launch and cook us half a dozen birds apiece for dinner.

WALTER H. YOUNG
A Merry Banker in the Far East (1916)

Beetle on a Pin

Looking back on his early years in the Consular Service in China, Edward Werner had vivid memories of some of his colleagues.

At Canton I served under the late Sir (then Mr.) Chaloner Alabaster, an official of the old gunboat policy, whose method was to put his case to the Chinese officials and, in the event of their not complying with his demands, to bang the table with his fist and threaten them with a British gunboat: a procedure then, but not now, possible and effective. Banging the table is regarded by the Chinese as a great insult, being supposed to be the equivalent, not only of an intention to bang, but of an actual banging of themselves. . . .

"The Buster," as he was familiarly called, was notoriously a hard task-master, difficult to get on with; but we hit it off exceedingly well, and he sent excellent reports about me to Peking. Certainly no one could have more conscientiously and industriously discharged the many duties attaching to the post than I did during those two strenuous years in that tropical climate and "prison" of Shamien.

His wife, Lady Alabaster, a most charming and kindhearted lady . . . was said to have had no less than fifty proposals of marriage before she accepted this physically insignificant and crippled dwarf. . . .

Her husband's stature (the result, it was said, of his shoulder having been broken through his nurse dropping him when he was a baby) was so diminutive that the amah once went and tucked him up in bed, mistaking him for one of his children! . . .

The "Buster" was not only thus physically deformed, but had a curious growl-like laugh or chuckle, which seemed to come from low down in one side of his throat – the side already lowered by the broken shoulder, and was perhaps conditioned by the physical deformity. On one occasion, at a large dance, when everyone present was sitting round the room between two dances, he (having, it was alleged, indulged somewhat freely during the evening) started walking, or rather hobbling, across the broad polished floor. Having reached the middle, he slipped and fell, and his broken shoulder preventing him from rising up again easily even when in his sober senses, he started twiddling round rapidly like a beetle on a pin, uttering all the while his curious gurgle-like chuckle. This escapade (or accident), getting noised abroad, is said to have stood in the way of the promotion to the high post he is said to have aimed at. . . .

The Portuguese Consul, a most charming and polite man (so polite that in accepting an invitation he always put "Mrs. and Mr." instead of "Mr. and Mrs."), his wife and daughter, one day asked some friends to a houseboat picnic on the river. His wife, having lost one hand, had a hook in its place, and his daughter had been born with one eye closed.

The huge houseboats used on the Canton river are generally towed by launches, but occasionally have to be poled by the boatmen. The latter do this by walking along from stem to stern on a narrow ledge which runs the length of the boat on the outside edge of the deck. In the present case, the party were sitting in wicker chairs on the deck, and one of the polers in passing lost his balance and, clutching hold of the back of the chair occupied by the Consul's wife, the latter turned a somersault backwards into the river, she, the chair, and the boatman disappearing beneath the surface. Seeing this, the one-eyed daughter was so astonished and alarmed that she jumped into the river on the other side of the boat, possibly imagining, in the bewilderment of the moment, that this might help to balance things (as it were). So the one-eyed daughter was in the river on the one side of the boat, and her one-armed mother in the river on the other side. But the latter had the presence of mind to raise her hook out of the water, and the French Consul, who was one of the guests, and had remained sitting in his chair, merely bent over and caught hold of the hook. Its possessor was then easily landed, or rather, shipped, and by means of a long boat-hook the daughter was also rescued. The poler subsequently appeared with a smiling face over the stern of the boat, having climbed up by the rudder.

So all was well that ended well (if somewhat damply), especially as the very polite Portuguese Consul . . . obtained for the French Consul, an Order of quite a high class for "gallantry in saving life!"

E.T.C. WERNER
Autumn Leaves (1928)

1893

Only a Girl

The Reverend Arthur Simpson journeyed through a number of "Missionary Lands" to see what progress was being made by the Church. While staying at Canton he spent a day visiting nearby villages.

As we landed at one of these villages, about six miles from Canton, we were astonished to find that we were as strange to these people as if we had come from another world. The children ran screaming into the houses, and the mothers were afraid to let us look inside lest we should "frighten the children." It was evident that some of them, at least, had never seen a foreigner before. Soon, however, they began to crowd around us, and ere long we were marching through the town with more than five hundred men, women and boys in our train. After we had scattered a few bits of sugar-cane in the crowd, which is their favorite sweet, they considered us quite safe, and perhaps even popular, and they showed us around.

The great sight of this village was the duck house. Here the ducks are incubated by artificial heat, and we saw great trays and boxes full of thousands of duck eggs in all stages of hatching. When the ducks are old enough, they are taken out to feed in great flocks. A duck boat is quite large and will hold many thousands of them. They simply sail up a little creek, and lay a plank to the shore, and the ducks just march out at call, and scatter in little companies over the rice fields, and spend the day in feeding on all the bugs, worms and insects to be found. They are very welcome visitors, for they destroy the pests that injure the crops, and the farmers and ducks are great friends. When evening comes, the duck shepherd calls in his flock, and they come quacking along as sensibly as well-trained sheep, and walk across the gang-plank to the ship, and each flock knows and goes to its own cabin or sleeping place, without the slightest trouble. The driver has a long whip, and they say there is great excitement when the ducks come to embark, for they know that the tardy ones and the last one will get a thrashing, and so they scramble and scream to get in first.

The first thing we saw at every village landing was the ancestral temple, or hall, where worship is regularly paid to the parents of the various households. Indeed, we found that usually each village belonged to a single family, all being related to one another and bearing the same name for countless generations. The village we landed at was La, and all were the children of La and successive Las, and so all assembled at the same shrine and burned their tapers to the same ancestors. We went into the temple and saluted the score or two of head men and others that were there, and as we looked at the countless tablets with the names of all their fathers, we began to feel something of the age and conservatism of China.

In one of the villages opposite Canton we went into a number of Chinese flower gardens, and laughed again and again at the odd shapes into which they had dwarfed and twisted every sort of plant and tree. Some were like dragons, others like men, women and gods. Some were comic, others religious; others, again, beautiful imitations of mountains, valleys and landscapes, with grottos, pagodas and houses here and there on the mountain side. But all were in miniature. Here were orange trees with fruit and flowers, and the trees were less than a foot high; forest trees, many years old, as big as rose bushes; boxwood plants cut to look like a great fat Buddha, or brother Jonathan, tall and lank, with an umbrella in his hand and his hat on one side of his head.

In another village was a great Buddhist temple full of lazy priests and sacred pigs and hens. Here is a regular pig-pen, with gigantic swine, so fat that they can scarcely move, which some one has rescued from the butcher's hands and dedicated to the gods, and here they are fed by all the pious worshippers who come, until their troughs are running over with rice and onions, and they are ready to die of corpulence. Here they live in peace till they die of old age . . .

But the saddest sight we saw that day, and the one that will live longest in our memory as a sort of Monograph of heathenism in its cruel horrors, was a little dead baby girl, floating with downward face on the water of the canal. All around were hundreds of boats, little family boats, full of men and women and children rowing and paddling about in the canal, but no one seemed to notice or care for her. Not a yard away was the boat from which, perhaps, she had fallen, but her little helpless hands had been stretched out to them in vain, and her little cries had been stilled by the waters of death ere they responded. *She was only a girl!* It was *"her fate"* to fall over, and why should they interfere? So our friends told us the Chinese really believed and acted. They assured us that if we were to fall into that canal, probably not a single hand would be moved to save us. It was our business, and why should they interfere? If we chose to drown, they were not going to hinder us; and if we chose to swim, why – all right.

REV. A.B. SIMPSON
Larger Outlooks on Missionary Lands (1893)

1893
John Chinaman

Thomas Dewar, a member of the famous Scotch whisky family, was travelling in the East for his health. Approaching Hong Kong his ship was caught in a typhoon – he called it a monsoon – with surprising results for the Chinese passengers on board.

... The wind freshened up more, and my friend Speedy told me in a most cold-blooded manner, "We'll have to look about us now, for we're going to tackle a monsoon!"

We did tackle it, or rather perhaps I should say it tackled us, and for over two days we had a very lively time of it. The poor Celestials were awfully frightened, and the scared look they had on their faces was quite comical to behold. The second night of the monsoon they took the matter into their own hands, and held a kind of prayer-meeting – supplicating their "Josses" to send fair weather. It was a very strange sight to see the whole 250 of them on their knees, holding a lighted taper stuck into a potato, and hard at it, pouring out their supplications, making a most indescribable and confused babel. After going at this for some time, they all got up and threw the tapers and potatoes into the sea, and then resumed the happy and contented smile that is peculiarly John Chinaman's own, for they were quite certain they had appeased the wrath of their "Josses," and that fine weather would soon follow. And so it did – the next day. But I don't think the tapers and potatoes had anything to do with it. The first officer very artfully made out that he had the most to do with it, for he knew how long he would be steering through this pretty monsoon, and that evening he harangued the 250 Chinamen very sternly ... but here I must make a little divergence to show where the *point* comes in.

Every Chinaman dies with the idea that he is going to be buried in his own country, and his compatriots do their best to carry out his ideas by shipping his remains ... but they are not over scrupulous as to how

148

COMING ON BOARD

they get them on board. Now, in the present instance, one Celestial, perhaps more timid than the rest, told the officer quietly and mysteriously that the "Josses" sent the storm because some of the Chinamen had smuggled some corpses on board without paying freight for them. He told him who they were, but begged and prayed most piteously that the source of information should not be divulged. The subject of the officer's harangue was the wickedness of displeasing the "Josses" by being dishonest, and he said he was quite certain that they had amongst their baggage some that had not been paid for, and that until the money had been paid over, bad weather would continue. All the luggage was examined, and sure enough in one carpet bag three skulls were found, in a dilapidated chest two or three limbs, and in an old champagne case an assortment of limbs and a skull. To teach them a lesson, he made them all pay something, and collected a good few pounds, then rated them very soundly, and said the "Josses" would send fine weather in the morning. By the early morning we had got clear of the monsoon, and were in lovely weather . . .

THOMAS R. DEWAR
A Ramble Round the Globe (1894)

1894

Sudden Death

Charles Halcombe of the Imperial Maritime Customs was living in Hong Kong when the colony received a most unwelcome visitor – the plague.

During the latter part of April 1894, we heard in Hongkong that a strange and dreadful disease had broken out in Canton, whose inhabitants suddenly became panic-stricken and fled to Hongkong in thousands – every steamer arriving from there being crowded each trip, until the colony was densely packed with them. Then the startling news was spread abroad that the death-dealing pestilence – in all respects analogous to the Great Plague of London in 1665 and 66 – was in our midst. . . .

A poor lean rat would creep out on the floor before you, and overcome with the disease, stagger and fall; then drag itself a little further away from its untenable hole, a little nearer you, as if for company, and die almost at your feet. That poor little thing was the first harbinger of death – a sure sign that the pestilence was stealing into your house; and you could not shut it out. Who would be the first? That was the awful question; and you all gathered together, and watched one another, looking for the first dreaded symptoms – a slight feeling of dizziness and faintness. . . .

Those who were able to fled from the colony, before it was too late and those who could not, went to their homes. Servants left their places and hurried off to join their families before death dispersed them. Two of my own servants went home and died: and several rats came out in my rooms all of which died from the plague – I buried them at once and took every precaution, burning sulphur and sandalwood continually, and using plenty of carbolic acid and chloryde of lime. But my wife and I fully expected every moment to be stricken with it, as I had marked symptoms and was very ill with a large boil for some time.

But in the midst of all this misery, desolation and death, some few heroic men worked and toiled for suffering humanity. . . .

Dr. Cantlie was absent on a holiday, at Pekin, when the epidemic broke out, but he at once hurried back directly he heard of it. Many a day have I met him hurrying along through the death-haunted streets, fearlessly going into the worst places and houses – into the most filthy dens of disease, where the pestilence was raging with dreadful potency – to tend poor penniless people from whom he would take no fee, whom he helped out of his own purse and provided with medicines. If ever a man deserved to receive the honour of knighthood, he does. . . .

Our English soldiers there also acted splendidly throughout: and went through some really dangerous and fulsome work. Many Chinese hid the bodies of their deceased relatives away in the houses so as to avoid the premises being cleaned and disinfected and the accumulated filth of years cleared away. In consequence search parties had to be organized to enter every house, and hundreds of corpses were found secreted in this manner and were buried. Great piles of refuse and garbage were cleaned out from some houses, that must have taken years to collect, where the germs of disease were cultivated. And the soldiers came forward and volunteered to clean the city out, when no one else would venture even near or in the vicinity of a plague-stricken house. One noble young British officer, whose name I am ashamed to say I have forgotten, fell a victim to the plague – sacrificing his promising life for the sake of the colony: he died after a hard day's work with his men. . . .

As all the hospitals soon became overcrowded with plague patients, mat-sheds had to be erected for their reception and treatment. At last, however, after thousands had been swept away, the colony began to shake itself free. Slowly and surely the dire pestilence was driven away, being met and courageously grappled with by the army of young English military volunteers who gallantly rose to the occasion and, acting the part of scavengers and heroes, routed out and burned tons and tons of filth and rubbish which had been accumulating for years. After the subtle poison in the air had sufficiently expended itself and was not further impregnated with exhalations from the putrid ground and the dirt-heaps covering it – hot-beds where the atomic germs had developed and multiplied – the epidemic began to abate. And by the month of August the colony and its inhabitants once more assumed its wonted appearance.

CHARLES J.H. HALCOMBE
The Mystic Flowery Land (1896)

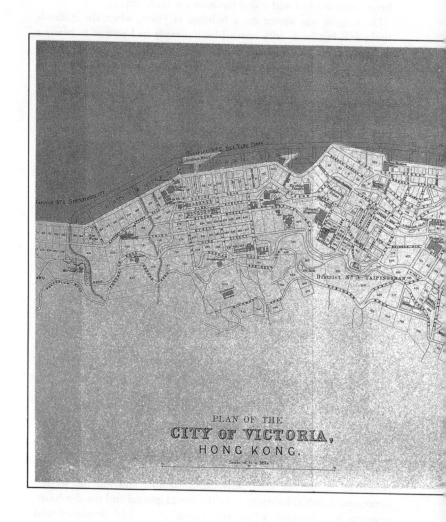

PLAN OF THE
CITY OF VICTORIA,
HONG KONG.

Scale of ½ a Mile

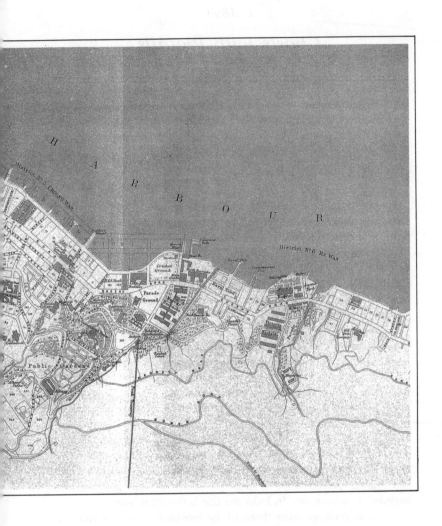

Ghosts with Pigtails

*While on leave from India, Captain George Younghusband visited
Singapore and then came to Hong Kong where he spent a few days.*

The steam-launch from the Hong Kong Hotel meets all ships, and no
sea-worn traveller can do better than step straight on board of it. The
hotel is one of the best I have come across in Asia, and recalls to
memory the large and well-managed hotels of Europe. The rooms are
excellent: large, well furnished, and well appointed. Ours was on the
fourth story, at a corner, where we caught every cooling breeze, and
from the veranda of which we could command a splendid view of the
harbour and mainland. . . .

In Singapore it is considered the height of wickedness to ride in a
rickshaw, and no resident would dream of appearing in one. At Hong
Kong, however, horsed conveyances are not obtainable on the spur of
the moment, and therefore the choice remains between riding in a
rickshaw or being carried in a "chair." Any one with the least proper
pride, however, will not be seen in a rickshaw, or certainly not a public
rickshaw. To be thoroughly *chic*, a "chair," the ancient "jampan" of
India, is quite necessary. We saw very few ladies in rickshaws; all were
being carried about in solemn pomp, at the rate of two miles an hour, in
chairs. Perhaps a rickshaw is looked upon as a fast and unladylike
conveyance; perchance it is regarded much as our grandmothers
regarded a hansom cab. In India the tide is the other way.

In the evening we drove down to the race-course – a very nice one
too: but where on earth the ponies, or horses, come from to race, it is
impossible to conjecture. During our stay in Hong Kong we saw, first
and last, perhaps a dozen ponies; and a man of ordinary activity could
have run faster than any one of these could gallop. The China pony is
not unlike the Kabuli pony, but with straight, heavy shoulder, and

absolutely impossible paces. A resident told me that he had had four in as many years, and none of them could stand on their legs at all, at any pace faster than a walk. Polo, of a sort, is played; but the ponies, as I said before, are impossible. . . .

The Sikh police are in full evidence in the streets, and, after dark, mount with carbines and ball ammunition. A policeman's life does not seem to suit our old friend the Singh. He is so large and lethargic by nature, that the professional dawdle of a policeman gives him a sloppy look. The damp heat, too, is against him, and he has the appearance of one whose back is about to break. As far as his duties go, he is, I believe, an eminent success.

The garrison consists of one British infantry regiment, one or two batteries, some sappers, and the Hong Kong Regiment. Here, as at Singapore, great groaning is going on over what is called the "military contribution," that is, the sum exacted from the colony for the support of the garrison. "We don't want any of your soldiers here – the fleet is enough for us," said a leading merchant to me. Of course, he knew best. Later, at dinner, I happened to ask why all the troops were garrisoned in the close, hot town, instead of on the airy and salubrious Peak. "Bless you, there are 200,000 Chinamen in this town to be kept in order!" said the same member. Whereat there was a general laugh all round. As at Singapore, a commander-in-chief sways the sceptre over this diminutive force; and a governor sways another sceptre over him. Looking out from our commanding position at the hotel, it was a somewhat striking fact that the only British men-of-war in harbour were an obsolete old wooden three-decker, built in the year A.D. 1, and called the *Victor Emmanuel*; and a diminutive gunboat, about the size of a junk. Close alongside H.M.S. *Victor Emmanuel* lay a fair-sized modern French man-of-war, which could have sunk her in three minutes; whilst three other good-sized war-vessels of the same nationality lay close by. If war had been declared whilst we were looking out of the window, it would have been a poor look-out for Hong Kong at the commencement of hostilities. Both entrances to the harbour are, however, no doubt thoroughly prepared with submarine mines, torpedoes, and the remaining delights of naval warfare; so that the Frenchman's triumph would be short. At the same time, I felt much in prospective for the proprietors of the Hong Kong Hotel: it is so very prominent, and just a nice range from the anchorage of the foreign men-of-war.

At the hotel all the servants, including the chambermaids, are Chinamen; and very good servants they seem to make. The hopeless squalor of an Indian hotel is entirely absent, and the Chinaman keeps everything as clean as an English servant. One Chinaman does as much work as three Indian servants, and draws from two to three times as much pay. The waiters wear long white nightgowns, and look like ghosts with pigtails.

There are some very good European shops in the town, and of course crowds of Chinese tradesmen. Evidently a chemist's shop pays well, for there are five within shouting distance of the hotel. We found nothing much to tempt us except a few small silver ornaments, a Chinese *chou* dog – quite black, tongue and all – and basket-chairs, which are made in every variety of form and shape. Many of the designs are beautiful, and the work is excellent. They cost from one to four dollars each. The *chou* dog cost a dollar and a half, and went back to India with us. A curious custom with regard to the coinage is met with. Such a large number of counterfeit dollars are in circulation that the bank punches its own brand on all the good dollars: this punching process, besides stamping some Chinese words on the silver, from the force of the blow makes the dollar into a little bowl. These "chopped" dollars, as they are called, with a handle fixed to them make unique spoons. . . .

Hong Kong is only three days' sail from Manilla; therefore, here are to be found Manilla cigars at their best and cheapest. They vary from one and a half dollars to six dollars a hundred. An excellent cigar can be had at the rate of three dollars a hundred. It seems impossible to get a good Manilla cigar in England, or in India; yet here they are, of the finest quality, and simply pining for purchasers. I have heard it gravely stated that there is opium in Manilla cigars, and that consequently they give you a headache. As my friend the tobacconist remarked, "they would be worth a shilling a-piece if there was opium in them: opium is as dear as gold."

CAPTAIN G.J. YOUNGHUSBAND
On Short Leave to Japan (1894)

1900

The Man of Science

By the age of thirty Elias Burton Holmes was already well-known in America as a successful public lecturer who brought back entertaining accounts – and photographs – from around the world. Now he was in Hong Kong to experience, on behalf of his audiences at home, what the place had to offer.

My first sortie is to the Chinese tailor to order suits of white, which are made in no time, for practically nothing – about one dollar and seventy-five cents a suit. The cost of laundering is only five cents each. We elbow our way in Queen's Road, the principal thoroughfare, through busy crowds, along the arcaded sidewalks; we see myriads of beautiful brown legs, with splendid brown bodies above them, bodies nude to the waist, backs streaming with warm rain, wide straw hats dripping water; calm coolie faces wet with sweat. Toil, toil on every side! for all these brown men are hauling jinrikishas or carrying chairs, suspended from long bamboo poles – the passing human panorama is all new to us, for the Chinese predominate to such an extent that it appears as if the white man were being crowded out. . . .

The first day of sight-seeing includes a 'rikisha tour wherever it is possible to go in a wheeled vehicle – along the water-front from end to end, from "Sugar House" to "Gas Works," and then up and down all the level streets in the lower town, then to the race-course and the cemeteries, Parsee, Catholic, Protestant, and Mohammedan. . . .

Through the kind offices of the consul-general we are put up for an indefinite period at the palatial Hongkong Club, where we meet men prominent in all the enterprises of the colony. We are presented to a doctor, who prescribes for us an easy chair out on the balcony, and a long cool glass of something. The long cool glass is one of the institutions of Hongkong. While the ice melts, the doctor confides to us the fact that he has had a hard day of scientific labor. "Just been

157

studying four Chinese plague patients, – dead ones of course," he calmly remarks, whereupon we are so impolite as to shrink instinctively from the man of science. "No danger," he continues, as he follows us into the library; "the plague seldom touches Europeans, and there is no use trying to avoid it. The servant who brings your morning tea and toast may have left a brother dying in a Chinese tenement. The papers report from twenty-five to thirty cases daily; these are the known cases only. Five times as many cases are jealously concealed." Then he relates startling incidents of the present outbreak. The night before he had stumbled over something in the roadway. It proved to be the head servant of a rich English family, stricken down by the bubonic terror as he was returning to serve dinner at their villa on the Peak. The morning of our arrival a jinrikisha coolie fell dead between the shafts, while running with a passenger. The dead man was picked up, placed in his own jinrikisha, and rushed away; the first ride he had ever had, and the last. "Therefore, why make yourselves miserable with worry? Take your chances cheerfully like the rest of us, and come to tiffin." "Tiffin," in the language of the East, means the midday meal. "But why do they hang the tablecloths to dry in the dining-room?" the griffin will ask as he perceives long white linen affairs suspended vertically from the ceiling. I must explain that "griffin" is the Far Eastern word for "tenderfoot." The griffin is bound to make mistakes. The supposed tablecloths are "punkas," Indian word for fans, huge, white, suspended wind-producers, which waving slowly to and fro keep the air constantly in circulation. Without the punka it would be impossible to eat. The superiority of this contrivance to the electric fan is at once apparent. The buzzing wheel of the latter projects a dangerous draft through the stagnant atmosphere of a hot room, ruffling our nerves, while the silent waving of the punka-wings produces the effect of a gentle breeze, which cools the room and soothes the senses. The punka is the delight of all save the poor punka-pullers, the miserable boys and men who stand outside on the sunny balcony and tug at the resisting ropes by means of which the motive power is transmitted. You can hire a boy to pull a punka-rope all day and part of the night for a monthly salary of about two dollars. The side streets of Hongkong are lined with sleepy Orientals, tugging rhythmically at ropes which dangle even from the windows of the topmost stories.

E. BURTON HOLMES
The Burton Holmes Lectures, Vol. V (1901)

1900

Bound Feet

The Natural Feet Society had asked Alicia Little – a writer and long-time resident of China – to tour the southern provinces and campaign against the ancient custom of footbinding. At Canton, Mrs. Little tried to enlist the support of the Viceroy, Li Hung Chang. (Li, a prominent figure in Chinese politics for over forty years, had led the "modern" party at Court which favoured learning from the West.)

... The chief feature of the visit to Canton consisted in an interview, accorded as soon as asked for, with the then Viceroy, Li Hung Chang. ... the British Consul, when asked in the first instance whether he could give an introduction or in any way facilitate it, pronounced it such an impossibility that a Chinese Viceroy should be willing to receive a lady, that he seemed to think it even unnecessary to say he could render no assistance in a matter so contrary to all decorum. Happily Mr. Volpicelli, Consul-General for Italy, residing in Hong-Kong, had thought otherwise, and already furnished me with a letter to his friend Lord Li – Li Hung Chang's adopted son. I therefore wrote to Lord Li indicating how much it would help forward the anti-footbinding movement, if I could gain any sign of approbation from the Viceroy, and asking whether he could in any way arrange it ... Lord Li immediately replied appointing a day and hour ... although without his knowing it the time he selected was singularly inconvenient, being that already appointed for a meeting of Chinese ladies. There had been before this a meeting of men and women at the Presbyterian Chapel ... and I have never addressed an audience, that seemed so much moved as that Cantonese audience, if one might judge by their laughter, generally a pretty fair indication in China, or by the way in which they all crowded up to the top of the chapel to pay each a small sum of money, and receive a paper indicating their association with the Natural Feet Society. It was impossible for the women to join there and then, as they

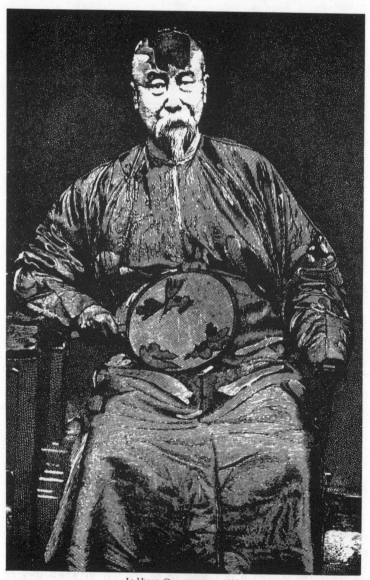

LI HUNG CHANG ABOUT 1900

could not get through the crowd of men, but the naval captain's wife took the opportunity afterwards for saying that she was going to let out her feet, had indeed already begun to do so, whilst an old woman of over seventy was eager to relate that, although no one had had courage to advise her to do so at her age, yet she had let out her feet; and though for some time she had certainly suffered very much, yet, determined to continue as an example to others, she was now thankful to say she suffered no more and could as we saw step out wonderfully well even considering her age alone.

The next day was settled for a meeting of ladies with bound feet, no others to be admitted. And then Lord Li appointed the very day and hour for an interview with the Viceroy, and to crown all it set to and poured – as it never can pour in England. Thus only nine Chinese ladies turned up, and even then we were astonished to see so many, for Chinese dread the rain even more than English cats do. I had only time to say a few words, before leaving them with many apologies, but there was again a proof of how little importance we instruments are in the world, for although the meeting would never have been called but for my visit to Canton, and the ladies had been invited to meet me, yet when I went away and left them, the other European ladies pleaded so efficaciously that all nine Chinese there and then decided not only to join our society but themselves actually to unbind . . . Meanwhile Dr. Fulton and I proceeded to the Viceroy's official residence . . .

We were shown at once into a side ante-room, passing by one in which a mandarin sat cowering in furs and much anxiety. The two interpreters joined us almost immediately, Lord Li and Dr. Mak, and very shortly word was sent that Li Hung Chang was ready to receive us, and after passing along a long corridor, a spacious courtyard on either side, and to the right an aviary full of birds, we were received by the great man standing at the door of his little reception room, a most imposing figure, six foot four in height, clad in an ermine-lined gown down to his feet, and a beautiful sable cape, with diamonds actually in the front of his cap as well as on his fingers. This at least my missionary friend told me with an American's quickness of sight for diamonds and sables. I only noticed his great height, uncommonly European type of feature, and piercing glance, as he received us most graciously, and waved us to seats at a round table in the middle of the room. There was one especially cushioned armchair for the old man, and an attendant stood close at hand to help him into and out of it. Lord Li sat down opposite, as we took our seats on either side of the Viceroy, Dr. Mak drew up another chair to his right and somewhat in the rear, and a line of men servants stood at 'tention all down one side of the room. This line of listening servants is what stands for public opinion and the press in China. It is also through them that the most important State secrets are known to the man in the street before diplomatists have even taken them in! . . .

. . . "No, I do not like to see little children suffer over having their feet bound," grumbled out the genial Viceroy. "But then I never do see them," he hastened to add. I told him his brother's descendants, his own relations were many of them not binding. He could not believe this, so I ventured to say something about his mother. "Oh, she only let out her feet when she was quite old," said Li Hung Chang. "I think all the women in the Li family have always been bound." Then as I looked discouraged, knowing it was not the case with the present generation, yet not liking to set the great man right about these family details, Lord Li politely interposed: "I can tell you of one who never has been and never will be, my own little girl." Li Hung Chang apparently thought it discreet not to seem to hear this, as he proceeded, "And you want me to unbind the feet of the women of China? No! now, that really is beyond my powers. . . ." The bright idea however occurred of asking him simply to write something on my fan as a recognition of the movement, and with the greatest good nature, he called two servants to lift him out of his arm-chair, for with his great height and advanced years he could not then stand up or sit down unaided, and walking to a writing table proceeded there and then to write an inscription, which has been shown at every anti-footbinding meeting since, and carried great weight. . . . Then he grumbled out, turning to me, "You know if you unbind the women's feet you'll make them so strong, and the men so strong too, that they will overturn the dynasty." I have often thought of this prediction of Li Hung Chang's since . . . That he has a charm none who talk with him can doubt, and the idea could not help crossing my mind how often Tse Hsi must regret that he is no longer her right-hand man, and that something or someone ever came between them. For with that imposing personality beside the throne the Dowager Empress must surely have felt a cheerier as well as a safer woman.

MRS. ARCHIBALD LITTLE
The Land of the Blue Gown (1902)

A Pile of Dollars

---

*World traveller C.D. MacKellar could not resist going to Macao even
though he disliked gambling.*

It is the thing to go from Hong-Kong to Macao, the Portuguese place,
for week-ends; but I went on a Tuesday. I left my room and all my
belongings in charge of my three Chinese boys. The steamboat took
three hours to reach Macao, was clean and good, and Captain Clarke
was most entertaining. . . . In the dining-saloon hung cutlasses and
loaded guns for the use of the passengers should the Chinese attempt
anything, and Chinese sailors, armed with sword, pistol, and gun, stood
on guard over the hatchways leading to the lower deck, where hundreds
of Chinese were padlocked down – for some of these might be
pirates. . . .

Captain Clarke kept a sharp look-out on all junks which came near
us.

The harbour of Macao looked very pretty as we entered it – the sweep
of it is supposed to resemble a miniature Bay of Naples. As a harbour it
is now no use, as it is silting up. . . .

. . . The Boa Vista Hotel is quite a good building and has prettily laid
out terraces descending to the sea. Captain Clarke, of the boat I came
over in, owns and runs it, and he and his wife seem to manage well –
though in truth it seemed really to be managed by Chinese "boys." My
bedroom window had a pleasant outlook over the town and
harbour. . . .

After dinner that evening I did what is the usual thing, and went to
the Chinese fantan or gambling-house. I walked down alone through a
street crowded with Chinese, lined with Chinese shops, open to the
street. Seeing some little bits of porcelain I liked, I went in and bought
them, but in pretending to give me back my change the Chinaman in
the shop kept back most of it. On my naturally objecting, he became

most insolent and called out things in Chinese to the others, and instantly the shop filled and they began to hustle me. I only realised then that I had done a silly thing coming out at night alone into this Chinese part. An old Chinaman, however, rushed in, harangued the others, pulled me out, and simply bundled me into the gambling-house, which was opposite, warning me to be careful what I did, and not to come out alone like that at night.

The fantan house was a dirty place, open in the roof to a room above, a rail running round this opening, and there above were the naval officers and the ladies letting down their money in a basket. I sat at the table amidst a mob of Chinese, with other excited half-naked Chinese sprawling over my back. The game was simple enough. I loathe gambling, do not like winning money (strange as it may seem!), and it does not amuse me in the least. I was doing it this night merely to see what the place was like and study the gambling Chinese. Yet, strange to say, whenever I put my money down I won, and so I scraped in quite a pile of dollars – I found afterwards I had enough to pay my total expenses in Macao! When tired of it, the heat, and the Chinese perfume, I departed, and was quite surprised that my former enemies in the street did not see that that was the time to molest me, overflowing with ill-gotten wealth as I was. Every one comes from Hong-Kong for the week-end or a few days to indulge in this pastime, but, according to my old-fashioned ideas, it is a strange taste that brings ladies into such a place.

The following morning I hired a rickshaw and two Chinese boys and explored Macao. The streets of the town are narrow and often steep. I dislike a rickshaw very much, and still more do I dislike being drawn about by a panting and perspiring runner; but, of course, here it is the usual thing.

I went first to the ruins of the church of San Paulo, the façade of which is alone remaining, and it is a conspicuous object from every quarter. It was destroyed by fire in 1835. It is approached by long, steep flights of steps under which is said to be a vault containing treasure . . .

I inspected a silk factory in a dirty Chinese village, where numbers of women were spinning – a curious sight . . .

. . . We stopped near the town to watch the funniest football match I had seen for long. Portuguese, English, and a Chinaman were playing. The latter, in his wide flapping trousers and his pigtail flying was very comical.

Then, as usual with me, I discarded the rickshaw and walked

everywhere – I always thought it was what legs were for. When strolling under the banyan trees on the Praya Granda ... a band of three Portuguese police with a Chinese prisoner caught up to us. The four of them and my coolie entering into an animated conversation, I asked what it was about, and learnt that the Chinese prisoner was being taken there and then to execution – to be beheaded. We accompanied them part of the way, whilst I asked questions, I bestowing cigarettes on them all, including the condemned man – who was perfectly at ease and quite cheerful, and smiled upon me in the most friendly way in thanking me for the cigarettes. They were most anxious I should go with them – I believe even the prisoner wanted it – but I was horrified when I realised the thing, and that the smiling, cigarette-smoking wretch was going to his death! To the great disappointment of my coolie I turned back ere we reached the place. There was something so careless and callous about it all – on this lovely, bright, sunshiny day, too. But it is a fact that death has little terror for a Chinaman, and this one did not seem to realise what it meant. . . .

When I departed from Macao at eight o'clock one morning, it was to enter into a dense fog, in which the steamboat lay at rest for nearly two hours, the Captain keeping a sharp look-out on the junks, whose sails

IN A MACAO GAMBLING HOUSE

now and then loomed near us through the grey blanket. It was a strange experience lying motionless there in that grey world, with hundreds of incessantly talking Chinese padlocked down on the deck below us. Suppose, in the fog, a swarm of yellow-faced figures had suddenly boarded and overpowered us, and liberated those hundreds below us? – it might easily have been. And though I like the Chinese, I have always said that I should have a horror of being put to death by them. I do not know why, but the repulsion at the idea is there.

When I reached the hotel at Hong-Kong I was welcomed by my three Chinese boys, conducted to my room, and there was surprised to find that, quite unasked for, all my belongings had been overhauled, my clothes washed and mended, and everything arranged in perfect order!

How delighted the good creatures were that I was pleased! And not a thing would they let me do for myself after that.

C.D. MACKELLAR
Scented Isles and Coral Gardens (1912)

1903

"Can Do"

While working in the South for the Chinese Imperial Customs, Oliver Ready discovered just how comfortable and well-run a bachelor's establishment could be.

The word "boy" bears no reference whatever to the individual's age, which may be anything between sixteen and sixty. It is merely a term applied by foreigners to their personal attendants.

The duties of the boy are those of the ordinary housekeeper in England, with several additions.

He looks after the other servants and is generally responsible for their good behaviour. He pays all wages and the accounts of the local tradespeople, on which, of course, he levies a recognised squeeze. He waits at table, answers the bell, makes the beds and brushes his master's clothes, in fact, makes himself generally useful.

As a rule, he accompanies his master to all dinner-parties to assist in waiting. Also, it is a common and recognised practice for the boy of a house where a big dinner or a dance is being held to borrow requisites from the boy of another house, and often without reference to the owner, so that when dining out you not infrequently drink from your own glasses, use your own knives and forks, see your own lamp on the dinner-table and are waited on by your own servant. . . .

The cook is, next to the boy, the most important of the other servants, and as a rule is fairly efficient, some indeed being excellent, although great care must be taken to guard against their natural love of filthiness. A kitchen into which the master or mistress of the house does not go once or twice every day should never be visited at all if one wishes to enjoy one's meals.

This is also a lucrative post, for besides wages and a heavy squeeze on every article brought into the kitchen, the remains of each meal, whether half a chicken, half a leg of mutton, or both, are regarded by the cook as his perquisite and carried off for sale to native restaurants, unless special orders have been given to the contrary. A reason for this is that in hot climates food, if not eaten at once, quickly becomes worse than useless. Also, owing to the cheapness of meat, eggs, vegetables, etc., it is by no means the serious loss that it would be at home, and so the householder is generally not sorry that the remains of each meal should disappear and thus get fresh food at every repast. . . .

In England a dinner-party must be arranged some days beforehand in order that the necessary preparations may be made, and it is practically impossible to suddenly announce at tea-time that there will be eight people to dinner instead of two.

This matter is certainly managed better in China.

Oftentimes on returning from office at five o'clock I have sent for the cook and said, "To-night eight piecee man catchee dinner. Can do, no can do?" and the reply has invariably been a laconic "Can do."

At once there would be great bustling but no confusion, and it has always seemed to me that these sudden demands on the kitchen staff, instead of evoking complaints and sullen looks, are regarded rather as a source of pleasurable excitement. "No. 2" hurries off to market and quickly returns with fish, chops, chickens, eggs and fruit. Meanwhile, the cook dashes another pint or two of water into the soup and gets a jam pudding well under way.

On returning from the club at seven o'clock you find that the boy has tastefully laid the table and decorated it with leaves and flowers. After seeing to the wine and cigars you go up to dress, and on receiving your guests at half-past seven the dinner is ready. . . .

Immediately under the boy for indoor work is the "house-coolie," whose business it is to swab floors, polish grates, light fires, trim lamps, clean knives and boots and make himself generally useful about the house. Oftentimes he is unable to speak any English, wears a short coat in contradistinction to the boy's long one, and while ranking below the boy is considerably above the other coolies as having better pay, pleasanter work and holding a position of trust.

At the chief entrance to most residences is a gatehouse, tenanted during the day by an old man who serves as gatekeeper, and who is responsible for keeping bad characters off the premises as well as for not allowing anything to be taken away. At sunset he goes home, being relieved by the night-watchman, who remains on duty till sunrise. He also is responsible for the general safety, and is not supposed to sleep during the night, but to be on guard. Every two hours, that is, at each of the five watches into which the night is divided, he should make a round of the outbuildings to satisfy himself that all's well. This he does not do quietly, but to the beating of a bamboo rattle, so that thieves may know he is on the lookout and run away. Sometimes in order to keep up his courage, I have even heard him shout "I see you," "I know who you are," "I'm coming," "Who's afraid?" etc.

Ridiculous as this may appear to English burglars it is yet very effective, though for a very curious reason.

China is the country of guilds, every trade being in the hands of a certain section of the population, who combine against all intruders. There is a guild of water-carriers, a guild of fortune-tellers, a guild of pipe-makers, and even a guild of *thieves*. This last is a recognised body, and is treated with by all householders, until it has become a kind of insurance agency against theft. All gatekeepers and night-watchmen pay a small monthly fee to this guild in order that no thieving may take place on the premises over which they have control, and the system works well, for not only is anything rarely stolen, but if, occasionally, something does go it is almost certain to have been taken by a free lance, who would be promptly done to death should he fall into the clutches of the guild thieves.

A friend of mine who employs many hundreds of coolies pays a regular monthly salary to the head of the thieves in that district. This man comes to the office on pay-days like other *employés* to draw his wages. If, however, anything has been missed from the factory during the month the value of it is deducted from his salary until the article is restored, which is invariably done.

I have heard of a case where a reforming spirit determined not to submit to such an iniquitous tax. The gatekeeper and night-watchman immediately resigned and could not be replaced, while by the end of the month most of his portable belongings had been surreptitiously removed. Thoroughly cowed, he recalled the two servants and instructed them to pay the tax, whereupon the stolen articles promptly reappeared and security was again restored. . . .

. . . at treaty-ports barbers are a convenient luxury, for at the cost of a few dollars a month one will come to your bedroom every morning at a stated time to perform the daily shave, as well as cut the hair when required. Oftentimes I have been still asleep when, leaving his shoes outside the door and creeping in noiselessly with bare feet, he has adjusted the towel, lathered and shaved me in bed without my having had more than a dim consciousness of what was going on.

Tailors are cheap and plentiful. A West-end cut is not achieved, but for flannels, light tweeds and all such clothes as are worn in the tropics, they are very passable.

"Boy."

"Sai."

"Talkee that tailor-man four o'clock come. Wantchee new clothes."

At four o'clock the tailor is there with a bundle of patterns from which you select a thin serge and a white flannel, and order a suit of each....

... after a good deal of haggling, eleven dollars and ten respectively are agreed upon, the clothes to be finished in two days.

"Can do."

Out comes the tape and he measures you all over, taking mental notes but writing nothing down, the Chinese having marvellous memories.

Next morning he appears with the garments loosely stitched together to try on, draws a chalk line here, puts in a pin there and hurries off.

The following day you discover both suits neatly folded up on your bed, and on inspection find them to be of good and comfortable fit.

OLIVER G. READY
Life and Sport in China (1903)

1905

The Hong Kong Season

The Reverend Edward Hardy was Chaplain to the British Forces in Hong Kong for over three years. This gave him time to become well acquainted with life in the colony.

Hong Kong is built as it were in three layers or storeys. Business is done on the ground floor, on the second storey are dwelling-houses and gardens, and to top-side, as the Peak is called, come in summer Europeans who can afford to be cool. The Peak . . . is connected to the town by a cable tramway. The journey occupies only seven minutes, but in less time than this a reputation may be slain, and "Heard in the tram" is the authority for many a lie. Those who travel up and down in the tram two or three or four times a day get very tired of each other. One can meet a person twice a day with breezy enthusiasm, but the third time the smile of recognition is sickly, and the fourth time there is an incipient growl. To those not accustomed to the tram the houses on either side look as if they were toppling over. New-comers hold on to their seats and murmur, "Oh my!" . . .

. . . At the Peak the thermometer is from six to eight degrees lower than at Victoria. There are fewer Chinese, and the nights are noiseless. There is, however, one great drawback to the Peak. Every now and then in spring and summer it is shrouded in a fog that suggests suicide, and mildews gowns, hats, and other vanities. This last is not altogether a disadvantage, as the airing of their clothes gives ladies something to do during the hot part of the day, when they cannot go out. If you live on the Peak your clothes rot; if you live below, you rot. . . .

. . . Of the civilians in Hong Kong, all that we shall say is that some are nicer than others. The number ones, twos, and even threes of the great commercial firms are sometimes social successes. There are distinctions, however, that are not easy to understand. Why should pig-iron turn up its nose at tenpenny nails? To this distant land people come with double names that sound formidable until it is discovered that the double-barrelled ones discharge very small shots at home. The Service people call the civilians dollar-snatchers, and the latter think of the former as dollar-lackers. Dancing days and nights begin with the three practice dances that precede the ball which is given by Scotch residents on each St. Andrew's night. The great difficulty men have is to get partners, so few unmarried girls are in the colony. Here it is men and not women who are wall-flowers.

If men cannot get partners for a dance unless they bespeak them days before, it is even more difficult to get them for life. Owing to this scarcity of wife material, as well as to impecuniosity, young European men, instead of marrying, form themselves into bachelor messes. Just before leaving Hong Kong, I dined at one of these establishments. It was monstrous. There were six men daring to have as nice a drawing room, as well arranged a table, and as good servants as any house I have seen run by that old institution – a wife. . . .

With the races the Hong Kong season closes, for soon after the weather begins to get warm. Great then is the disappointment of the ladies if the race-days are cold or wet, or otherwise unsuitable to the costumes they have planned and perhaps imported ten thousand miles for this occasion. . . .

I never could care which horse came in first, but the human races always amused me. I liked looking at Chinese jugglers pretending to run swords through boys; at dentists making believe that they draw teeth and put them in again; at the curious arts of medicine-sellers; at the solemn efforts of Indian soldiers to be jolly and funny to a tom-tom accompaniment. I treated myself to an entrance ticket, price one cent, to several shows containing such things as a duck with three legs, an optical illusion which made a human head look as if it were separated from the trunk, and a deformed dwarf that seemed to be only half human. Do the Chinese ignore Western inventions? Certainly not, for I saw them at these races paying cash to get electrical shocks and to hear phonographic wonders. . . .

The Chinese highly approve of the tramway cars, lavatories, and fire-engines of the West, but many of our contrivances are, in the opinion of the educated, curious rather than useful, and in that of the ignorant, connected with magic, and with magic Confucius warned them to have nothing to do. Whatever he may pretend for the sake of advantage, the most unprogressive yellow man despises the most inventive white man. The inventiveness of the latter is, in the eyes of the former, no more worthy of respect than is the cunning of a fox or the strength of an elephant.

Still, we never know what a Chinese is feeling under his cloak of stolidity. One did allow himself this expression of surprise when he saw for the first time a train on the new railway at Canton, "No pullee, no pushee, but go like hellee!" The huge steamers, too, that glide into Hong Kong, with apparently nothing to move them, seem very magical. . . .

The Chinese and our interpretation of things are so different! Here is an illustration. To bring me to conduct Divine Service at two forts at Hong Kong, a steam launch used to be hired by Government. Orders were given to the Chinese cockswain, and these he wrote in his own language on a piece of paper. A friend of mine finding one of these papers and knowing Chinese, thus translated it to me, "To fetch the old man who tells stories to the soldiers in fort ___." The Chinese thought that my craft was the same as that of his countrymen, who earn a living by spinning yarns to the crowd at street corners. After all, the Gospel is "the old, old story."

The Chinese must misunderstand us as often as we misunderstand them. The regimental pet of the Royal Welsh Regiment is a large white goat. When a battalion of the regiment was in Hong Kong the animal used to be led before the band by its silver-mounted head-collar every Sunday when they marched to the parade service. It was, indeed, the most regular church-goer in Hong Kong. A crowd of Chinese, many of them visitors to Hong Kong, would wait outside the Church to see the battalion march up. One day the general's wife, observing these people looking at the goat, remarked to the writer, "The Chinese must think that we worship that goat!" "Certainly," I answered; "with far less to go upon a Western globe-trotter would dub the Chinese goat worshippers."

THE REV. E.J. HARDY
John Chinaman at Home (1905)

c. 1906

Such a Reputation

In Hong Kong, visiting American F. Dumont Smith considered the qualities of the Chinese and made some far-sighted predictions.

Just across from my room a great stone block is building. The stagings are of bamboo lashed together, not a nail in them. Shelters of matting keep off the sun and rain. The blocks are hoisted by hand and the work goes on slowly but steadily and cheaply twelve hours a day and no Sundays. The cooly moves slowly but he never stops. He neither hastens nor pauses.

What are coolies as distinguished from other Chinese? They are what we call at home "common laborers," if such a thing exists in America.

They are just muscle. They are born to toil, to carry burdens, to pull rickshaws, to do the menial work, to bear without alleviation the Primal Curse. Never can they rise or change their condition. They cannot take the examinations for public employment. They and their women and children for all time must do the same. The brothels of the East are recruited from his daughters if they are comely. The others must labor as their brothers and husbands do, at labor that seems inhuman, fit only for beasts. Their rank and station is fixed; there is no escape from it. They sell themselves in far-off lands to toil that is almost certain death, such employment as the Panama Canal, for a pittance paid in advance to their families, to a father or mother too old to work. They are the most industrious, faithful, frugal self-denying class in the world. . . .

Some facts about the Chinese stand out with such startling clarity, they are so certain and well attested, that you cannot escape them; and one is their honesty. You may ask any man who has dealt with them and he will tell you the same, that they are the most absolutely honest and reliable race in the world. A Chinese merchant will commit suicide if he cannot meet his obligations. He will suffer any loss, he will sell himself into slavery rather than fail of his word. China is the only country in the world that has no law for the collection of debt, – needs none. This statement rests not upon a preponderance of the evidence: it is unanimous; there is no dispute about it. Every man in the East will tell you that he had rather deal with the Chinese than any other people in the world. They are slow in a bargain, they weigh every penny, but their word once given, that ends it. You need no bond, no guaranty; he will die before he will shirk one jot of his promise. Those who deal with the Japanese demand an iron-clad bank guaranty and watch them besides. With the Chinese, the naked word is enough – no writing, no

A COOLIE

bond, just his word. I could tell of a hundred stories I have heard that illustrate this; stories of loss and suffering borne uncomplainingly as a matter of course in the fulfillment of a contract. Just this morning the United States District Judge for the District of Shanghai, in a suit between two Americans and a Chinese, where the evidence rested solely on the word of the Chinese disputed by both Americans, gave judgement for the Chinese, and in doing so said: "It is a well-known fact that Chinese merchants and business men are honest and trustworthy and faithful in the performance of their obligations under their contracts."

Certainly it is a great thing to have established such a reputation with all the nations that deal here, so that the word of one of them is taken by an alien judge against that of his countryman. So that Chinese has become a synonym for honesty. No little thing, that. "Better is a good name than great riches." The Chinese has it. He is no fool; he is just as acute, as far-seeing, just as shrewd at a bargain, and he has more honesty than any of the people who deal with him; and there he holds an advantage. In the long run he will get his own again. He is recovering his own trade, and he will retake Hong Kong and Shanghai some day as he has retaken Macao. All over the East the cashiers are Chinese. Even in Japan, in banks and hotels, the boys who handle the money are Chinese. Not only is he honest, but he is the swiftest and most accurate accountant in the world. He can count money faster than the expert teller of a New York bank; he can compute as rapidly as a machine, and he never makes a mistake. He has a natural head for figures, and some day he will be what the Phœnician was once, the merchant of the world. He knows the game, he has patience, courtesy, he can figure a profit closer than a Jew or a Scotchman. Inch by inch he is regaining his trade, by reason of these qualities.

F. DUMONT SMITH
Blue Waters and Green and
The Far East Today (1907)

1908

Chinese New Year

An experienced traveller who had been to Hong Kong before, Count Fritz von Hochberg took his companions under his wing and guided them around the festive city.

We were told we should be at Hong-Kong at seven o'clock in the morning. Of course I never believed a word of it, having travelled too much to be taken in by what captains say, and so, to Healy's horror, I refused to get up before eight, although both he and the servants came in several times, declaring that the harbour was well in sight. Well, let it be! And so while I was slowly dressing I enjoyed the *stationary* pretty sight of the harbour entrance (seen from the cabin window), for of course, as always, we were late. Then there were the endless formalities of quarantine, etc., etc., to go through, so that we really only moved on about 9 o'clock; and when I appeared on deck, where the silly wretches had been shivering since dawn, as, of course again, it was bitterly cold about this time of the year here, we were only just slowly gliding into the real harbour and never really dropped the anchor for good before half-past ten, and then it was at least half-past eleven before the tenders came and we could have our luggage moved on to them, and finally could say good-bye to captain and officers and steam towards land. It was cold, as I have said, and a grey winter's day, and the harbour absolutely deserted of the numberless and very picturesque large and small djunks usually there, on account of the Chinese New Year. But all the same it had the same fascination for me it always has had, this harbour, which I really think is one of the prettiest I know, surrounded by all those hills and hilly islands and the town of Hong-Kong, climbing with its many buildings, villas, and gardens up to the Peak, and Kowloonen, the native and merchant city . . .

We've been told the King Edward Hotel is the best. I, obstinate of course as I am, want to stick to the Hong-Kong Hotel, but give in to Healy, Miss Elliott and Miss Christal, and we walk to the hotel; there are no real distances in Hong-Kong. But it is difficult to tear oneself, and especially me, away from all the fascinating attractions of the Chinese harbour life. I love the Chinese. The enchanting djunks all tied to the piers for the New Year's week, when no Chinese will do any work, but everybody has to don new clothes and give themselves up to frolicking and the letting-off of as many crackers as his purse will allow him. And yet all the fascinating, though not always strictly clean nor odoriferous life that is going on in these djunks, from which I always find it so difficult to tear myself away, is the same. The cooking, washing, dressing of those fascinating Chinese doll-children, and their delightful ways and plays! Very unwillingly I follow the others into the lugubrious-looking hotel, where a dirty-looking Greek takes us to see some just as lugubrious rooms. Of course, it is a puzzle for him, poor devil, why being two women and two men, we are not satisfied with only two double-bedded rooms, but, quite apart from that, the rooms are really too dark and dirty for words. Poor Miss E. is in despair. "What can we do – all our luggage has been brought here?" So I just whisper to her, "Don't say or ask anything, but follow me." And not heeding the Greek manager, who shouts after me, "Shall I register your name?" (which I know he doesn't know), I walked out of the hotel, followed in dumb astonishment by the trio, and I made them step at the next corner into rikshahs, and off to the Hong-Kong we went. "But what are you going to do?" "Simply see whether the Hong-Kong Hotel's rooms are better, and if so, send for our luggage." And on we trot. Of course they are better, they all agree. It is more old-fashioned, but very nice and clean, and has pretty balconied rooms over-looking part of the harbour in front and up to the dear Peak behind. So we register our rooms here, send for our luggage and descend for an excellent tiffin, served with the noiseless swiftness only Chinese know how to achieve.

The hotel was crammed full, and we were lucky to get such good rooms. After lunch I took the trio under my wing, and we started for a stroll through the streets, sending the children, or making them, walk in front of us (I mean Miss Christal and Healy, while Miss E. and I followed in the rear) so that they shouldn't get lost or into mischief, for the streets were packed with merry-making Chinese, burning thousands of crackers, which make a deafening noise and smoke. It was a lovely picture to see them all in their many-coloured new silk garments, with irreproachable freshly-plaited pig-tails and spotless white-soled flannel or

A Toy Seller

felt boots. But especially delightful were the fascinating children, who were decked out in every colour of the rainbow and had such queer garments. Apple-green satin trousers, and pink, gold-embroidered coats, or all clad in cornflower blue silk. . . .

As it began to get dark and cool the streets got empty, and as all the shops were closed, the place, just now so gay and bright, looked wintry and desolate, with its high grey stone facades, and we too turned in to have a welcome cup of tea beside a blazing fire, which was really very much needed; but not before we had stopped for quite a long time watching some boys playing the new game craze of China, a sort of shuttle-cock played with the feet. It was really very pretty and amusing to watch them, and how well and agile they were at it! I wonder how long it will take for this Chinese game to come over to Europe and become the same craze there as Diabolo is at present, which of course is one of the oldest Chinese games. H. couldn't resist, and, to the delight of all the Chinese boys, joined in the game, and very successfully even. . . .

The next afternoon we went up in the Funicular to the Peak, and I again had the same tumbling-over sensation as I had thirteen years ago, as the cars are built in such an extraordinary way. They are all right on the level, but not on the steep hill, where one hangs on to one's seat in such a backward fashion, that the scenery, which is otherwise very fine, all seems to fall over till one is quite giddy. It was bitterly cold up there, but the view was splendid . . .

Another day we went for a long walk half up the Peak, and always alongside of the hill on a road that had been most ingeniously cut out of the rock, at least partly. Through beautiful trees one looked down on one's right to the lovely harbour with its many boats and djunks, and as it was late when we had started it began to get quite dark before we returned, and all the many lights in the town and harbour began to be lit. One really could not see where the city itself ended and the djunks and boats commenced; it stretched for ever a star-like view at our feet, and looked most lovely.

COUNT FRITZ VON HOCHBERG
An Eastern Voyage (1910)

c. 1908

The Spell of Hypnotism

American traveller John Stuart Thomson spent three years in China and, more than once, came face to face with the Mysterious Orient.

China too produces its gum-shoe men of nocturnal prowlings. It was the hot season at the Hong-Kong Club, every roomer sleeping with only the half door closed. The electric fans worked loud enough to drown the foot of a thief, or possibly he carried a sleeping draft in his handkerchief. Into six rooms he crawled night after night. He doubtless carried the long Punjaub knife. Gold studs were removed from shirts; watches were taken from under pillows, and rings from bureau tops. How could it all be done with so formidable Sikh *chowkidars* on guard at the door all night! Weeks went by and there was no trace. The Chinese bath boys, the older tea boys, every one's private boy, were in turn marched up to be put through no simple inquisition of "Third Degree" behind the stone walls at the top of Wyndham and Mosque Streets. Then Blass, who was on a seven year indenture in the East, and who was a wonderful fellow scientifically, remembered that his ring had a flaw in the ruby. It is a way pigeon rubies have for catching thieves, and that is why Burmans call only the pink gems good luck stones. The pawn-shops were again searched, even to distant Yamati and the mainland. The ring was found, but horrors! the Chinese broker attacked our faith in those perfect guardians of our eastern homes, the Sikhs. He identified one of our own *chowkidars* as the guilty party. The latter confessed to pounding the gold to bullion and throwing the watch works in the harbor from a sampan. He also said he knew why he could safely move around our rooms, but that it was "Indian knowledge" which he would never betray. Let the curious therefore debate whether it was ether, hypnotism or mere luck six times unbroken. Those who had studs stolen were of no use as witnesses, for there was no recovered gold to identify, but Blass was witness enough, and the Indian got as fair a trial as a white man. We think less of Sikhs now, but Rasil Singh, behind the jail walls on Mosque Street, thinks more of us.

The most sensational performance in the all-wonderful East is the act entitled: "The Murder of the Child Lo." I witnessed it on the mountain lawn of the Royal Artillery mess at Hong-Kong. There was certainly no subterranean passage. We hemmed in the performer. First he proceeded with snake and other tricks, until in the high quiet above the city, the attention of all was riveted. Near him on the grass was an upturned empty hamper. Seated at our feet was one stray Chinese child. He called him; seemed soon to quarrel with him; – some one said it was the conjurer's ward. His temper rose as the child seemed to be obdurate. With a growl of a tiger he grasped the boy and threw the basket over him. Holding it with one hand, he muttered solemnly; he was swearing the clan vow of murder. Before we realized it, he drew a sword, and thrust it again and again through the basket, the most heartrending, smothered cries beneath gradually dying to the death whimper. From the sword seemed to drip blood. The conjurer's mad eyes gleamed. He leaned on his sword, as satisfied with his work as one possessed of a fiend. In the awful silence, we looked from the terrace to the heathen hills where rules the Abrahamic code that a child always belongs to its parents, even for death if so decreed. There was a general sigh, and a flutter like leaves as he released us from the spell of hypnotism. Returning reason made us try to reach him, to avenge brutality. He anticipated this; he kicked the basket over. There was nothing beneath it. A terrible silence settled down and held our hands. We looked at one another, all believing that this was a magician, instead of a rascal, like unto whom there was never an equal. The child had vanished like air, and the dry wicker was as empty as it first had been when we gathered round it on the lawn. The magician had no assistants among us. Suddenly the child, with a cry of joy, burst from our midst into the arms of the wonder-weaver. We had seen the most famous act of legerdemain in the world, and understanding it not, but having experienced it, declare it to have been hypnotism.

They may talk of a thermometer on a flat roof in Bagdad registering 150 in the sun, but please remember that the Tigris Valley has nothing like the humidity which accompanies heat at Hong-Kong, and it is humidity only which kills and which tells you of its heartless intent while it is doing the killing. The barometer is scanned at the newspaper offices to see if there is any chance of a typhoon breaking the awful still glow. It is painful to hear a 'rickisha move along at mid-day; what fool can be daring a sunstroke! Every one keeps changes of clothes at the office, for the journey to business in a jolting sedan chair has brought out the perspiration which has wet one's Chifu silk coat through and through. Relays are hired for your punkah-coolie force, who are on night work. You keep your shoes near your bed to throw at a delinquent, who, as soon as he thinks you are asleep, stops pulling the rope of the ceiling-fan, and falls asleep himself, utterly indifferent to the fact that the lack of a breeze will at once wake you up. It is stifling under your mosquito curtain and you tear it down, trusting to the punkah breeze to alarm the flying cockroaches and other winged pests. You raise the temperature of your bath, for your diminishing vitality will not stand the slightly cooled water from the cistern of your home, or the artesian water of the club. Day by day the pavements and walls grow more dazzling in the sun; night by night your head swims and you think you will swoon away for ever. If only you could, and the torture of recoveries not be repeated. You grow terrorized, and the sight of the blue walls of a Christian's cemetery in exile gives you a panic. You are fearing that after all you will not be able to pull through. They are sending the patients who have been operated upon, from the hospitals on the peak by ships to Wei-Hai-Wei and Chifu, as their wounds will not heal here in the south. The barometer lowers and you have high hopes, but still no rain comes. . . .

The wind at last rises with the voice of an angel, and the harbor in welcoming joy has leaped up with white arms. It is growing darker even at four o'clock, and the burned hills are not so glaringly red and white. There are shadows spotting them. Coolies come out of their cellar retreats and are gathering at the curbs, a *high-ya* upon their voices and a new soul in their eyes. . . . Of a sudden a darkness, like later evening, closes in. The drops strike like shots on the wide grass Hupeh hats of the coolies and on the starched blue Nankeen blinds of the sedan chairs. It pelts; it comes in spears and sheets; the earth drinks and rises in a glorious perfume. . . . How it rains! The gulleys and gorges roar in the night. Thirty inches fall in twenty-four hours. The great white Praya has been converted into a lake, which, as it drains into the sea, makes of the long revetment walls a waterfall of wonderful width. The mounted army officers dash through the flood and remind one another: "How like it is to Calcutta's maidan in August." The unpaved country roads become a viscid pudding and your house coolies at last have a good excuse for delaying the supplies for your dinner.

... The last week of April, 1908, was unprecedented for rainfall in southern China. Fifty inches fell, making seventy inches for the year, which is twice what Shanghai and ten times what Peking gets. Canton and its villages were under two feet of water. The creeks flowing into the Sikiang (West River) rose with their parent and submerged rice fields, trees and huts. Millions die yearly of famine because China persists in a devotion to rice. ... If China would only take to raising grain on higher land!

JOHN STUART THOMSON
The Chinese (1910)

1911

Pirates at Last

When Sybil Ready and her friend Miss Gordon came to visit Sybil's brother Oliver (a Commissioner with the Chinese Imperial Customs) they found the country in turmoil. Revolution had just broken out in China, while along the river at Kong-moon where the Customs bungalow was situated, pirates were on the rampage.

DECEMBER 7th. This morning still no report of the safety of the Missionaries, so all our gunboats have gone up-river and the *On-Lee* had to sail for Hong Kong, with an escort for part of the way only, which was considered most dangerous. We shall be without any guard to-night, but one torpedo-boat is to be back early to-morrow.

About 2 a.m. I was awakened by the opening of our garden gate, then hasty steps (European shoes) up our garden path, round the house, then Oliver's window thrown open and excited voices. No doubt at all, pirates at last and this is a warning! Off go the footsteps, bang goes the gate and out of bed I jump. I'm not going to be found unprepared so, making a hasty toilet, I go to Oliver to ask the reason of the visitor. . . . It was Captain Leith of the gunboat *Moorhen* calling to see if we were all right, as he had been kept down-river by great disturbances, so, if we were, he wanted to go up-river to join the torpedo-boats, as there were terrible happenings near Wuchow.

After the excitement of Captain Leith's visit it was some time before I could compose myself and get off to sleep. At last I must have fallen into a heavy slumber as I suddenly awoke with the idea that we were being bombarded. I listened; certainly it was not a dream, but the near firing of rifles and much shouting, followed by a loud battering on the front-door. Without the loss of a moment I put on the few garments that were always hanging by my bedside in case of an emergency, and rushed into the passage, where I found Oliver and Miss Gordon, as well as the four Chinese servants, viz. the Boy, the old Coolie, the Cook and the

Gardener. These four had all quickly come in from their little huts . . .

Oliver, with a revolver in his hand, was standing on guard by the front-door, which of course was bolted and barred, demanding in an angry voice "Who are you?" The reply was a burst of Chinese and renewed knocking as if with the butt-ends of rifles. Oliver, turning to us said "For Heaven's sake defend the other doors." The two doors indicated were situated on the side of the Bungalow away from the Custom House, and as yet had not been attacked. The cook, gardener and old coolie piled furniture and packing-cases in front of them, the shutters needing no attention, as they had all been well fastened when darkness fell. Miss Gordon and I each seized a revolver and the Boy, white as death, with a stern and immovable countenance, took a rifle, whereupon the thought flashed through my mind "Has he ever handled a rifle before?"; while the three others armed themselves with whatever they could lay hands on. The awful word *Pirates* was whispered amongst us. I cried out to my brother "Where is our guard and what are they doing?" No sooner had the words been spoken than a renewed fusilade answered the question. Oliver remained stationary at the door, longing no doubt to open it and help beat back the attack, but he had us to consider, and well he knew that if the door were opened but an inch, the Bungalow would soon be ransacked, and we (I dare not think of it) at the mercy of those devils.

The Bungalow now seemed surrounded, firing increasing on all sides. . . . The turmoil was indescribable.

Suddenly, with a suddenness almost painful, there came a lull, the shouting and shooting ceased and only the occasional crack of a rifle in the distance could be heard – and then the clear hooting of a gunboat rent the air. Yes, a gunboat, and we were saved!

A few minutes later another knock came on the door, but a friendly one this time. It was Otte, and it was he who had rallied our guard and with them had put up such a splendid fight. The gunboat turned out to be a Chinese gunboat. The officers soon came ashore, made many and great apologies and said for the future a still stricter watch should be kept on our compound. . . .

It was generally believed that the cause of this sudden attack on us was that the pirates living far off in the mountains, having heard of the recruiting of the pirates around Kong-moon Port, decided to attack the Customs in the hope of obtaining rifles and revolvers, it being well-known that many fire-arms had recently been confiscated from passing junks.

AN OLD PAGODA

DECEMBER 10th. . . . Having been invited several times by friends to make a trip to Macao, we had decided to start on Monday, but on Sunday evening Mr. Volkmann called to say a Chinese passenger junk had been pirated on its way to that port, all the cargo and over two thousand dollars taken, one man killed and four wounded. The junk was, as usual, being towed by a steam-launch. We were to have started at 9 a.m., but have now given it up, not wishing to be pirated . . .

As we could not go to Macao we had a nice walk. Work seemed going on briskly all around. In a great many fields they were threshing the rice . . . Quantities of buffaloes were to be seen, but none very near. Most of them had small children on their backs. On our way home we were greeted by a nice, smiling Chinese woman, with a great waving of hands and a few words. We gathered she was asking if we came from far-off England. She simply shouted at us, hoping so to make us understand. On our return we went to look at the shipping from the Bund, when another Chinese woman came up and evidently wished to talk. They are beginning to look upon us in a more friendly light, so different from when we first came; then a smile never crossed their faces.

Captain Davies called almost immediately after tiffin. He thinks things are improving a little and says the River is certainly quieter higher up, but he went on to say two pirates had been caught and executed on the river-bank just above the Missionaries' houses. It is horrible to think that men, even if pirates, have been beheaded on the very path where we walk almost daily.

SYBIL READY
My Visit to China and Japan (1937)

1915

Secret Communication

*Winifred Clift and her husband normally lived up-country in China,
but when her doctor ordered a rest they came to stay on a small island
near wartime Hong Kong.*

War telegrams had reached us even in our inland home, but . . . it
seemed to bring the whole thing nearer to us when we steamed out of
the Canton delta towards Hong Kong Harbour and were met by the
British patrol-boat. A benevolent looking man in the lightest of summer
garments and a khaki sun hat megaphoned – "Any European
passengers?" (The chief officer had been down to the saloon to ask us
our nationality and had been told "English") – "Br-r-ritish" he yelled. He
was a Scotchman – we might have known it.

Having duly hoisted the flag for the day we went on our way. Without
that flag, the boat was in danger of being fired upon from the forts.
Only once, I believe, since the war began has a boat really been fired on
and that was a Japanese which for reasons best known to herself refused
to stop at the order of the patrol and persisted in steaming straight
ahead.

No steamer may enter or leave the harbour after 6 p.m. during this
time of war, so we were anchored by the praya by 5.30, but the island
launch had left and there was nothing for it but to spend the night on
board and wait for the morning. At dawn the next day we were on
shore and making our way through the fresh, clean streets. There were
people about already – white, weary-faced volunteers just off duty, some
of them dragging tired limbs back to their rooms or hotels. In an hour
or two they will be at work again in bank, and office and shop, and
your wants will be attended to by a man who looks like a footballer who
has brushed his hair too carefully – for they are often in uniform all the
time, a dark yellow-brown khaki with loose knickerbockers exposing the
knees.

The work has not been without cost to men who, already worn out by the oppressive heat of a tropical summer, have pluckily taken their places without a grumble when the call came.

Every night without fail, great searchlights with their fiery glance sweep land and sea till dawn. The great shafts of light come creeping over Lantau and down the mountain side towards the island, give us a friendly glance where we sit drinking coffee in the moonlight, and sweep on – and we have the comforting assurance that for a distance of thirty miles they can see every single ship that passes, and not only see her but *know who and what she is*. . . .

Here are some of the little incidents whispered in the colony just now – A good German pastor belonging to one of the missions working in the colony duly signed the document required of him in order that he might be allowed to stay at his work . . . He had undertaken not to communicate anything concerning the war, etc., to any other "nationals." I don't know the exact wording, but it is easily understood that he mistook "nationals" for nationalities, and believed that he was quite within the bounds of his promise when he wrote – well, quite freely, shall we say – on the subject of the war to one of his fellow countrymen in Switzerland. Imagine his amazement when he was confronted by a stern official seated at a table on which were spread out – *his own letters*. He is now required to report himself every forty-eight hours at the nearest police-station.

Not so innocent was the German who went to the largest bookshop in the colony and requested the man who served him to forward by post the book which he had just purchased for a friend. While the bookseller's back was turned the German quietly opened the volume and slipped something between its pages. The shop man caught a slight movement, but said nothing, wrapped up and addressed the parcel, bowed the purchaser out of the shop – and went straight to the telephone to ring up the police.

"I may be quite wrong" he said, "but I think if you open that parcel you will find a secret communication with Germany inside." He was not mistaken – the little ruse had failed completely. All the same it was a clever plan. A parcel from the noted bookshop would pass at once while anything mailed by the German might have been suspected.

A wealthy and well-known German, a naturalised British subject, went for a pleasant little trip to Macao. Whilst there he took the opportunity of cabling a long and informing message in code to Germany. This was at the very beginning of the war, before it was known that cable communication with Germany was impossible. What could be safer than a code message from the Portuguese Colony? But he did not know that every cable from Macao must pass through Hong Kong and that the Hong Kong authorities had the key to the code he used. They waited patiently for this loyal British subject to return to the colony which had made him rich – and as he stepped on shore he was arrested. The sentence I suppose was imprisonment for life.

Every day we hungrily gather a few crumbs of news from the papers – it cannot be called more, and like every one else we sigh – "When will it end?"

C. WINIFRED LECHMERE CLIFT
Annals of an Isle in the Pacific (1915)

1923

Government House

Charles Hardinge Drage was posted to the China Station to join the sloop H.M.S. Bluebell as First Lieutenant. Arriving in Hong Kong he found his new ship undergoing a refit, which left him free to accept a temporary position as A.D.C. to the Governor, Sir Reginald Stubbs, while the usual occupant of that post was on leave.

Nov. 10th – The "Fantôme" (the Guinnesses yacht) arrived and I went on board to ask them to lunch at G.H. I found Fane, whom I had known at the Embassy in Berlin, another young man, Nancy Tennant and the three Guinness flappers. Mr. and Mrs. Guinness came to lunch and afterwards we all went to the races in Happy Valley, where I gave them lots of bad tips.

Nov. 11th. – Armistice Day. With H.E. to the Cathedral Service and then to the Cenotaph where he deposited a wreath. The ceremonial was quite impressive. In the afternoon I took old Lady Hammond up to the Peak, going up and down by the Peak Tramway, the front seat in which is reserved, by the way, for H.E. and his staff if on duty.

Nov. 12th. – A busy day. With H.E. to the races, then on to present prizes at the Garrison football final and then after dinner to watch the finals of the Garrison boxing. They have the "Pari-Mutuel" here and, for place betting, pay on the first three if there are six or more runners. In the last race there were this number and H.E. sent me to back them all at $5 for a place and cleared $40 on the deal.

Nov. 13th. – In the afternoon I played tennis. In the dog watches H.E. presented a shield to the Hong Kong rifle team who have won the inter-port competition (Hong Kong, Shanghai, Penang and Singapore). In the evening there was a big dinner (31 all told) for the Guinnesses and local celebrities. Afterwards the elders played bridge and the rest danced to a gramophone in the ballroom. Everything went off well. . . . I danced with Nancy Tennant, who has come on a lot since I last saw her in

London, with the Guinness girls and with some amusing married women and enjoyed it.

Nov. 14th. – During lunch Sir Claud Severn (the Colonial Secretary) rang up to say that a Japanese steamer had gone ashore 12 miles from Canton and was being attacked by pirates. I rang up the Commodore, who said that the *Cicula* was being sent from Canton to her assistance.

In the afternoon H.E. walked into my office and offered me the temporary job of Private Secretary at $3,000 a year, to start when Cross, who is getting married, leaves for his honeymoon. This would be very nice but I doubt if it can be arranged.

Nov. 15th. – I saw the skipper and the Commodore and arranged to stay on at Government House as Private Secretary until the end of our refit. . . .

Nov. 19th. – With H.E. and members of the Council to lunch with a big Chinese merchant, called Sui Min Chen, at his house behind Old Kowloon. It was a pretty place built round a flower-filled garden and full of lovely silks and lovely china but disfigured by a profusion of painted mirrors and some Turkey carpets that made one feel positively ill. The meal was very good, especially the birds' nest soup with pigeons' eggs, the shark's fin and the ducks' tongues with snow fungus. Our Chinese hosts were charming and the whole show most enjoyable. . . .

Nov. 22nd. – Went down to the *Bluebell* as usual in the forenoon and was greeted with the news that Patrick Smith, the "No. 1" of the *Tarantula* and rather a pal of mine, had died of cholera. The pilot is quite cut up about it. Went to "Flower Street" and bought a wreath for the funeral. . . .

Nov. 23rd. – Neville got back early and took over A.D.C. again, so I became Private Secretary. The Japanese training squadron arrived at 08.00 but Neville organised everything. He is jolly good at his job. . . . I spent all the forenoon in the ship, where the work is going on well. In the afternoon Cross (the late Private Secretary) got married. . . . The reception was held at Government House.

Nov. 24th. – In the afternoon Fletcher took me in his car for a run to Repulse Bay . . .

That night there was a dinner for Vice-Admiral Saito, and the Japanese officers. It went off all right, but they were an inhuman lot – except for one who arrived rather tight and explained that he had been at a Jap dinner since 17.00 and had been dressed by the geishas only just in time for this one. I made one bad break; their dinner rig is frock coats and medals and I asked one (thinking that he was wearing an overcoat and had mess dress underneath) if he would not take his coat off?

Nov. 25th. – In the afternoon I played tennis with Mme. Krémer and some of the French Colony at the Ladies Recreation Club. The most amusing person was a Mme. FitzHenry, who might have stepped straight out of La Vie Parisienne – golden hair pulled back to reveal exceedingly pretty ears, large blue eyes, long lashes, a tip-tilted nose and a perfect complexion. As Private Secretary I have not done much work so far, except to draw up some suggestions ... and write a burlesque intelligence report on the suspicious activities of the yacht "Fantôme" and the Guinness family. This latter effort was in the somewhat heavy style of the reports that emanate from the Political Intelligence Bureau in Singapore and, to my horror, H.E. minuted it to the Executive Council. . . .

Nov. 30th. – The *Hawkins* came in with the C. in C. and the old boy turned up at G.H. for lunch. To my surprise, instead of exploding with wrath at finding me at G.H., he was extremely nice about it and offered to let me stay. He talked a lot about steps to be taken against the pirates, but H.E. does not expect that much will actually be done. . . .

We dined with Stephens (the "taipan" of the Hong Kong and Shanghai Bank) for the St. Andrew's Night Ball. Before dinner we were given "athelbrose", a semi-solid mixture of whiskey and honey, so strong it made you blink. Stephens has some interesting little portraits of Chinese notables of the last century by an artist called Chinnery. The Ball was very well organised but crowded. . . . After supper I took H.E. home and then came back to see the fun. The chaplain from the *Tamar* was hitting it up and might have been taken for an example of the "Catholic and Alcoholic Church". . . .

Dec. 1st. – Woke up feeling rather the worse for wear and with a busy day ahead of me. With H.E. to lunch with Sir Paul Chater, a coloured magnate and the multi-millionaire of Hong Kong. He has a lovely house full of wonderful china, and gave us an excellent meal with superlative wine. . . . His collection of china is well-known and, though much of it is said to be faked, the pieces are really beautiful, but the furnishing of the rest of the house is in atrocious taste.

Then on to the races, which were much as on other days. After dinner to a jolly little dance in the *Carlisle*.

COMMANDER C.H. DRAGE
The 1914–1933 Diaries (manuscript)

1923

Fragile Guide

Revolution was again in the air at Canton. Nevertheless, with only a female guide for company, Grace Thompson Seton, American author and explorer, ventured into the city to learn more about the home life of Cantonese women.

It was a long ride back to Shameen. But as always, I found the streets of Canton a never-failing delight. . . .

It was a strange medley that assailed the senses, not always pleasantly. The brutality of the pig traffic made the air hideous for a while, as I passed a dock upon which the pigs were being unloaded from a boat where they had been stacked up like so much cord wood, twenty or thirty feet deep. One hates to think of the underpigs. Each pig is confined in a loose, wicker cage; a protesting leg thrust from it rarely escapes being broken. At the market these animals are weighed, and, after being sold, their legs are tied together, a pole put through them, then upside down, their heads waggling painfully, they are carried away, squealing with what protest is left in them, to be butchered by their new owners.

Later that afternoon, a Y.W.C.A. worker, who modestly requests to be unnamed, arranged a series of visits to the homes of her friends. It was a fascinating experience, to meet these dozen hostesses each offering me tea in a different background. From the small three-room "flat" of the young bride who had succeeded in breaking away from tradition, and separating her life from her husband's family, we visited compounds of increasing comfort and elegance, to the beautiful home and gardens of a high official. . . . No hint of the grace and treasures of a home is given by the high blank walls that surround it. One could travel the streets of a Chinese city from dawn till dark, along a dreary pattern of dirty walled-in roads and never dream of the glories hidden from view, not a dozen feet away.

Three things I found in every home – flowering plants, a shrine for the Ancestral Tablets and the most gracious hospitality. While I was drinking my twelfth cup of tea and the hostess was telling me that her husband would not allow her to go into the streets on account of the soldiers, I was brought back sharply to a realization of the Revolution by noises of a street fight going on beyond the walls of a tiny garden where we were. Angry voices arose and the spatter of Mausers. Then silence.

Darkness had suddenly fallen. It was more than time for us to seek the protected Island of Shameen before the sunset gates were closed. In the street we found our chair-bearers mutinous. They had been frightened by the brawl between a looted shop-keeper and three soldiers, who had done the looting, and whom some guards of the Merchants' Protective Association had driven off.

The Y.W.C.A. worker was calm and firm for so gentle a creature. She argued with the sullen bearers, eight of them, four for each chair, but they were obdurate, demanded their money, and proposed to leave us stranded miles from Shameen.

For two women to be afoot in those dark alley-like streets, under the circumstances, was highly dangerous. Kidnapping was not unknown. A strong hand could so easily reach out and drag us into a black doorway. We should never be heard of again. A concealed cellar or the bottom of a filthy canal are good hiding places for dead bodies. I regretted my money and my rings . . . My pretty, little fragile guide was carrying on a battle of words with the eight ruffians. I brought to the rescue the only ally we had.

"Promise them much *cumshaw*. Tell them the Consul-General may have them all shot if they do not bring me back. Make the best bargain you can, but bribe them sufficiently to make double-quick time too or the gates will be closed for the night."

Greed won. It was a wicked trip, jolting over the stones, swinging around corners and passing strange shadows lurking in dark places. We got past one barrier just in time and twenty minutes later arrived at Shameen Gate to find it closed!

The guard, however, had orders to admit me. The flame of adventure burned low within me that night, and I parted from those chair-bearers and from the native city with no feelings of regret whatsoever.

GRACE THOMPSON SETON
Chinese Lanterns (1924)

The House of Lin

Back in the early 1800s a member of Nora Waln's family had traded and become friends with the Lins on the China coast. The Lins kept the memory of this American friendship alive through succeeding generations, and when Nora Waln was at college she received an unexpected invitation to visit them in Canton. While in China she met the Englishman who became her husband. She also met the great revolutionary leader Sun Yat-sen.

Shameen is small. Society is formal. All the community walk on the Bund to take the air every evening before dinner. I walked there each evening with my husband. Yet no person smiled or spoke until we had met properly. The Shameen ladies waited until they had given me time to settle into my house. Then, hatted and white-kid-gloved, they left cards in the little box that was on our gate when we arrived.

I demurred at doing it, but I had to go around in my best hat and white kid gloves and poke my cards and my husband's cards in correct number in the boxes on their gates. Then we were invited to dinners at which we were carefully seated according to "rank," the highest places belonging to Government Officials in precedence of the dates of the establishment of their service, and the next places to merchants according to the date of the establishment of their firm's China trade. Afterwards, those people to whom we had been introduced at the dinners bowed when we walked on the Bund. I did not meet any Chinese people in the homes in which we were entertained. . . .

My husband was almost entirely occupied by the delicate political situation. I seldom saw him outside the brief hour he always kept for me just before dinner. Then we usually walked on the Bund so that he could get exercise and air as well as conversation with me.

I had much leisure. I had no Western friends. I spent my time mostly on my verandah, visiting with the river people, or in the House of Lin. . . .

Neither Mai-da nor I ever assumed any regular tasks. But sometimes we assisted Su-ling by pouring tea and passing cake. She was "at home" four afternoons each week. Few of the older republicans came to her drawing-rooms, but they were filled with young Chinese men and women of means who had been educated in Western universities.

These were bright, attractive, energetic young people at loose ends. They were from all the provinces. They had gathered at Canton because, on return from Western schools, they could not fit themselves into their homesteads and because Canton was the headquarters of the republican movement. They spoke in English because they had no common Chinese dialect. . . .

One afternoon, Sun Yat-sen came. He stood by Su-ling's tea-table and asked her for tea. As he was recognised, talk ceased, cups and plates were put down. For forty years, longer than the lifetime of any of this group, he had devoted his life to an attempt to elevate China to a state of unity, freedom, and independence. He had accomplished the overthrow of the decadent Manchu dynasty; but again and again, within touch of the establishment of a national Republic, he had failed.

Yet there was no smirch on his reputation. His life was an open book. These young people held him in the deepest veneration. With his hand resting on the back of Su-ling's exotic cubist painted chair, he asked for three minutes of silence, for self-examination, for consideration of the doctrine of republicanism, and for self-determination. The silence was emotional, yet peaceful and profound. At the end of it, he made the finest call to leadership of the masses that it has ever been my privilege to hear. . . .

His speech was conversational. Yet it rang a louder call to unselfish service than any dramatic oratory could have done. . . .

Sun Yat-sen was unquestionably the leader of the Kuomintang Party, with power to give membership to what other groups he chose. As each new organisation was formed it was given membership in the national party. Organisations were formed almost as soon as anyone in Su-ling's crowd suggested a name. . . .

The news spread north that a returned student had but to appear in Su-ling's drawing-room to find his or her life work. The Western-educated students flocked to Canton. The Russian advisers, experts in each type of organisation, came from Moscow and trained this new leadership for specific, usually propagandistic, enterprises.

It is so easy to become interested in one group to the exclusion of all others. When I had poured tea at Su-ling's I was quite certain that the

Kuomintang was the only active party in Canton. Then one morning I went with my cook to market.

He had just purchased two live ducks and instructed his apprentice to carry one under each arm, when a Yunnanese soldier entered the market and demanded the contents of the shopkeeper's till. The man was slow in unlocking it. To quicken him, the soldier pulled the trigger of his gun.

Cook's apprentice was frightened to forgetfulness of the ducks. They flew squawking out of the shop. Cook sat down flat, upsetting his basket of vegetables. I found myself under the counter. Blood from the merchant's forearm dripped on my head, but I waited there until the soldier had emptied the cash box, Cook's purse, and mine.

On the way home, Cook told me that these Yunnanese soldiers were hired henchmen that Sun Yat-sen had brought to Canton to police the city some years ago, and that what I had witnessed was a frequent occurrence. He said that the merchants were arming themselves against both the Yunnanese and the new youthful activities of the Kuomintang.

Four days later, Cook borrowed my chair-bearers. He wanted them to help him carry home a week's supply of food. He explained that it was necessary because the markets were closing. Fighting between the Merchant Guilds and the Kuomintang would start that night. The merchants had sandbags, bricks and solid iron gates ready to barricade all the business section of the city. This could easily be done at Canton because the business section is a complete unit. . . .

The rumble of guns began just before daybreak. Battles by night and sniping by day continued most of the week. Stray bullets fell on Shameen but the only damage done on our sandbar was a bullet hole in the fire engine.

The river people gave me news of the progress of the war and told me how the merchants were routed. The barbers belong to no recognized guild. They were forgotten in the merchants' alliance, so were not loyal, and yet were not suspected of treachery. They were inside the barricades. A bribe was passed in to them. They punctured the water mains; then set fire to a dozen shops.

The merchants surrendered their weapons. The Kuomintang helped to put out the fire and clear away the barricades. We had peace again.

NORA WALN
The House of Exile (1933)

c. 1924-25

Timid Tourists

American travel writer Harry A. Franck was planning to do a book
on southern China, so he took his family (his wife, two children and
his mother) and rented an apartment in the suburbs of Canton.

The dangers of life in Canton were much impressed upon us,
especially before we got there. At Hong Kong a letter came out to us
before our steamer from Shanghai could dock warning me not to bring
my family to Canton until I had come up and investigated for myself, as
the writer would not be responsible for what might happen. I came, saw,
and laughed, and we settled down for the short winter. But the outside
world retained its hint of terror when the name of Canton was
mentioned. Now and again the place was deluged with a round-the-
world tourist party. The American consul in Hong Kong would let only
a fraction of them go up the river, as he feared the effect on Canton if
several hundred ascended upon it at once; but there was no great
difficulty in restricting the party, I understand, because of the dread
most of these unseasoned travelers have of wantonly risking their
precious lives. Those brave enough to come arrived by the regular day
steamer at 3:30 in the afternoon, and by special arrangement with
another British boat that usually left at five they managed to remain
until 5:30, which gave them ample time, of course, to know all about
Canton. Half of them were rushed out to the Flowery Pagoda by
automobiles, the rest coming more slowly in chairs. There loads were
exchanged, and while those who had been whisked out by gasoline and
had finished their seeing took the chairs back, so that they, too, could
have their share of that vivid, unique experience of the East, those who
had arrived by chair saw the same sights and were motored back to the
Bund in time for the steamer. . . . Now and again I took the trouble to
go on board the boat for a few moments before it sailed and, being often
mistaken for a member of the party, I got many a story of the horrors of

life in Canton, as seen so vividly in a short two hours . . . and then as the whistle sounded I would leave the flabbergasted tourists open-mouthed with my bravery as I walked ashore with the casual assurance that I lived in a far more Chinese part of that dreadful city than their guides had dared show them. . . .

To be sure, the first view of the "rats in a sewer" is not unnaturally terrifying. Not only the tourist bureaus, fearful of the awful publicity that would follow a scratch on the nose of one of their precious charges, but Hong Kong, eager for their trade, fill these poor human sheep with incredible tales of the dangers of Canton. There is really not much need of this, for the Canton shopkeepers do not get much out of them; they not only do not dare go into those dreadfully narrow streets where the good shops are, but no time is left them for unguided activities. . . .

The sight of a party of tourists shopping along the China coast is not one to be passed lightly by. Most of them drop in and ask prices just as they would at home, calmly paying at least three or four times as much as the shopkeeper would have been delighted to receive. . . . On those gala days shops catering to such trade do not wish to be bothered with local shoppers, even old foreign residents who have long been customers. I know of an American woman who came to pay a bill on one of those rare days when tourists were buying in Canton and was quickly told that she did not owe anything – true, the debt amounted to only $5 Canton currency, but the Chinese do not let money slip lightly through their fingers – in order not to have her hanging around and perhaps hinting the truth when she saw the robbery being practised on the simple tourists. I am reminded of a group of American tourists of the least amiable type who, happening to drop into a famous curio-shop in an important south coast city just in time to impress into service as interpreter a fellow-countrywoman long resident there, concluded purchases totaling several thousand dollars, during which they had been anything but courteous either to the shopkeeper or to the impressed go-between, by flashing forth the sum named in good American green-backs. The merchant, who had of course been thinking in "Mex" if not indeed in the still cheaper local dollars, turned an expressionless face toward the interpreter, who had her revenge merely by gazing back at him without the flicker of an eyelid as he slowly dropped the money into his Chinese till. . . .

However, to come back to our timid tourists; there were of course dangers in Canton. We heard so many rumors of them that firecrackers were somewhat disturbing in the middle of the night, when a string of them sounds so much like the rat-a-tat of machine-guns we were always half expecting, the big ones like the boom of cannon. There were constant brawls among the motley collection of soldiery overrunning the place, endless injustices to the Cantonese people; but the dangers to foreigners were really not great. For the Chinese it was another story; kidnapping, assassination, unjust punishment, military confiscation, wanton destruction, were the common lot. . . .

Kidnapping being a favorite Chinese sport, it was surprising to find no apparent tendency to steal the children of foreigners, surely a rich possibility. Some of the crimes might have been imported directly from our own cities, as when two men posing as electric-light inspectors were let into the home of well-to-do people near us and proceeded to rob them. The little boy of the family came home just then, sized up the situation with Chinese quickness, and got the police. The sequel had nothing in common with New York; no bail, no lawyers, no expert alienists, no months of delay, no acquittal on insufficient evidence or reversal of the decision by a higher court. . . . The men were paraded through the streets for a few hours as soon as an announcement of their crime could be hastily written and appended to them, and then were shot out in the open space in front of our gate, left there the rest of the day with the same rude placard still beside them, and toward dusk were carried away in slap-dash coffins. . . . But even though there were unpleasant sights and sounds, and consuls spent much time in warning those who would not listen, the foreigner really had less reason to worry about his wife and children anywhere in the streets of Canton than in any one of the first hundred American cities.

HARRY A. FRANCK
Roving through Southern China (1925)

"Pleasant Surplise"

<hr>

British lecturer and broadcaster Clifford Collinson and his friend George teamed up with an American acquaintance Elias B. Howard to go sightseeing. Together they hired a guide and set off in sedan chairs.

Yung Mak kept looking at his watch ... being anxious, as he explained, that we should visit another place before we returned to the hotel for tiffin. But in answer to my question as to what it was he wished us to see, he only returned a mysterious smile.

Once more, therefore, we climbed into our chairs and went a-burrowing through the alleys of Canton, twisting and turning until I lost all sense of direction, but emerging finally into an open space surrounded by buildings and mean-looking booths. At the far side of the square there stood a small knot of people, and in front of them, on the ground, lay a shapeless figure. Yung Mak, urging his overburdened steed, drew abreast of me, and, pointing towards the little crowd, cried:

"Too late; so solly; please esscuse."

"Too late for what?" I queried.

"Liver pilate – choppee off head!"

"River pirate?" I exclaimed. "Head chopped off? Gosh! Does Mr. Howard know?"

"No, no," replied Yung Mak, shaking his head. "Pleasant surplise."

By this time our jogging bearers had carried us much nearer to the scene of execution, and the prone figure had revealed itself to be a headless corpse with blood pouring from the stump of the severed neck. Even as we approached, the executioner, an enormous fellow grasping a sword in one hamlike hand, bent down and picked up the severed head by the hair. The whole dreadful scene was so utterly unexpected, that our chairs were dumped down close to the corpse before any of us realized the full significance of what we saw. Yung Mak, addressing himself to Elias B., was full of apologies for that we had arrived too late to witness the actual decapitation of this river pirate, but, perking up a little bit, explained that if we cared to wait, we should see an even more delightful spectacle – that of the cutting off of the arms and legs, and, finally, the beheading of a man who had murdered his brother. Even now, as Yung Mak pointed out, his spectators were beginning to gather for this notable event – the punishment named "*linchi*", which is reserved for the most terrible of all crimes – that against the sacred family. Whilst our guide was talking, I looked round at the natives. Hardly any of them even spared a glance for the dead man, and many of them had resumed their chaffering at the stalls near by. To the Chinese, death is merely an incident, and their only interest in an execution is to note whether the victim meets his end with proper stoicism and sang-froid.

But in spite of Yung Mak's promise of further entertainment, Howard had had enough ... His face had turned a ghastly green and he displayed every symptom of becoming violently sick. . . .

After tiffin – which Howard missed entirely – we set forth again upon our travels, visiting first the Wa-tap or "Flowery Pagoda", a magnificent nine-storied octagonal erection nearly three hundred feet in height and dating back to the sixth century. . . .

To me, our actual objectives, although extremely interesting, were by no means so fascinating as the crowded alleys through which we passed to reach them. Seated in our chairs, and borne at a level which was higher than the heads of the swarming natives, one caught tantalizing glimpses of a thousand things of interest – many of which, however, were so strange as to be unintelligible. Travelling in single file it was impossible, of course, to communicate with one another. Howard led the way, I came second, George was third, and the three Orientals brought up the rear on their little donkeys. Our palanquins were fitted with canopies and short side-curtains, and a door in front effectually closed us in.

It was while we were on our way from the Flowery Pagoda to the Temple of Shing-wong-min that the speed of our passage considerably increased and that, simultaneously, I heard loud cries of "Oi" from George behind me. . . .

I looked backwards to see George's face, now glistening with perspiration and absolutely purple with rage, glaring at me from his front window, whilst below the chair George's legs ... were paddling swiftly in an effort to keep pace with the hurrying steps of his sweating coolies. . . . But help was at hand. Yung Mak, seeing that something was amiss, spurred his steed forward, and, espying George's predicament, brought his palanquin to a sudden halt. Turning round, I was just in time to see George's bearers lower the chair suddenly to the ground – and to witness the totally unexpected apparition of George's head as it burst through the top of the descending canopy.

When at last we managed to extricate him from the ruins of his chair, and he had calmed down a little, he explained that, on rising from his seat to rearrange his cushion, the floor-boards had given way beneath his weight, dropping him through, with the result that for the last half-mile he had been running within the four sides of his sedan and shouting to attract the attention of his not only deaf, but, apparently, daft fellow travellers. . . .

The next morning we caught the eight a.m. boat back to Hong Kong
. . .

On the following night we all went to a Chinese theatre, a substantial-looking building, the frontage of which was plastered with long narrow posters covered with brightly-coloured Chinese characters. Entering, we found ourselves in a well-lighted hall with a stage at the far end and filled with wooden benches occupied, for the most part, by a somewhat malodorous audience of Chinamen.

The performance had already commenced – two whole days ago – and we tiptoed lightly to vacant seats at the end of one of the rear benches. But we need not have troubled to do any tiptoe business because, regardless of the actors, the members of the audience were chattering and laughing, whilst white-coated boys, carrying trays of cakes and sweetmeats, wandered about in the brightly-lighted auditorium, crying their wares with shrill voices.

What the play was about I have not the faintest idea. The stage itself was merely a wooden platform with blank canvas screens behind. . . . and in the centre an insecure-looking structure, composed of . . . tables and chairs, piled up one on top of the other, represented the towering heights of a precipitous mountain. At the moment of our entrance the heroine – a young man dressed as a woman, for all female rôles are played by men on the Chinese stage – was climbing up this flimsy erection in a desperate attempt to escape the clutches of the villain – Yung Mak knew he was the villain because his nose was painted white
. . .

Later, after the mountain had been cleared away by the scene-shifters,

AT A CHINESE THEATRE

there was a wonderful fight between the hero, wearing a gorgeous gold-embroidered costume, and six opponents, whom he tackled one at a time. All were armed with long two-handed swords. . . . Meanwhile, scene-shifters walked on and off the stage and amongst the actors, moving chairs and tables about or just having a look round – but Yung Mak, sitting next to me, said that I must pretend not to see them because they were supposed to be invisible.

. . . A white-clad Chinese boy – a young student – sitting next to me, did his best to explain about the play, but his English was very rudimentary, and the only thing I clearly understood after half an hour's difficult conversation was that the action of the play was supposed to take place, for the most part, in a brothel. . . . The theatre in China ranks low; and the social position of an actor was, until quite recently, comparable with that of a barber.

On the last night but one of our stay in Hong-Kong there was a lunar eclipse, which created a good deal of consternation amongst the Chinese, who thought that the end of the world was at hand. And so relieved were they the next morning to find that everything was still normal, that they celebrated their deliverance by indulging in an orgy of fireworks. The Chinese are great on fireworks, the favourite kind being immensely long strings of crackers which are hung from roof to pavement. . . .

The Chinese are a noisy people – most Orientals are – and the deafening pandemonium not only, according to their beliefs, exorcizes the foul spirits of evil, but is to them as the sweetest music. Incidentally, from a purely hygienic point of view, the sulphur fumes, penetrating into every cranny, undoubtedly help to exorcize the foul spirits of disease – which is all to the good.

CLIFFORD W. COLLINSON
Half the Seas Over (1933)

Night Life

James Hutchison of the American Tobacco Company had previously spent six years in China, mainly in the north. Now back again in Asia, and passing through Hong Kong, he found British ways stranger to him than those of the Chinese.

Early in September I took the Dollar line to Hongkong. British Hongkong must be the tidiest of all the tidy cities of the world, and the most completely inconsistent. It looked in the early morning as if overnight a corps of efficient charwomen had given it a thorough sweeping. Even the foliage of the undergrowth and trees softening the contours of the hills seemed to have been dusted and polished to silvery high-lights against the vivid green. And like good boys and girls, the foreign element went to bed at 10 o'clock, at which hour everything closed by law. Yet the Chinese shops on the sides of the stone steps at the bottom of the hills were brown with dust and smelled to heaven. And the night life among the native residents was only starting at midnight and was about as free and unmoral as in New York during prohibition.

Before going to Canton I attended a Chinese dinner that was supposed to start at 9 P.M. Knowing the Chinese custom, I arrived at 10. The banquet room of the restaurant, located two blocks back from the water front, took up an entire square. Ten or twelve tables of *ma chiang* and *twenty-one* were in full swing. One side of the room was taken up with a row of black-wood *k'angs*, on each of which an opium smoking outfit was neatly arranged. Occasionally one of the slender silken gowned guests would leave off gambling to lie down and relax with a smoke. I wandered around watching, wondering hungrily when dinner was to begin. Finally, around eleven-thirty, I asked the company's number one, who was concentrated on a *ma chiang* game. He pointed to a door at one side. I entered and found a long table piled with food, then suddenly realized that the meal went on all evening and that guests drifted in and out, eating when they felt like it. A Southern custom that was new to me. The food, too, was different from that of the North, with many thin soups and fish and highly seasoned sauce dishes – like the Southerners themselves, a thin, nervous diet.

While I was seated at the dining table, the air was rent with a terrific noise as if a light artillery had let loose. I looked around but no one was paying attention. I asked my neighbor what had happened. He shrugged his shoulders, "Perhaps a wedding – shooting off giant crackers." I looked at my watch – it was half an hour to midnight. I walked to the window and gazed out – the streets below were as light as day, echoing with the clatter of pedestrians' wooden clogs, motor cars, rickshas and chairs. Chinese night life was at its height. I stared up toward the peak – a few lights blinked here and there against the black mass silhouetted against the sky. The British were tucked in their beds, quietly sleeping.

Some one had told me the day before that the English imposed a fine for taking off one's coat in public – even on the hottest day. I thought of all the formal cleanliness I had seen, of the 10 o'clock curfew, then of the tremendous racket going around me and the open consumption of opium. What a curious mixture of contradictions the Englishman is – morality as such plays no part in his life – he is ruled by the one and only law of "it's done or it isn't done".

JAMES LAFAYETTE HUTCHISON
China Hand (1936)

1932

Conspiracy of Silence

As a traveller Ramnath Biswas belonged in a class of his own: his incredible global journey of 51,000 miles on a bicycle lasted eight years. Here, still comparatively inexperienced after only six months on the road from his native India, Biswas arrived at Canton.

It was the New Year's Day, 1932. I had completed the first half year of my projected Round-the-world-tour on push-byke. Yet I had only seen a little corner of the globe and that too not a very unfamiliar one. But today the ancient City of Canton lay in front of me, like a beakon of light as if ready to light my way into the mysteries of the Celestial Empire. It was about noon when I reached the city of Sun-Yat-Sen. I was tired, after spending three days on my push-byke and three nights in poor peasants' huts, all the way from Hong Kong. But the thought of exploring the Celestial Empire and of having already reached the glorious city of revolutionary patriotism bucked me up. I looked forward to a friendly welcome in this land of the great republican of the East.

Queerly enough the whole city turned icy cold. No one would speak to me and nobody would listen to me! No one was obliging enough to show me the way or direct me to a hotel. Not even the local police would have a word. An inexplicable conspiracy of silence greeted me from all sides!

"Well, it's all in a traveller's life time," thought I and dragged my push-byke on. By the riverside I found a number of hotels and asked for a room at the first I came across. "No room" was the curt reply, not even flavoured with a courteous "sorry!" The same cold greeting at the second hotel and again at the third – and so on to the twentieth.

I turned round disgusted. I was burning with thirst and getting into a cafe asked for a cup of tea. There were many other customers around and all were served in good time. But not I! None cared to attend to me.

With a rebellious spirit I came out and went on knocking from door to door and from street to street. I was bent on finding out the British Consulate. It was at night-fall when I succeeded in getting in touch with the consul. He listened to my story but he himself could not explain it. His only advice was "Go back to Hong Kong and then home!" Finally he turned me over to an unfriendly Chinese instructing him to arrange for my stay for the night. We made another long detour from hotel to hotel until at last an abominable hole of a cellar was arranged for.

Close to the cellar was a drumful of urine. The air was vitiated. An unbearably obnoxious smell filled the room. Some grub, fit for street curs, was shoved in and the door banged from the outside. It was lucky I was faint with hunger and fatigue. I devoured the "food" and in a minute lay fast asleep.

The morning came and I jumped up and out of the cellar. I asked for a little water to wash my face. Of course no-body listened. So out on to the streets. There I washed my hands and face from a street tap. I felt better now and decided to make another round of the town. I might get better luck! Who knows? But the same conspiracy of silence greeted me from all sides!

It was about ten o'clock when, all exhausted, I was standing by the side of the Sun-Yat-Sen Park. I stood there for a long time, thinking and thinking. Should I go back? But it would mean good-bye to my travel, farewell to my "Round-the-world-on-a-push-byke" project! I felt too unnerved to make up my mind.

"Keiling Kuei! Wei Keiling Kuei!" It was a distant shout from the left. It sounded nearer and nearer. It came quite close and seemed to be meant for me and I turned round. What a luck! It was an old Chinese friend from Singapore.

"You Keiling Kuei, what brings you here, old chum?"

"The devil himself has led me here – the most god forsaken place" I said. And I told him my whole story. How he laughed! I felt like blowing his head off for him.

"Why, old man," he started again, "you look a perfect Jappon Kuei! I wouldn't be surprised if you were shot and killed by one of my people!"

"Get out of your joke," I said, "tell me what it all means."

He began to explain. "We Chinese are burning with hatred for the Japanese militarists. We hate to look at them. None of us would speak to them. In fact we would drive them out of our fair land had not our government and our generalissimo held us in check. They say we are not strong enough yet. The way you have dressed yourself is the way of the Japanese peasant. You look exactly like him. Our people naturally take you for a Jappon Kuei. That explains the boycott, the insult and the malicious maltreatment you have suffered. Come on, let me overhaul you, and you will see how our people like you and love you as a little brother."

So he led me to a tailor's shop, had a badge made out with the words "Hindu-Yangtze-Saikai" displayed prominently and pinned it to my shirt. It cost me 40 cents. The words meant "Hindu World Tourist." Then we both came out on the streets.

Now I was embarrassed the other way round, and over-whelmed with warm sympathy and sincere regrets from all sides. Greetings of welcome and good wishes rained on me wherever I went. Yes, I was treated like a real little brother. And when I returned to the hotel, the owner received me with a warm shake of hands and a broad smile. How he regretted yesterday's maltreatment and kept repeating "Thank God, you are no Jappon Kuei. We all love you. But how we hate them. They have devoured our Manchuria. And now they are preparing to devour us all."

He himself removed my luggage to the best room in the hotel, led me to a luxurious bath room and when I had finished my bath treated me to a sumptuous meal.

In the afternoon my old friend called again and we both went for an outing. We entered the best hotel in the town – the Asia Hotel, where the owner invited me to a free meal and tea. Everywhere, in the hotels, in the streets and parks, in the market places and shops, men and women, old and young, all received me with warm affection, talking and chatting all the time.

The next day was a Sunday – the day on which the Cantonese patriots gather in front of the marble statue of Sun-Yat-Sen to pay their homage to his memory. My friends took me there. It was a solemn ceremony. Thousands of men and women knelt silently before the statue, their faces illuminated with a grim determination to follow him and to rebuild a free and strong China.

From there we went to see the Sun-Yat-Sen University. Some young students led us to a hall and requested me to speak to them about India. In ten minutes the hall was filled with young boys and girls. A student introduced me as a Hindu traveller and co-patriot of poet Tagore.

I didn't know what to say to them. I was no public speaker. But when I got up I found all I said about our poor old India got tinged with a sadness and brought out a picture of humiliation. . . . I ended by hoping that the sacrifices of the ancient peoples of the two great countries, India and China, would not be in vain . . .

As I sat down I was greeted with a prolonged applause. I was introduced to a number of foreign professors and treated to a delicate dish. At the table everyone ate with the "stick" Chinese fashion. But I had to use my fingers. There was a roar of laughter, but good humoured.

As we left, my friend said, "So now you know the Hindu is our friend and little brother, but the 'Jappon Kuei' is our hated enemy for he, more than any one else today, is out to enslave us, to crush our movement for liberation."

RAMNATH BISWAS
China Defies Death (1944)

c. 1933

What a Racket!

William Martin was a man of many parts: university professor,
League of Nations official, journalist, and former Foreign Editor of the
Journal de Genève. He was also a perceptive traveller.

If you reach Hongkong after dark you will rub your eyes – where does
the sky come to an end? Those scintillating lights, are they of earth or
heaven? Are those streams of stars, prolonging the Milky Way, really a
city? They must be, for at eleven o'clock they all go out. Morals are
morals in the British colonies.

In the daytime the effect is no less impressive. Behind a quay of
European type there is the busy life of the indigenous towns: streets
mounting by stairs, sedan chairs, banners floating in the wind –
authentic China. But a China of macadam roads, all climbing toward
the Peak, whence you may look out over one of the finest landscapes in
the world. The Europeans would not say "See Naples and die" if they
had seen Kowloon Bay with its encircling mountains. And it is
impossible to feel much pity for the Chinese émigrés who nurse their
grievances here, in their luxurious villas, as they watch the sun go down
in its glory.

The British are artists, but they are, above all, traders and strategists.
To get a good view of Hongkong it is necessary to see it from across the
water, from Kowloon; and it is also necessary to have Kowloon, with its
docks and railway station, its monumental hotels and its hinterland, in
order to dominate the Bay.

It is from Kowloon that the train starts for Canton, running beside
the estuary of the Pearl River, up which the Europeans have always gone
to compel the Chinese to trade with them. Canton is the porch of
China, and the Pearl River is its threshold. That is why the British have
planted themselves there. . . .

When two Chinese meet, a few moments' talk is enough to reveal where they come from. And if they are both from Fukien or Chekiang, Szechuan or Shansi, if they like their glazed duck, their sharks' fins or bamboo shoots cooked in the same way, they feel themselves to be fellow-countrymen, like a couple of Finns or Spaniards meeting far from home. If they speak different dialects and do not like the same dishes, they will not unbend to one another.

. . . All over China the people live largely out of doors; in Canton in the evening you have to play leap-frog in the streets over the sleepers. Don't walk with your head in the air; watch where you go, or you will be stepping on people's hands or stumbling over their faces. They must be tired, these people, and their consciences must be at rest, for them to be able to sleep like this on the ground, on the bare ground, indifferent to all the noise.

And what a racket! China is the capital of the country of noise; but, for noise, Canton is the capital of China. The chauffeurs drive with one hand on the wheel and the other incessantly working their motor-horn; every shop has its gramophone yelling or its loud-speaker speaking its loudest; the coolies sing to keep their spirits up; hawkers shout to make you buy, and passers by shout louder to make themselves heard.

Deafened and exhausted, do you think of going back to your hotel for a rest? What a mistake! You will find them all there, the hawkers, the coolies, the gramophones, droning electric fans, singing-birds, grasshoppers for luck, who raise their voices too; you will find open-work doors and Chinese who talk in the passages the whole night long. When do these people sleep? And if Chinese seek happiness in marriage the occasion is marked by unending discharges of crackers, right in your ears.

The Chinese hotels are not at all bad; they are decidedly better than most of the foreign ones in the country. You ask for a room and they give you four. A "room with two beds" in a Chinese hotel is two little single-bedded rooms opening on to a sitting-room, with a monumental bathroom, all on the tenth floor – for Canton is modern, and modern in China means American.

When you go back four boys spring up to serve you. One opens the door, the second gets a bath ready – no matter what the time is, day or night; the third brings you tea, and the fourth rushes to the fans.

There is one thing that a Chinese will never understand, that people may object to draughts!

If you want a little peace and quiet, or even fresh air, do not take refuge in your room, where the noise will soon drive you out again. Go to Shameen – in the International Concession.

The foreigners of Shanghai are proud to think that all the commercial and social and artistic activity of the town, in a word, all its life, is concentrated in the Concessions. In Canton it is the opposite. The Concession resembles a convent. Under the great trees by the side of the canal porters "take it easy," lounging in the fresh air; lovers come and go; dogs chase one another; here and there a British or French soldier rubs up his kit. Nobody goes by, there is not a sound to be heard except from the birds in the trees. It is a charming spot from which life has withdrawn. Shameen is a museum, in which privileges are exhibited like curiosities from the past.

Now cross the bridge that separates this oasis from Canton. To right and left are massed sampans, intertwined like the straw of a hat. I am told that they get out every now and then to go fishing. How do they manage it? . . .

It is hot in Canton in June. For protection the houses are dressed up with long laths – and the people are undressed. Children under ten go completely naked; coolies wear nothing but shorts; the rest of the population are in pyjamas. If you go to dine with a great personage and are invited to take your coat off, do not attempt to say it is unnecessary. You will be making all the rest keep their robes on . . .

. . . Canton is the only city in which a foreigner will find Chinese homes open to him, and I retain a grateful recollection of exquisite and delightful lunches that I was given in the home of the Mayor of Canton, in a villa completely buried in flowers . . .

The complications of etiquette here are such as only a Chinese can cope with. The guest is perfectly free to do as he chooses. He may turn up a couple of hours late, or not at all; he may leave before a meal; his host will never take offence. In China there is a long exchange of civilities before the meal; the invitation will be for six and dinner will begin at nine. But when the last mouthful has been swallowed the guest will take his leave.

. . . The master of the house takes his guests to their seats, himself serving each of them with hot rice wine from a little cruet. The place of honour is the seat facing him, and a contest of retiring modesty goes on for the seats by his side, which are the places of least distinction.

Hot wine, fortunately of no great strength, for a lot of it is drunk, plays an important part in a Chinese meal. After each dish, and they are countless, healths are drunk, and one solemnly shows the bottom of one's empty glass, with a little bow. . . .

Twenty-six courses – and that is only a simple meal. Everybody eats out of the same dish . . . Everything is thoroughly done and has its full flavour. But – flavour of what? Birds' nests, pigeons' eggs, ducks, resins, chickens' giblets, ducks' tongues, bamboo shoots, buds of kidney beans, pine kernel or sunflower seeds, preserved lotus seeds, melon pips, and so on, and so on; dessert half-way through, fish at the end. How to manage it all? . . .

Each guest helps his neighbour, with his own chopsticks or spoon. Between the courses boys hand round boiling napkins, for wiping hands and faces. When it is all over mouths are rinsed over the spittoons.

. . . Canton is the only town in China in which one may now see thoroughly Chinese women dressed in the European style. In any other part of China, if one sees an almond-eyed woman in a low-necked dress she is sure to be a Japanese, a Korean, or of mixed blood. In Canton she will generally be Chinese. . . .

The evolution is rather to be dreaded, as the Chinese women, whose high necks and robes slit above the knee lend them such charm and elegance, are generally ill-served by European dress. As for hats, they are a disaster. If the Chinese women could see what is in their own interest, they would do anything rather than imitate their Western sisters. But, alas! fashion seems to be winning the day; and we shall perhaps see the disappearance of the style of dress that makes the Chinese women of to-day the prettiest in the world.

WILLIAM MARTIN
Understand the Chinese (1934)
Trans. E.W. Dickes

c. 1936

On the Water-Front

Although a Chinese, C.S. See was visiting China as a foreigner. He came from Malaya, and at the age of twenty-five was enjoying his first-ever trip abroad.

Canton has nearly half a dozen huge restaurants, probably some of the largest in China. One of these typical eating houses is the magnificent Mun Yuen Restaurant situated on Mun Yuen Cheng Road. It has two floors covering a very wide area and contains over twenty large rooms. Considering the severe depression the writer was surprised to find every room taken up by diners . . . Many of the waitresses have good voices and these are much in demand as they move around the room pouring rice or some other wine into the glasses; they too are capable of answering all kinds of questions whether funny or personal, and they are supposed to light the cigarettes of their customers. They are friendly and courteous and chat to every customer and occasionally steal a few of his water-melon seeds. When the dinner is over these waitresses come in with huge piles of face towels under their arms and these are rinsed in perfumed and warmed "Florida" water for the customers' use – this has become a custom in most Chinese restaurants in recent years. . . .

In these large restaurants in Canton one also finds mah-jong parties and opium smoking saloons where trained girls help to prepare the drug and the pipes and are able to entertain their customers with stories and legends of old China.

One night in Canton the author's eyes were attracted by numberless lights on the sea side of the Bund. It was interesting to find on the shore endless poorly-lighted stalls selling coffee, rice or fruits, all kinds of peddlars, hawkers, sugar-cane vendors, quack physicians selling medicine for all ailments and quack dentists whose only stock-in-trade seemed to be a heap of teeth which they had extracted from their previous clients. The art of dentistry is an easy thing with them, and has none of the complications of modern science. The patient sits on a stool, about eight inches high, and by sheer force the dentist manages to extract diseased teeth.

This part of the water-front in Canton is most spectacular by night. Paraded along the side and stretched for thousands of yards there is to be seen nightly a long line of house-boats, all tied to one another temporarily.

At sunrise not a single boat or sampan remains here. For, as early as three or four o'clock in the morning, in good weather or in storm, these boats unfasten their ropes or chains and go out to the sea to their daily business of catching fish, whilst others get their livelihood by transporting cargo.

A visitor to this part of Canton will see thousands of men, women, and children, the women predominating, all standing on the water-front looking at one another or at passers-by. The girls are called "hum-swee-mooi" in Chinese, Cantonese dialect, which literally translated means, "the salt-water girls." They live a peculiar and hard existence. During the day they row far out to sea to catch fish. In the evening on their return to the shore they first sell their fish and then put on their gayest clothes. Many of them parade the water-front for immoral purposes.

The writer had never been inside a house-boat and when he went round the house-boats he was surprised to see that almost all the boats, which looked so humble with their thatched awnings from outside, were exquisitely decorated inside. The materials used for adorning the interior of these house-boats are specially made and are certainly expensive: the variegated colours and designs look like the artistic panellings of a mansion.

These humble house-boats, which go out to sea in the morning and return in the evening, to pass a few hours of the night by the shore, even have electric lights to illuminate the interior of their cabins. Some of these boats become night clubs where mah-jong and card games are played, whilst many are hired out as opium smoking dens.

It was a cool and pleasant afternoon when we were strolling amongst the tall pine trees which line the embankment of the delta at Shameen in Canton. We had originally planned to spend only a few minutes there, but were induced to pass a whole afternoon discovering this part of Canton whose aesthetic beauty appealed strangely to us.

This splendid spot borders a beautiful portion of the foreign concession of Shameen wherein are situated all the leading business houses, import and export firms, and the foreign banks and consulates. . . .

The sky was overcast and it was therefore not hot and glaring. We saw women and children plying their crafts selling pork, vegetables, sweetmeats and all kinds of things as they shouted or sang advertising their wares.

Then there came a long line of junks, boats, and sampans, all linked to one another, not unlike a procession. It was a peculiar sight, for these crafts not only carried passengers and cargoes but also had floating shops and barbers' saloons on them. When they stopped at each halting place their hawkers would rush out to sell certain special things brought from up-river and the barbers secured a lot of business. . . .

A charming young woman passed along in her sampan and as she dipped her oars into the water she was shouting "Ice-cream, ice-cream." The place seemed to us like a veritable river "city" with all manners of crafts and people passing up and down stream.

Not being able to resist the urge any longer we hailed a passing sampan rowed by a middle-aged woman with a long pig-tailed queue. We imagined ourselves in a gondola in Venice and were allowed to cherish this little dream as the lady at the helm turned out to be an excellent and accomplished songstress who entertained us with Chinese songs. We attracted considerable attention and even little boys and girls of no more than five summers followed us in a procession as they paddled their little canoes and tried hard to catch up with us. We were worried about the safety of these little children as some of them could not swim if their canoes capsized, but they were well prepared as everyone of them was chained to a heavy block of wood. If they fell into the water they were taught to catch hold of the wooden "buoy." At night they use these blocks as pillows. . . .

We began to wonder at the philosophy of life of this curious class of people. . . . We noticed a woman selling a few poor radishes and asked her about herself: she replied that she had been rowing the whole day and had covered about twelve miles. On our asking her how much she had sold that day, she replied that she had only taken five cash the whole day – less than two Straits cents – and she had a whole family of seven children and an aged grandmother depending on her!

C.S. SEE
A Chinese Sees the World (1937)

c. 1936

A Wonderful Dragon

What French playwright Francis de Croisset saw in Canton and Macao must have appeared to him like scenes from a living theatre, all too often played as tragedy.

I went for a stroll in Canton with a Chinese student.

. . . I was appalled. Everything which, before my visit, had made me so fond of this land of poets, painters, architects and sculptors, was repudiated by these very men who are in charge of it.

The last remaining shrines have been defiled and are now used as garages, restaurants and shops. There was one temple which had been spared, because no use could be found for it. The powers that be then decided to pull it down. It so happened that I was there when, amid the cheers of the mob, the pickaxes began to chip away the pink plaster scales of a wonderful dragon belonging to the fourteenth century. Frescoes in green, strawberry and pale yellow portraying birds and flowers were similarly defaced in the name of progress. A Buddha, made of ordinary material but exquisitely carved, was hacked to pieces under my very eyes by those strange workmen who were possessed by the lust for destruction. I, the only foreigner, was the only one among them all to suffer from this act of sacrilege.

"We've got to do away with the things which caused our misfortune," said the student, who, having been to America, thought himself up to date. "My country is decaying because of its superstitious beliefs. You have a French saying: There are some dead who must be killed. We are acting on it."

"What will you put in the place of the things which you are destroying?"

"Technical achievements: railways, factories, aerodromes."

"And your religion?"

"It doesn't fit in with progress."

221

A CHINESE TEMPLE

"And your works of art?"
"We'll produce fresh ones, and anyhow, that's not very important."

At Canton there are two kinds of sampans, those with permanent moorings and those that are "rovers."

The former . . . a regular floating town . . . is the pleasure district, where the ladies of easy virtue reside and receive their visitors and where in the evening young men-about-town like to gamble, make love and have a good time generally. . . .

The "rovers" seldom venture into the ultra-smart quarter containing the moored sampans, and then only on the plea that they are showing tourists round. It should not be forgotten that the ladies who reside in these stationary house-boats form the gentlefolk of their small world and

fornicate only with the Chinese. Any intercourse with a foreigner would at once cause them to lose their social standing, whereas the women on the "roving" sampans for a low fee grant their favours to the sailors and soldiers of the "heathen nations."

Whichever kind of boat she may belong to, not one of these ladies hails from Canton. To tell the truth, nothing is known about their earliest years, and all that can be said with any certainty is that from century to century, from mother to daughter, they live and die on the sampans. . . .

Each sampan, for the sake of decorum, displayed in the foreground only a small parlour showily tricked out with gilded frames, mirrors and glass trinkets. Mats were scattered about, and mottoes on hanging strips of silk also caught the eye.

A little farther to the rear there were glimpses of a back room and a bed which, at the right time, could be concealed by a dimity curtain.

Each sampan is shared by two or three women. The parlour, a prim-and-proper apartment, has no knowledge of the back room. . . . this love mart suggested anything but love.

On the sampans some Chinese were playing at mah-jongg, sipping green tea the while; others were smoking or lolling on sofas; not one of them was taking any notice of the women who, sitting stock-still and with taut bosom in their dappled gowns, with their little painted faces turned towards the canal, seemed to have been left there all night by mistake. Now and then one of them would get up to follow a customer into the private room, to fetch the tea-tray or hand round some kickshaws. But as soon as her task was over, she resumed the stock-still posture which made her look like a little, good-tempered idol.

Slowly our boat glided past the sampans. As we went by, I vainly tried to catch a stray glimpse of a kiss, a caress or a meaning smile. No, these girls were just menials, menials clad like flowers.

. . . Macao, under Portuguese control, the city to which Camoens imparted renown, is a kind of liberty hall. Opium, and also fan-tan, the Chinese pastime, are allowed there. Thus, a week-end at Macao is what all gamblers, and hence all Chinese, hanker after.

. . . The boats sail punctually enough, but they are not always sure of getting there because the sea is infested with pirates. . . .

Of course, all the passengers hope to win a fortune, and for this purpose they take some money with them. More often than not, by the time they come back they have been relieved of it after playing fan-tan all night. Accordingly, the pirates prefer to swoop upon the boat-loads of hopeful passengers bound for Macao than upon the rueful trippers who are returning home. . . .

We had scarcely got clear of the Pearl River than the weather changed. A sudden storm arose and the boat began to roll.

"The pirates leave boats alone when it's stormy," said the Captain to me. "We're in luck's way."

. . . Macao entranced me. It is a startling, delightful little town, in which a few Portuguese churches and houses of the sixteenth century served as a reminder of those who founded it but which otherwise is motley and strident, while the scents and smells with which it is laden convey perfectly the stench of China. . . .

Every night Macao grimly sets out to have fun. That is its job.

Restaurants, gambling-houses, dance-halls, brothels and opium-dens are crowded together, higgledy-piggledy. There is a ceaseless ant-like hubbub of people rushing to and fro, jostling each other, going in and coming out. . . .

Everybody at Macao gambles: the painted flapper who is not a school-girl but a prostitute, and who, between two brief spells of dalliance, wagers as much as she can earn in a night; the mandarin who has lost all his money and stakes his rings; the society woman on the balcony who throws banknotes into the cup without even bothering to count them; the rickshaw coolie who pockets his tip and then has a flutter with it; the beggar who has just managed to cadge a coin and now, no longer cringing, stakes it with a lordly air; the croupier himself who, the moment he goes off duty, rushes to the neighbouring fan-tan table to try his luck there, and finally the old woman who, with nothing left to wager, to my amazement took out three gold teeth, which, with a gaping smile, she staked and lost.

FRANCIS DE CROISSET
The Wounded Dragon (1937)
Trans. Paul Selver

1937

Nobodies

Twenty-four-year-old Charles Thomas had been in the Royal Navy for three years when he was posted to Hong Kong; here he served as a Wireless Telegraphist at the Navy Wireless Station. Soon after arriving in the colony Thomas wrote this letter home.

HONG KONG
14th August 1937.

Every European here is waited upon hand and foot. I am myself I admit. It goes to the heads of the people who in England are nobodies. Dockyard people, petty government officials, and the like, who have created a caste which is nauseous to say the least. Naturally this caste is not recognised by the higher caste of officers and their wives and higher Government officials, nor do either caste recognise yet another group of Army family society. The sailor stands aloof – a society of his own.

Today in the Kowloon post office an American tourist turned to me and said "Say how d'ya spell Cholera?" I thought he said colliery and said "Do you mean the coalmine?" "No, guess I refer to the disease" he replied. I obliged with the spelling. It is only an American who would ask that in a public post office.

The cholera epidemic is spreading and emergency inoculation measures have been instituted. I was inoculated on Tuesday. Strange to say the Roman Catholic Church officials have issued a decree allowing followers of their religion to eat meat on Fridays instead of fish, because the latter is the chief source of infection. . . .

I read of an amusing incident in Canton very much like the "Mikado" opera. The Central Government ordered the expulsion of all the White Russians (Tsarists) on the grounds that they were pro Japanese in sympathies. Well the Cantonese authorities expelled them alright but told them that as far as they were concerned they could return again straight away because the order had been carried out and obeyed. So the Russians travelled by steamer to Hong Kong and caught the next train back from Kowloon to Canton. Honour satisfied all round in true comic opera style.

Out in the streets China carries on. The old men sit on the pavements smoking their long pipes and philosophically regarding the passers by, the women cook their rice on the small fires in the gutters and the children in amazing numbers play their queer card games. Soon the chopsticks will come out, the families will squat round in circles and China will eat her last meal of the day. Afterwards they will stretch out their mats and sleep impervious to the patter of feet by them and the rattle of the buses and tramcars in the roadway. God only knows what life holds for these people!

CHARLES RICHARD THOMAS
Correspondence (manuscript)

1939

"Tipperary"

It was twenty years since Carveth Wells, author, lecturer and explorer, had last been in Hong Kong. Then the Great War had just come to an end: now another was already at hand.

We sailed from Shanghai on September 1st and, as we reached the open sea a British cruiser came along as escort and remained close by all the way to Hongkong. Whether or not this escort had been requested no one could tell, but it was comforting to know that the British fleet was co-operating with us in the Pacific. At eight o'clock that night the captain informed us that Polish cities were being bombed by Germany and that war was almost certain to be declared. The next day, instead of seeing numerous vessels, as is customary on the run between Shanghai and Hongkong, we found the sea deserted. But on the horizon we could make out a comforting patch of smoke that remained with us all day long. It was our unexpected but welcome British cruiser.

For the first time, except for an occasional dance band, the ship's radio was silent. The instant any voice began to speak, it was drowned out by a powerful station which filled the air with static, and we went to bed that night wondering what the morrow might bring forth.

At seven o'clock in the morning the *President Pierce* stopped her engines. A British man-of-war dashed alongside and ordered us to follow her into Hongkong. A mine-field had already been laid and the entrance to the Hongkong harbour was closed by a great submarine net. No one could say that the British navy had been caught napping.

On each side of the narrow entrance to the inner harbour was a small British gunboat. Not until we were within a few yards of the net and had come to a dead stop did one of the gunboats slowly tow an end of the net away to make an opening just wide enough to admit our vessel. We sailed into the harbour and the net was immediately closed after us.

228

From the water, Hongkong looks like a giant layer cake, rising from the esplanade and business quarter at the base, tier after tier, to the top of the Peak. The icing on top is formed by the Governor's mansion and the lovely villas of Hongkong's wealthy residents who live 1800 feet above sea-level in an atmosphere about eight degrees cooler than the business quarter. . . .

After an absence of twenty years, I think the most striking change that I noticed was in the dress of the modern Chinese girl. The dance hour at tea or cocktail time in the Hongkong Hotel presents one of the most fascinating scenes in the Far East – that is, if you are interested in pretty Chinese girls. Unbecoming trousers have given way to the slit skirt, which seems to have been purposely designed to show off the charming legs of Chinese women. The modern Chinese girl, with Madame Chiang Kai-shek as an example, looks forward to a career that only liberty and complete freedom can offer her. Twenty years ago, young Chinese girls, with their feet bound until their tiny shoes were not much longer than one inch, were a common sight; but I failed to see one such girl this time, although, of course, I saw many elderly women with bound feet.

But the Chinese still use rickshas and sedan chairs in Hongkong, and I could not notice any diminution in the number of Chinese who spend their lives as beasts of burden. The ricksha has practically vanished in Japan, yet the vehicle originally came from Yokohama, where it was invented by an American missionary in 1869. The missionary's wife was an invalid; in order to give her an airing, he converted an old perambulator into the first ricksha. A Japanese improved and patented the invention and, in so doing, started a special race of mankind, the ricksha puller.

Hongkong was teeming with excitement on Sunday evening, September 3rd. War had been talked about, of course, but when newsboys began racing through the streets at seven o'clock, with the official news that it had been declared, it came as a shock, especially to those who, like myself, had experienced the last World War. Almost instantly the streets were thronged with excited people, telling one another the dreadful news as if it were something to be glad about. I could not understand this until I began talking to some Englishmen in the lobby of the Hongkong Hotel. One of them said: "I'm glad the suspense is over. Damn Hitler anyway. Now we know where we are; it's Germany or the British Empire. This time, by God, we'll finish the job we left undone in 1918. Treaty of Versailles too harsh, they told us. Not harsh enough, by a damn sight."

"What's Japan going to do?" I enquired. This was exactly two weeks after Germany had signed her pact with Soviet Russia.

"Japan!" replied the Englishman. "We thought she was going to grab Hongkong a month ago. She had thirty thousand troops ready to do it when Germany double-crossed her. Since then we haven't heard any more about it."

We ourselves had motored all over Hongkong and had seen the preparations that had been made to receive the Japanese. Wherever there was a beach upon which a landing could be made, barbed-wire entanglements had been erected and numerous machine-gun nests and field guns trained seawards. Every few hundred yards along the roads we came upon a gun emplacement behind a wall of sandbags. All these were in addition to the permanent fortifications, which were so well concealed that it was impossible to tell whether or not the place really was fortified.

Remembering a conversation I had had with a Japanese in which he had told me that when the time came Japan would capture Hongkong in two days, I asked an Englishman the same question and received the reply: "One day."

Apparently at that time Hongkong was supposed to be practically without any anti-aircraft defences and it was expected that the city would be wiped out by bombing.

As we left the Hongkong Hotel to return to the *President Pierce*, the lobby was filled with Englishmen singing the old songs of 1914, especially "Tipperary."

When we reached the dock where the *President Pierce* was tied up alongside, we saw that something unusual had happened. British soldiers had taken charge of the gangplank and a fierce argument was in progress between them and some American sailors who were objecting to the British going aboard the vessel. Presumably, a vessel in a foreign port is subject to the laws of that port, but this was not the view of the Americans. An ugly situation was arising, but the arrival of a British officer, who poured oil on the troubled water, saved the day. It appeared that six Germans were missing from their houses when the British military police, within thirty minutes of the declaration of war, had arrived to arrest them. Knowing that there was an American vessel in port, the military demanded the right to search the vessel, with or without the co-operation of the American crew. A German doctor and his wife were quickly discovered, but since they were over military age they were permitted to remain on the ship and make their way as best they could to Germany. After five hours' search, only three of the other Germans had been found and arrested. One was still at large.

In the meantime the boat had been held up for hours and the captain, who was thoroughly exasperated at having his vessel turned into a haven of refuge by a bunch of Nazis, gave an undertaking to the British authorities that the missing German, if found to have stowed away, would be returned to Hongkong on the next boat. Without such an assurance, the *President Pierce* would have been held until the man was found.

Finally, at 2.30 a.m., we sailed for Manila, but long after we had passed out of the harbour and beyond the submarine net, we saw how well guarded was the approach to Hongkong. Several times from the pitch darkness the silver beam of a searchlight would suddenly illuminate the ship and then go out. Swift motor torpedo-boats would dash toward us, take a look and disappear again into the darkness. Instead of hauling down our flag at night, a special searchlight was rigged so that the Stars and Stripes could plainly be seen floating at the mast-head, while the whole vessel seemed purposely to be illuminated until we must have looked, as the captain remarked, "like a Christmas tree."

The next day at breakfast who should turn up but the missing Nazi! Dressed only in a shirt and trousers, he walked into the dining-room and immediately started boasting about the sinking of the *Athenia* and generally making himself objectionable. Misled by the strict neutrality of the officers and crew, he had concluded that he would be greeted as a hero, but I'm glad to say that he was quickly disillusioned by the captain, who kept his word and returned the man to Hongkong.

CARVETH WELLS
North of Singapore (1940)

1941

In the War

Three years earlier when her father was posted from England to the Naval Dockyard in Hong Kong, Barbara Redwood, with her mother and sisters, had accompanied him. After his untimely death in 1940 the family stayed on rather than risk the journey back to war-torn Europe. Now twenty-three and a stenographer with the government, Barbara Redwood watched the war come to Hong Kong.

Dec. 8th. Monday. Was raked out of bed this a.m. at 6.30 – to be at office at 7. At 10 to 8 Bevan said war had been declared between Britain & America, & Japan, & just after 8 o'clock the air raid syrens sounded. At about 10.30 the all clear went & it was said 1 bomb had dropped in Sspo. [Sham Shui Po] causing many casualties. At 1.30 the syrens went again & there was quite alot of A.A. fire. I thought they were all bombs at first. I saw 3 'planes high up being chased away to Lyemoon. It's hardly worth writing diary because I can't visualize us ever getting out of this, but I want to *try* to believe in a future. Kai Tak has been bombed & I'm thinking of Arthur & Sid. . . . I'm home now till 7 o'clock. Scared & gloomy. I feel sure we'll have raids every night & day, & in the night much worse than in the day. . . .

Dec. 9th. Tuesday. 2 false alarms, 1 last night and one early this morning, & 6 alerts throughout the morning. Not much damage, mostly propaganda leaflets dropped which means, I fear, that we may expect heavier raids in due course. Didn't expect to get a peaceful night last night – it was moonlight. . . . Japs. are said to be at Taipo (according to London news). Also some Japs. were ambushed and mostly annihilated on Castle Peak Rd, where the boys are. Can't properly imagine it. . . .

Dec. 10th. Wednesday. Sid has been wounded. Bullet through shoulder. He told Hosp. to phone Mum who went up to see him. In afternoon I went into town . . . & I was able to get in to see Sid. . . . He is very shocked & upset & didn't look his old self . . . He's worried about the 2 men he had with him, – no news of them. They went on ahead when he got entangled in a creeper plant & was sniped. . . . Went in Battery St. tunnel in alarm when on way into town. It was more orderly than I had expected & quite cool. Dropped in to Olive's office but she wasn't there. Peaceful night but 3 raids in afternoon. News is that Japs. have sunk "Prince of Wales" & "Repulse" by bombs – hard to believe. Japs. seem to be starting well, though here we sunk boats of an attempted landing at Tide Cove.

Dec. 11th Thursday. . . . Worked from 7 last night till 7 this morning, but actually slept from 4.30 to 6.45. . . . No raids during night, but shells are coming over now, but so far not doing much damage.

. . . Slept some of morning and a little in afternoon, when they dropped about 17 bombs in Wanchai area. One near Football Club – Amah took me downstairs to 1st fl: Then I went over to office and worked on till about 12, when had chance to doss down. It seemed so queer – me retiring behind screen on camp bed, with Cole on a bed nearby, looking kind of helpless the way men always look to me when they're asleep . . . Office may be moving to C.S.O. Tunnel. Kowloon mostly evacuated.

Dec. 12th. Friday. The rumour about Jordan [Band Master of Royal Scots] was confirmed today, he was shot by one of our own sentries – being deaf, he apparently didn't hear the challenge. Mum got up to see Sid this morning & he is walking about now & hopes to be back with his unit within a few days. . . . But we have apparently abandoned Kowloon & unless a miracle happens are going to be shelled to bits. There is talk that Chinese guerillas are coming up behind the Japs. & are now at Taipo, but I'm afraid to believe anything so heartening. I can see absolutely no escape – but we didn't have to stay, & at least this *is* something & we are in the war with the folks at home.

B.C. REDWOOD
Diary (manuscript)

1941

Surrender

The end of the battle was not long in coming. Charles Ford, a Regimental Sergeant Major in the Royal Artillery, kept a record of his experiences in the days before that fateful Christmas.

23/12/41. To town again this afternoon, and as is usual when I go out all sorts of fun and games start. I set out for the Peak, but as the Japs were knocking hell out of that I went down to get cables away first, and was just in time to be "in" on the shelling of Garden Rd-Des Voeux Rd-Queens Rd junction. While the shelling was at its height I sheltered in the Supreme court building. Even Justice has its merits, but that didn't stop the Jap Artillery from dropping two heavy shells on top of the building. Having visited Battle H.Q., where the panic shows evident signs of increasing I decide, in a moment of generosity, to take my escort and driver to a meal in the Hong Kong Hotel. As soon as this meal is over we get roped in to arrest armed deserters . . . who are sheltering in Air Raid Shelters. . . . Being unsuccessful in my efforts to scrounge any cigarettes or beer for the troops we return to Fort Davis at about 8:30 p.m. We never got to the Peak for all the approach roads were blown and the Naafi destroyed during the afternoon's shelling. However, the cables were accepted "subject to heavy delay". I wonder how soon it will be before my wife and daughter know that I am alive and well at least until today.

24/12/41. The Japs have consolidated their positions right across the island but a message from B.H.Q. says that the Japs have been seen retreating northward from Kowloon and that only "pockets" remain on the island. We are exhorted to hold on for a few more days only before relief by Chiang-Kai-Shek's army. During the afternoon a force of 50 gunners from Mt. Davis and Jubilee, under Lt. D. Clayton and B.S.M. Barlow are sent to Happy Valley for "mopping up" operations. . . . It being Xmas I decide to be Santa Claus tomorrow and take the rations over to 3rd. Battery at Aberdeen, and with this pious thought in my heart I retire to bed; but not before I have "half-hitched" a couple of bottles of beer . . .

25/12/41. Xmas Day, and, I imagine, the most memorable one of all time. I begin the day by wishing my family in Australia very heartfelt compliments of the season. . . . The sun is brilliant and a truce is declared until 12 noon. I set my course for Aberdeen at about 10.30 a.m. but as soon as I get near Waterfall Bay a couple of bombs and the answering crack of our 4.5's tells the world that the truce is no longer in operation. . . . On arrival at the battery, being Xmas, I am greeted by a bottle of beer and smiling faces. I visit every man in the fort, a chat here, a story there, but happiness everywhere. They invite me to tiffin, sausages, tea, bread, biscuits, butter and cheese, oh yes, and a bottle of beer. At 2.30 p.m. I take my farewell . . . I walk to Waterfall Bay and am picked up by a police car. The driver gives me three apples. Fruit, of all things, one is mine, the others I share with the cooks on my return at 3.30 p.m. and at 3.35 I hear that we are going to surrender. This is confirmed at 4.00 p.m. from B.H.Q. and we have progressed from fighting troops of the British Army to prisoners of war in the hands of the Imperial Army of Japan. This is a bitter moment, for none ever expected Hong Kong to surrender, and men are crying . . . Many of the men are all for fighting on, but where organised resistance has failed, indiscriminate bands cannot succeed in an island so small as this.

R.S.M. CHARLES FORD
The Battle for Hong Kong (manuscript)

1942

Bid for Freedom

---

*After the fall of Hong Kong, E.D. Crossley, a pilot with the Royal
New Zealand Air Force, was interned by the Japanese at Kowloon.
Crossley - later awarded the M.C. - decided with two fellow
prisoners to escape.*

The greatest difficulty we had to face in planning an escape from this
camp lay in the fact that the only way out was through China. We
knew neither the land nor its people, but we had heard that bandits
infested the surrounding countryside. In addition, the Japs had spies in
our camp.

An exchange of some Chinese sweets for a bottle of soya-bean sauce
was to help me a lot. I made the exchange with a Chinese who put me
in touch with a British Army officer in the camp who spoke Cantonese.
This officer, who had an extraordinary Oxford accent and wore a
monocle, was an Army doctor, married to a Chinese who was a friend
of the owner of the soya-bean sauce.

He and I compared notes and plans for almost three weeks. . . .

One by one our plans went astray, until in the end our position
looked hopeless. More and more sentries were posted round the camp,
and the barbed wire was first doubled and then tripled. An outside
contact we had managed to make came to nothing, and the attempt we
finally made to escape was a desperate bid for freedom at any cost rather
than the result of any carefully prearranged plan.

I had by chance met in the camp an Army captain who knew the
layout of what were called the new territories of Hongkong - a strip of
land extending about twenty miles inland. The captain joined the doctor
and myself, and the three of us made the break together. . . .

Five minutes after we got outside the compound the sentries spotted us
and immediately opened fire. Bullets were flying in all directions, but I
feel sure now . . . that the shots were fired indiscriminately. Although

236

we had been told that the Japanese would shoot escaping prisoners on sight, we wore our uniforms.

Our prison camp was on a small promontory on the China coast opposite the island of Hongkong. After we got outside the compound we entered the sea and swam across the bay, of which the promontory formed one end. The swim took about forty minutes. We still had to cross that brilliantly-lit main road, and so, on leaving the water, we crept along by the side of the road in the hope of finding a suitably shaded spot to cross. While we were doing this two native dogs barked, and as we threw ourselves into a ditch a Japanese patrol passed at the double. We waited until we thought the Japs could no longer hear us, and then climbed on to the road, crossed it, and made our way into the surrounding hills. . . .

. . . For the next few days we marched over hills and through swampy valleys. Our food-supply, which consisted at the time of our escape of two tins of bully, a tin of cheese, and a tin of sardines – sardines were worth about £30 a tin – had run out and we were getting very hungry.

Then, one very cold misty night in the hills, we met a Chinese who spoke excellent English. He told us he was a pro-British guerrilla operating in the surrounding country, and said that if we cared to wait a few hours he would find food . . . Earlier that day we had passed through a village where we paid a thousand dollars in Hongkong currency for a guide for the afternoon. We surmised that this fellow, having seen our money there, had followed us.

The whole thing seemed a bit suspect, but we decided to accept the fellow's offer. It had been raining continuously for two days and we were wet, tired, and hungry. This possibility of assistance, therefore, was one we were not prepared to give up. The Chinese took us to a cleft in the hills and told us to wait for two or three hours while he made the necessary arrangements.

We must then have dropped off to sleep, for the next thing I remember was seeing a man waving a dagger and shouting "Yakpunchai!" (Cantonese for "We are Japanese men"). One of my friends, Tony, was on the ground with four men beating him up. The only weapon at hand was a pole, sharpened at one end, which we had found in the hills. I picked this up and drove it into the stomach of the nearest of our assailants. As he collapsed, two more of the bandits – there must have been eight or nine of them altogether – turned to deal with me, but at this moment Doug, the third member of our party, appeared, from where I don't know, and smashed one of them over the head with a bayonet, which he had apparently taken from an earlier opponent. Between us, Doug and I managed to account for about four of them, and the others ran away.

When we picked Tony up we found he had two terrific gashes across the scalp and all the tendons of his right arm were severed. He was only semi-conscious, but we patched him up the best way we could with a couple of field dressings which we happened to have, and as soon as possible went on our way again.

Tony in the next few days performed miracles. The pain in his arm must have been great, but not once did I hear him complain. Doug, who was an Army doctor, managed to keep the wounds clean until we were able to get Tony to hospital some two weeks later, and this although we had only one bottle of permanganate and sometimes had to wash the wounds in stagnant water.

The day after this encounter one of Doug's knees packed up on him, and I contracted dysentery. And so when a couple of nights later we fell in with more bandits we were in no condition to oppose them. This time there were about sixty of them, and if we had resisted we would probably all have been killed. After they had stripped us of everything of value, the bandits, however, were not at all sure what to do with us. They held us for twenty-four hours, then let us go.

Within four hours of leaving them we ran full into another bunch. This crowd were armed with Mausers, but for reasons which will appear presently it would be unfair to describe them as bandits. They were mainly Chinese negroes and most of them seemed to have relatives in Jamaica. Their leader was named Lee – Mr. Lee. He wore Chinese trousers with a coat and waistcoat in European style and a slouch felt hat. Round his waist were three rows of bullets and a Mauser hung on either side. He had two gold watches on one arm and magnificent rings on every finger. When we first met I offered him my Onoto fountain pen as a peace offering, but he gave it back to me, saying it was too cheap!

He told us his was one of the many unrecognized guerrilla bands in South China. He depended on village folk to assist him with supplies. If they refused, he burned their villages down. All in all, he was as bloodthirsty an old rogue as you could ever hope to meet. But, once having satisfied himself we were really escaped prisoners, he seemed to take a great fancy to us. Indeed, he invited us to remain with him, promising that he would make our fortunes within twelve months. His offer tempted all three of us – the life looked good to us – and it was with much reluctance that we refused it. . . .

It wasn't so easy to leave Mr. Lee, and when we did finally say good-bye to him we did so with genuine regret. He gave us a guide, and on our first day's journey we covered nearly thirty miles. This march brought us to the headquarters of a Captain Wong, who welcomed us heartily. Captain Wong's job was to embarrass the Jap lines of communication and to train young men for guerrilla warfare under his command. These trainees were no more than twelve or fifteen years of age, but their discipline and self-denial were incredible. In the short time we were at this camp, they destroyed four Japanese lorries, killed 130-odd infantrymen, and captured a considerable quantity of arms and equipment.

Captain Wong agreed to have us conducted through the Jap lines to Free China or the first unit of the regular Chinese Army, whichever was the nearer. We crossed the Canton-Kowloon railway by night, and were then passed from village to village, the inhabitants of which fed and cared for us as we went.

The time of our journey was the Chinese New Year and many of the villages we passed through had in celebration been freshly white-washed and decorated with picturesque signs. These villages were in enemy-held territory and much evidence of the Jap occupation was to be seen. The poverty was indescribable. Many villages were burned out, and fields, from which the cattle had been driven away, were empty. We heard stories of women and children being raped and murdered and of young men being conscripted into the Jap labour corps, yet everywhere we found a will to resist. I am sure the Chinese have no such word as defeat in their vocabulary. . . .

In Canton, the capital of Kwantung, which we eventually reached, we were taken to a Catholic hospital run by Father Ma, who took us down to a newly constructed eating house, and ordered what he thought a reasonable meal. There were at least eight plates of soong, the Chinese equivalent of the English meat dish, and we must have had these filled at least three times. Father Ma then ordered sumpu, a reasonable rice wine. When we had all had four glasses of this, Father Ma was becoming visibly excited and we were becoming visibly intoxicated. Before we left the restaurant Tony had liberally bespattered the good father with quantities of rice and sumpu. We left Tony in that Catholic hospital and I have not seen him since.

E.D. CROSSLEY
"Episode in China"
Korero Vol. 3, No. 2, 1945

Glossary

Abacus *or* **Swan-P'an** – calculating tray. A wooden frame in which are fixed a number of beads strung upon parallel wires. It is used by the Chinese for all kinds of arithmetical calculations. The system is one of decimals . . .

Amah – a nurse; from the Portuguese *ama.*

Ancestral Worship – a Chinese religious ceremony performed on stated occasions before tablets inscribed with the names of deceased ancestors, and consisting of prayers, prostrations, and offerings of food and paper-money to the spirits of the dead. . . .

Arec-Nut – *see* Betel-Nut.

Bamboo – the bamboo is the common instrument for flogging criminals in China, and consists of a strip of split bamboo planed down smooth. . . . Until the reign of K'ang Hsi, all strokes were given across the back; but that Emperor removed the *locus operandi* lower down . . .

Bazaar – from the Persian *bazar* a market.

Betel-Nut – the leaf of the *sirih* or betelpepper smeared with chunam, or lime, and tobacco, and the nut of the areca palm, chewed together by the Chinese and other eastern nations.

Bocca Tigris – *see* Bogue, The.

Bogue, The – "Tiger's Gate," otherwise called Bocca Tigris. The principal embouchure of the Canton river . . .

Book of Rites – *see* Rites, Book of.

Boy – the common term . . . for a servant, such as a house-boy, office-boy, etc.

Bund – the common term . . . for a quay . . .

Buttons – the knobs adopted by the Manchu dynasty to indicate rank and worn at the top of the official hat. . . .

Cash – . . . the only coin cast in China, one thousand of which were originally equal to one tael or Chinese ounce of silver. Each cash has a square hole in the middle for convenience in carrying a large quantity . . .

Celestial Empire – a common name for China, taken probably from the phrase Heavenly Dynasty, which has been for many centuries in use amongst the Chinese themselves . . . [hence "Celestials"].

Chop – a mark, number, or brand.

Chop-Boats – lighters or cargo-boats. Literally, "water-melon boats," from the resemblance of the roof to half a water-melon.

240

Chop-Sticks – hasteners. The bamboo or ivory sticks which take the place of knives and forks among the Chinese.

Chow or Chow-Chow – food of any kind. Pidgin term invented by Europeans probably in imitation of Chinese sounds. A *chow-chow* amah is a wet nurse.

Chowkidar – a watchman.

Clans (Chinese) – hamlets, villages, and sometimes even country towns, are inhabited by people of one common surname and ancestry, forming a tribe or clan.

Compradore – negotiator of purchases. From the Portuguese *comprar* to buy. The name given to the Chinese agent through whose means foreign merchants in China effect their purchases and sales.

Confucius – the great ethical, not religious, teacher of China. Flourished B.C. 551–479.

Coolie – the menial of the east.

Cue – the tail of hair worn by every Chinaman. Introduced into China by the present (Manchu) dynasty only about 250 years ago . . . It is said to have been originally adopted by the Manchus in imitation of a horse's tail, as a graceful tribute to the animal to which they owed so much.

Cumshaw – a present of any kind. . . . Often used by Chinese beggars to foreigners in the same sense as "baksheesh" . . .

Dezembargador – chief judge.

East India Company – first established a factory at Canton in 1684.

Empress Dowager – the mother of the . . . Emperor T'ung Chih . . . said to have been sold as a slave-girl at the age of 14, in consequence of the poverty of her parents. She was . . . a concubine of the Emperor Hsien Feng . . . Is popularly known as Her Imperial Majesty Buddha.

Factories, The – so called from their being the residence of *factors*, or agents of the East India Company, and not because anything was manufactured there. The former residences of foreigners in the western suburbs of Canton.

Fanqui or Fan Kuei-Tzu – foreign devils, i.e. foreigners. An absurd attempt was once made to shew that the epithet "devils" was applied to foreigners more as a "term of endearment" than anything else, on the ground that the Chinese have good devils as well as bad in their unseen universe . . .

Fans – . . . fans are used by the Chinese, men and women alike, from the highest officials down to the lowest coolie, and even by the very soldiers in the ranks. . . . They are made to serve the same purpose as an album among friends of a literary turn, who paint flowers upon them for each other and inscribe verses . . . They are also used to circulate the news of any important event among the people at large . . .

Fantan – the celebrated method of gambling with cash, common in China. . . . A pile of the coin is covered with a bowl, and the players stake on what the remainder will be when the heap has been divided by 4 – namely 1, 2, 3, nothing.

Feng-Shui *or* **Fung-Shwuy** - wind and water, or that which cannot be seen, and that which cannot be grasped. The great geomantic system of the Chinese, by the *science* of which it is possible to determine the desirability of sites . . . For a grave, a wide river in front, a high cliff behind, with enclosing hills to the right and left, would constitute a first-class geomantic position.

Flowery Land, The - a common Chinese name for China, similar to *la belle France*, and not necessarily implying the presence of flowers.

Geisha - a Japanese singing or dancing-girl.

Geomancy - *see* Feng-Shui.

Golden Lilies - a poetical name for the cramped feet of Chinese women.

Griffin - a new arrival in the East; equivalent to a "freshman" at Oxford. . . . Also, a racing pony that runs for the first time.

Hakkas - strangers. A race said to have migrated from the north of China . . . to the Kuang-tung province . . .

Hong - a row, or series. Chinese warehouses were so called because consisting of a succession of rooms, and the old "factories" being similarly built, the Chinese called each block a *hong*. Now used of all kinds of mercantile houses.

Hong Merchants - the security merchants of former days, who, for the privilege of trading with foreigners coming to Canton, became security to the mandarins for their payment of duties and their good behaviour while on shore. Monopoly broken up by Treaty of Nanking 1842.

Hoppo, The - the . . . Superintendent of Customs at Canton has been so called for many years.

Jade - . . . a species of nephrite, the green and white kind of which . . . is highly valued by the Chinese. Rings, bracelets, vases, and various other ornaments are made of this stone, which is also largely imitated.

Jinricksha *or* **Jinrikisha** - the man's strength cart. A small gig, invented about 1872 and constructed to carry one or more persons, drawn by a coolie in shafts and sometimes pushed by another from behind.

Joss - a Chinese idol; also applied to the Christian God. The word is a corruption of the Portuguese *Deos*, God, and has come to be used in pidgin-English in the sense of luck.

Junk - only the larger kind of Chinese sailing-vessels should be so called; but the term is now used of all sea-going boats and of the more bulky of the river craft.

Kang *or* **K'ang** - a brick bed, with a fire underneath it.

Keiling Kuei - *see* Klings, The.

Klings, The - the common term in the Straits Settlements for all Indians.

Kuomintang - originally the Revolutionary League formed (1905) under the leadership of Sun Yat-sen; reorganised (1911) as the National People's Party (Kuomintang). Communist members admitted from 1923. After Sun's death (1925) his military adviser Chiang Kai-shek became leader; in 1927 right wing elements led by Chiang took control of the party and formed a Nationalist Government.

Ladrones, The – "The Pirates." The group of islands which includes Hongkong has been so called . . . due to the piratical disposition of their inhabitants.

Ling Che or Ling Ch'ih – the "ignominious slashing" or so-called "lingering death," which should, strictly speaking, consist in a fearful mutilation of the limbs before giving the *coup de grâce*, but which is now generally modified into a few cuts on the body just before decapitation. Is the punishment for parricide and similar heinous crimes.

Linguists – English-speaking Chinese, of more or less capabilities, employed as interpreters for the local dialects. The intermediaries of trade between foreigners and Chinese in the old days were so called.

Ma Chiang or Mah-Jong – a Chinese table game employing pieces shaped like dominoes.

Mafoo – horse-man. The Chinese groom or "horse-boy."

Maidan – an open space, an esplanade, parade-ground or green, in or adjoining a town.

Mandarin – any Chinese official, civil or military, who wears a button may be so called. From the Portuguese *mandar* to command. *See also* Button.

Middle Kingdom, The – a translation of the common Chinese name for China; it being generally believed that China is situated at the centre of the earth, surrounded by the Four Seas, beyond which lie a number of small islands inhabited by the red-haired barbarians who come to the Middle Kingdom to trade.

Monsoon – from the Arabic *mausim* "season;" the season winds.

Moormen – a common term in Canton for the miscellaneous natives of India who go there to trade.

New Year, China – . . . may be any date between 22 January and 20 February, inclusive. This is the season chosen for the great annual holiday of the Chinese. . . . On New Year's Day, absolutely no work is done from one end of the Empire to the other. Fire-crackers, feasting, and congratulatory visits are substituted for the ordinary routine of life.

Opium – . . . it is the dried juice of the unripe capsules of the . . . Common Poppy . . . It is acknowledged beyond doubt that long before the English had intercourse with China, or had anything to do with the cultivation of opium, the drug used to be carried in quantities overland from India by way of Burma, Yunnan, etc.

Paddy – . . . rice as it grows in the *paddy-fields*.

Pagoda – . . . a circular or octagonal building, always of an odd number of storeys, originally raised over relics of Buddha, bones of Buddhist saints, etc., but now built chiefly in connection with Feng-Shui.

Palanquin – a box-litter for travelling in, with a pole projecting before and behind, which is borne on the shoulders of 4 or 6 men.

Pariah – . . . pariah dogs, *i.e.*, dogs with no owners, are not uncommon in large Chinese towns.

Parsee or Parsi – descendants of the Persians, of which Parsi is the old form, who left their native country and settled in India to avoid Mahommedan persecution. . . . Bombay Parsees are established in business at several of the Treaty Ports, notably Canton, Amoy . . . dealing chiefly in opium.

Penang Lawyer – a large heavy walking stick with a big knob sold at Penang and in the Straits generally.

Piá – half-breed.

Pidgin – business of any kind, from which word the term *pidgin* is said to be derived through the Chinese imitation of our word, i.e. business, bizzin, pishin, pidgin.

Pidgin-English – the *lingua franca* of China, used by foreigners of all nationalities who do not talk Chinese in speaking to native servants, shop-keepers, chair-coolies, sailors, etc. Also frequently spoken to each other by Chinamen of different parts of the Empire whose dialects are mutually unfamiliar . . .

Pigtail – *see* Cue.

Praya – a quay or esplanade. From the Portuguese *praia*, a shore or beach.

Punjaub – the name of the country between the Indus and the Sutlej [in North West India].

Punkah – a Hindi word (pankha) meaning a "fan." Introduced into China by Europeans, and now known to the Chinese as "wind fan," but rarely seen even in the wealthiest native establishments . . .

Queue – *see* Cue.

Rattan – the common cane is so called. From the Malay *rotan*.

Rickshaw – *see* Jinricksha.

Rites, Book of – . . . contains a number of rules for the performance of ceremonies and "the guidance of individual conduct under a great variety of conditions and circumstances."

Sampan – a Chinese boat of any kind, short of a junk, may be so called.

Samshoo – . . . a general name among foreigners for Chinese fermented liquors of all kinds . . .

Savvy or Sabe – from the Portuguese *saber* to know.
  "My savvy" = "I understand" or "I know."

Sedan Chairs – the Emperor alone is entitled to employ 16 bearers for carrying his chair; a prince of the blood 8; the highest provincial authorities also 8 . . . Chinese etiquette makes it necessary to get out of a chair to speak with a passing acquaintance. . . .

Shameen – sand flat. Formerly a mere mudbank in the river close to the city of Canton, but . . . formed into an artificial island with an embankment of granite all round; the expense of this ($325,000) being borne by the British and French Governments in the proportion of four to one, according to which ratio the whole area was subsequently divided between the two countries.

Sikh – the distinctive name of the disciples of Nanak Shah who in the 16th century established that sect, which eventually rose to warlike predominance in the Punjaub.

Sola Topee – *see* Topee, Sola.

Son of Heaven – . . . the title *par excellence* of the Emperor of China, who is supposed to hold his commission direct from on high.

Soy – this word is from the Japanese *shoyu*, a kind of sauce made from fermented wheat and beans. Has been wrongly derived by some from the first syllable of Soyer, the great gastronomer of that name.

Squeeze – originally, the *commission* which Chinese servants, fully in accordance with Chinese custom, charged their European masters on all articles purchased. Now extensively applied . . . to peculation of any kind.

Swan-P'an *or* **Suan-P'an** – *see* Abacus.

Tagalo – one of the dialects of the Philippine Islands . . . spoken in Manila.

Tail – *see* Cue.

Taipan – great manager. The head of, or partner in, a foreign house of business. The beggars and little boys all over the south of China shout "Taipan! Taipan!" to any foreigner from whom they wish to extract a gratuity . . .

Tiffin – the mid-day meal; luncheon. . . .

Topee, Sola – a pith helmet, worn as a precaution against sunstroke. From the Hindi *shola*, a pithy reed, and *topee* a hat. Occasionally wrongly written *solar*, because supposed to have some connexion with the sun.

Typhoon *or* **Tyfoon** – a cyclone, or revolving storm of immense force . . .

Viceroy – or Governor-General of one or more provinces, within which he has the general control of all affairs civil and military, subject only to the approval of the Throne.

Victoria – the city of Hong Kong, on the north shore of the island.

Whampoa – yellow reach. Strictly speaking the port of Canton, from which it is about 12 miles distant. That foreign steamers proceed farther up the river than this point is a privilege accorded by the Chinese authorities in the interests of trade, and might be taken away at a moment's notice . . .

Yamun *or* **Yamen** – the official and private residence of any Mandarin who holds a seal.

Zenana – the apartments of a house in which the women of the family are secluded.

HERBERT A. GILES
A Glossary of Reference on Subjects connected with the Far East (1878)

COL. HENRY YULE and A.C. BURNELL
Hobson-Jobson (1886)

Background Events

1816	Lord Amherst's Embassy to China
1823	Robert Morrison's Chinese-English dictionary published
1824	American trading firm, Russell & Co., established at Canton
1827	The *Canton Register* – first English newspaper in the Far East – founded by James Matheson
1831	Trade at Canton temporarily halted following "insolent acts" by Chinese
1832	Firm of Jardine, Matheson, & Co. founded
1833	East India Company's Charter expires – company loses its advantages in China trade
1835	St. Paul's Church, Macao, burned down: only facade survives fire
1836	Two inches of snow fall at Canton (8th February)
1839	Chinese destroy 20,000 chests of foreign-owned opium: start of First Opium War (1839–1842)
1840	British forces establish headquarters on Hong Kong island and blockade Canton
1841	Chinese destroy the foreign factories at Canton British forces besiege Canton – Chinese pay $6m to ransom the city Hong Kong island annexed by Britain
1842	Anglo-Chinese peace restored with Treaty of Nanking: confirms Hong Kong ceded to Britain; provides for opening of five Treaty Ports including Canton
1844	First steamship passenger service between Canton and Hong Kong
1848	Portuguese expel Chinese officials from Macao
1849	Governor Ferreira do Amaral of Macao assassinated by Chinese
1851	Start of Taiping Rebellion (1851–1864)
1854	Fatshan and Kowloon captured by Taiping rebels; Canton blockaded Substantial Chinese emigration begins through Hong Kong to Australia, California, and West Indies Population of Hong Kong 56,000
1855	British forces from Hong Kong move to protect Canton from Taiping rebels

1856	The affair of the *Arrow* leads to renewed hostilities by Anglo-French forces: start of Second Opium War (1856–1858)
	Foreign factories at Canton again destroyed by Chinese
1857	British docks and stores at Whampoa burned by Chinese
	Unsuccessful attempt to murder foreign community in Hong Kong with poisoned bread
	British destroy Chinese war junks at Fatshan Creek
1858	Anglo-French forces capture Canton: beginning of four-year occupation
	Peace restored with Treaty of Tientsin: opium trade legalised and missionary activity allowed
1859	Imperial Maritime Customs Service established at Canton
	Reclamation work begins to create island of Shameen for foreign residents at Canton
1860	Kowloon Peninsula ceded to Britain by Convention of Peking
1861	Empress Dowager Tzu-hsi becomes effective ruler of China (1861–1908)
	Island of Shameen completed and ceded to Britain and France
	Foreign occupation of Canton ends
	Chamber of Commerce formed in Hong Kong
1862	A typhoon causes 50,000 deaths in and around Canton
	Indian police recruits first drafted into Hong Kong
	Formation of Hong Kong Volunteer Corps
	First Hong Kong postage stamps issued
1863	Foundation laid for Roman Catholic cathedral at Canton
	Reports of English and Americans serving on pirate junks in the area
1864	Taiping Rebellion crushed after 13 years and up to 30 million deaths
	Gas street-lighting introduced at Hong Kong
	Hongkong & Shanghai Banking Corporation founded
1865	Population of Hong Kong 125,000 (4,000 non-Chinese)
1866	Birth of Sun Yat-sen
1867	Chinese start blockade of Hong Kong to force local junk trade back to Canton (1867–1886)
	Hong Kong's trade with Japan worth $6m
	Severe typhoon demolishes Praya sea wall at Hong Kong
1869	Opening of Suez Canal
1870	Tientsin massacre: serious threat of violence to foreigners throughout China
1872	Tung Wah Hospital opened in Hong Kong (using Chinese medicine)
1874	Government Civil Hospital opened
	Extensive typhoon damage in Hong Kong

1875	Macao coolie-traffic suppressed
1877	First Chinese Minister accredited to London
1878	Canton severely damaged by a tornado; Hong Kong suffers serious fire
1881	Telephones installed in Hong Kong Population of Hong Kong 160,000 (10,000 non-Chinese)
1884	France and China at war; Shameen attacked by Chinese mob and partly burned
1887	China confirms permanent occupation of Macao by Portugal Chinese Chamber of Commerce formed in Hong Kong
1888	Completion of the High Level Tramway in Hong Kong (first cable railway in Asia)
1890	Electric street-lighting introduced in Hong Kong
1891	Serious anti-foreign riots in China
1894	Japan declares war on China U.S.A. and China agree to halt coolie immigration for ten years Epidemic of bubonic plague: up to 100,000 people die in Canton; thousands more in Hong Kong
1895	Japan wins war with China Missionaries attacked at Fatshan
1896	Nation-wide postal service established in China Sun Yat-sen banished from Hong Kong for conspiracy against Canton authorities
1898	Hong Kong's New Territories leased for 99 years Star Ferry Company incorporated
1900	Boxer uprising
1901	Population of Hong Kong – including the New Territories – is 400,000 (20,000 non-Chinese)
1902	Footbinding in China denounced by the Throne
1904	Electric tram service introduced from Kennedy Town to Shaukiwan Electric street-lighting installed at Shameen
1905	Traditional system of literary examinations for government office abolished throughout China China boycotts American goods Sun Yat-sen leads anti-Manchu movement (the Revolutionary League) Hong Kong experiences frequent earth tremors
1906	Opium dens closed in China Telephone service introduced in Canton Hong Kong hit by worst typhoon since 1874: 10,000 die in and around Hong Kong
1908	Death of the Emperor Kuang-hsu and the Empress Dowager Tzu-hsi
1910	Opium dens closed in Hong Kong

1911	Revolution breaks out in China; Canton proclaims the "Republic of Kuangtung"
	Republic of China established (at Nanking)
	Completion of the Kowloon-Canton railway
1912	Sun Yat-sen becomes Provisional President of Southern Provinces
	Abdication of the Manchu Dynasty
	Sun resigns in favour of Yuan Shih-kai
	Hong Kong University opened
1913	Chinese Republic recognised by the U.S.A.
1914	Outbreak of the Great War in Europe
1915	Typhoon refuge at Mong Kok Tsui completed
1917	China declares war on Germany
1921	Formation of the Chinese Communist Party
	Parliament at Canton elects Sun Yat-sen "President of China"
	Population of Hong Kong 625,000 (15,000 non-Chinese)
1922	H.R.H. the Prince of Wales visits Hong Kong
1923	Foreign forces protect customs facilities at Canton from Sun Yat-sen threat
1925	Death of Sun Yat-sen
	Start of 16-month anti-imperialist strike and boycott affecting Hong Kong and Canton; Shameen besieged
1926	*Coup d'état* at Canton by General Chiang Kai-shek
1927	Civil war begins in China
	Heavy fighting in Canton after November and December *coups*: thousands flee to Hong Kong as refugees
	Start of anti-Japanese boycott in Canton
1928	Development of Kai Tak airfield begins
1931	Japanese occupy Manchuria
	Population of Hong Kong 850,000
1932	Chinese communists declare war on Japan
1934	Start of the Red Army's "Long March"
1937	Start of second Sino-Japanese war: communists and nationalists cooperate in face of common enemy
	Population of Hong Kong reaches one million
1938	Japanese troops occupy Canton
	500,000 Chinese refugees enter Hong Kong
1939	Hainan island captured by Japanese
	World War II begins in Europe
1941	Population of Hong Kong 1.6 million
	Japanese occupy Kowloon and Hong Kong
1945	Japanese surrender

Acknowledgements

Grateful acknowledgements are due to the following publishers, authors and others:

A & C Black Ltd.
John Chinaman at Home by The Rev. E.J. Hardy
The Land of the Blue Gown by Mrs. Archibald Little

The Bodley Head Ltd.
Chinese Lanterns by Grace Thompson Seton
The Chinese by John Stuart Thomson

Chapman & Hall Ltd.
Life and Sport in China by Oliver G. Ready

J. M. Dent & Sons Ltd.
An Eastern Voyage by Count Fritz von Hochberg

Hutchinson Publishing Group Ltd.
Half the Seas Over by Clifford W. Collinson
The House of Exile by Nora Waln
North of Singapore by Carveth Wells

MPH Magazines (S) Pte. Ltd.
A Chinese Sees the World by C.S. See

Methuen & Co. Ltd.
Understand the Chinese by William Martin

John Murray (Publishers) Ltd.
Scented Isles and Coral Gardens by C.D. MacKellar

The Department of Documents, Imperial War Museum, together with the following:

> **Mrs. B.C. Anslow (née Redwood)**, for permission to quote from her manuscript *Diary*.

> **Mrs. E.M. Drage**, for permission to quote from the manuscript *1914-1933 Diaries* of Commander C.H. Drage R.N.

> **Major E.C. Ford (Rtd.)**, for permission to quote from his manuscript journal *The Battle for Hong Kong*.

> **Mr. R. Thomas**, for permission to quote from the manuscript *Correspondence* of Mr. C.R. Thomas.

The British Library
The National Library, Singapore
National University of Singapore Library

Every effort has been made to trace the owners of copyright material; however if any other acknowledgements are due but have been omitted the Compiler offers his sincere apologies.

The illustrations, which have been selected for their interest and are broadly contemporary with the tales alongside them, come from the following works:

Anon: *China and the Chinese* (1844)

William Blakeney: *On the Coasts of Cathay and Cipango* (1902)

Mrs. Brassey: *A Voyage in the "Sunbeam"* (1878)

Charles H. Eden: *China* (1877)

A.W. Habersham: *My Last Cruise* (1858)

C.V. Lloyd: *From Hongkong to Canton* (1902)

E.D.G. Prime: *Around the World* (1874)

E.R. Scidmore: *China, the Long-Lived Empire* (1900)

J. Thomson: *The Straits of Malacca, Indo-China, and China* (1875)

J.R. Young: *Round the World with General Grant* (1879)

Index

Abacus, 52
Aberdeen, 235
Adventure(s), 27, 76, 126
Ah Kum, 109–12
Aide-de-camp, 72–4
Air raids, 232–3
Alabaster, Sir Chaloner & Lady, 143
Amah(s), 108, 124
American consul, 200
American factory or hong, 23, 37
American missionary, 229
American sailors, 230
American tourist(s), 201, 226
American(s), 97, 176, 201, 226
Ancestors, 146
Ancestral tablets, 196
Anti-footbinding movement, 159
Archdeacon Gray, 93, 105
Artists, 40–1
Asiatics, 63
Attack, 97, 186

Bamboo(s), 18, 21, 47, 174
Bandits, 236–8
Barbarian(s), 23, 51–2, 126
Barbers, 169, 220
Barracoons, 95
Beggar(s), 23, 109
Bicycle or Byke, 131, 210–11
Biswas, Ramnath, 210, 213
Boca Tigre, 28
Bomb(s), 232–3, 235
Book of Rites, 72, 73
Bookshop, 190
Bound feet (see also Feet), 161, 229
Bowring, Dr., 94
Boy(s), 166, 167–8
Brassey, Mrs., 115
Bride, 121
British (see also English), 209
British army, 235
British consul(ate), 159, 211
British empire, 43
British government, 43
British navy, 228
British soldiers (see also Soldiers), 230
Buddha, 221

Camoëns, 94, 224
Cantlie, Dr., 151
Carabâo, 141
Carnegie, Andrew, 116, 118
Carriage, 115
Caste, 226
Cat(s), 116–7
Chairs (see also Sedan Chairs), 154, 196,
    204–5
Champagne, 107
Chater, Sir Paul, 194
Chiang Kai Shek's army, 234
Children, 32, 78, 140, 145, 182
Chinaman(men), 36, 113, 156, 163
Chinese, 44, 51, 73, 84, 116, 118, 129, 151,
    174–6, 207, 214
Chinese ladies, women, girls, 122, 217, 229
Chinese negroes, 238
Chinnery, 40, 194
Cholera, 193, 226
Chop-sticks, 56, 74, 108
Christianity, 44
Christian(s), 45, 84, 128
Christmas Day, 118, 235
Church, 40, 118, 164, 173
Cigar(s), 156
Citadel, 17
City of the Dead, 92
Clift, C. Winifred Lechmere, 189, 191
Climate, 72, 79, 88
Cockroaches, 28, 183
Collinson, Clifford W., 203, 207
Colonies, 42–3, 214
Concubines, 84
Confucius, 172
Conjurer, 182
Convert(s), 84, 86
Cook, 58–9, 167–8, 199
Cooke, George Wingrove, 66, 68
Coolie(s), 95–6, 110, 118, 168, 174
Corpse(s), 56, 92–3, 149, 151, 203
Court, 102–3, 129
Courtesy, 107
Crackers, 178, 207, 209, 215
Cradock, Lt. C., 137, 138
Crime(s), 20–1, 102–3, 202, 204
Croisset, Francis de, 221, 225

Crossley, E.D., 236, 239
Cumming, C.F. Gordon, 121, 124
Curio-shop, 201
Curiosities, 63, 120
Custom, 47, 140, 208, 209, 218

Dangers, 200-2
Death, 129, 150-1, 165, 204
Dentist(s), 218-9
Dewar, Thomas, 148, 149
Diamonds, 161
Dinner(s), 167-8, 197, 208, 216
Disease, 150-1
Doctor, 87-8, 129, 151, 157, 236, 238
Dog(s), 38, 82, 84, 116-7, 156, 237
Dollars, 156
Dowager Empress, 162
Drage, Commander C.H., 192, 194
Dragon, 221
Dress, 122, 217, 229
Ducks, 33, 145-6, 199
Ducks' tongues, 33, 193
Dynamite, 139

Eclipse, 207
Ellis, Henry T., 65
Emperor, 69, 71
England, 43
English or Englishmen (see also British), 16, 44, 45, 67, 209
English and Irish wives, 84
English merchants, 40
English oaths, 84
English residents, 65
English soldiers (see also Soldiers), 151
Escape, 77, 99, 236-7
Etiquette, 106, 216
European women, 47, 84
European(s), 41, 48-9, 66-7, 158, 226
Execution, 70-1, 165, 203-4
Execution ground, 70, 111-2
Exercise, 51, 82
Expense, 49

Factory, 29
Family, 64, 113, 146, 204
Fan, 162
Fanquis, Fanquai, Fankwae, 29, 125, 132, 133
Fantan house, 164
Fashion, 217
Fate, 71, 101, 147
Fatshan, 81, 83, 131-3
Feast, 58-9
Feet (see also Bound Feet), 123, 161-2
Fever, 53-4
Field, Henry M., 102, 105

Finger-nails, 110-12, 122
Firecrackers (see also Crackers), 201
Fishing, 139
Flogging(s), 32, 69
Flower Street, 193
Fog, 165-6, 171
Football match, 164
Forbes, Robert B., 37, 38, 39
Ford, R.S.M. Charles, 234, 235
Foreign devil(s), 26, 82, 126, 128, 135
Franck, Harry A., 200, 202
French consul, 144
Frenchmen, 67
Fruit, 48
Funicular (see also Tram), 180

Gambling, 117, 164, 208
Game-pie, 141
Gaoler(s), 66-8
Garrison, 41, 43, 155
Gatekeeper, 168-9
Geomancer(s), 92-3
German(s), 119, 190, 230-1
Goat, 173
Golden lily, 123
Government House, 114, 119, 192-4
Governor, 41, 72-3, 93
Grave, 92-3, 100-1
Gray, Archdeacon, 93, 105
Gray, Mrs., 106, 108
Greek, 178
Griffin, 158
Guerillas, 233, 237-9
Guide, 109-12, 116, 125-7, 204
Guilds, 169
Guinnesses, 192
Gunboat(s), 143, 155, 228
Gun(s), 199, 230

Halcombe, Charles J.H., 150, 151
Hall, Capt. Basil, 15, 19
Happy Valley, 192
Harbour(s), 43, 155, 177, 180, 189, 228, 231
Hardy, Rev. E.J., 171, 173
Hat(s), 122
Headache, 124
Heat, 182
Henry, B.C., 134, 136
Hero(es), 151, 206
Hindu, 212-3
Hingston, James, 109, 112
Hochberg, Count Fritz von, 177, 180
Holmes, E. Burton, 157, 158
Honesty, 174, 176
Hong, 29
Hong Kong & Shanghai Bank, 194
Hong merchants, 23, 26, 27, 37, 38
Hongkong Club, 157, 181

Hospitality, 124, 196
Hostess(es), 195-6
Host(s), 121-2, 124
Hotel(s), 210, 211, 212, 215
  Asia, 212
  Boa Vista, 163
  Hongkong, 114, 154, 155, 178, 229
  King Edward, 177
Houqua or Howqua, 38, 106-8
House(s), 40, 62, 124
Humidity, 182
Hunter, W.C., 23, 26, 38
Hutchison, James Lafayette, 208, 209
Hypnotism, 182

Ice, 49
Imperial Army of Japan, 235
Indian, 115, 181
Inn, 134-6
Insult(s), 17, 56, 143, 212
Italian consul, 159

Japanese or Japs, 175, 193, 211, 229, 230,
  232-3, 234, 236-7, 239
Jappon Kuei (see also Japanese), 211, 213
Jewellery, 122
Jinrikisha (see also Rickshaws), 158
Jones-Parry, Capt. S.H., 119, 120
Josses, 148, 149
Judge(s), 102-3, 176
Junk, 20-1, 46, 56-60
Justice, 18, 102-5

Kai Tak, 232
Kitchen, 38, 167
Kowloon, 214, 233, 234
Kuomintang, 198-9

Laird, E.K., 94, 96
Lantau, 190
Laurie, P.G., 72, 74
Lay, G. Tradescant, 34, 36
Leper(s), 100, 110
Li Hung Chang, 159-62
Libraries, 31
Lin, Commissioner, 37
Lindley, A.F., 75, 77
Lintin, 27
Little, Mrs. Archibald, 159, 162
Loviot, Fanny, 55, 61
Low, Harriet, 27, 30
Lunch(eon), 106-7, 121, 141
Luxuries, 74, 87-8
Lyster, Thomas, 78, 80

Macaists, 62-3
MacKellar, C.D., 163, 166

Magic, 172
Magician, 182
Magistrate, 104
Mah-jong or Ma chiang, 208, 218, 219, 224
Manchu Dynasty, 198
Mandarin(s), 15, 17, 25, 27, 67, 70
Mangiapan, Francisco, 20, 22
Marie, 76-7
Marriage, 76, 215
Martin, R.M., 42, 43
Martin, William, 214, 217
Mauser(s), 196, 238
Maxwell, Capt., 15-7
Meadows, Thomas Taylor, 51, 52
Men-about-town, 222
Men-of-war, 120, 155, 228
Missionaries, 44-5, 81-4
Mob, 125-6
Morse, Edward S., 125, 128
Mosquito curtains or nets, 28, 82, 183
Mosquitoes, 83, 140
Mourning, 72, 74, 121, 122
Mundy, Walter William, 97, 99
Music, 79, 118

Nails (see also Finger-nails), 51
Natural Feet Society, 159
Naval officers, 65, 164
Nazis, 231
New Territories, 236
New Year, 177-9, 239
Night life, 208-9
Noise, 215

Opium, 28, 37-9, 71, 72, 73, 156, 208, 209
Orientals, 71, 158, 207
Ox, 36

Paddy-fields, 140
Pagodas, 28, 118, 204
Painters, 40
Palanquins, 109, 110, 204-5
Peak, 171, 180, 192, 209, 214, 229
Pearl River, 214, 224
Pei-quei, 73-4
Peninsular and Oriental, 119
Petitions, 23-6
Pfeiffer, Ida, 46, 50
Photography, 120
Pickpocket, 19
Picnic, 144
Pidgin or Pigeon, 15-6, 23, 114
Pig(s), 146, 195
Pirate(s), 49-50, 55-60, 69, 97-9, 186,
  188, 203-4, 224
Pistols, 46
Piton, Rev. C., 100, 101
Plague, 150-1, 158

254

Pleasure district, 222
Poison, 31, 67
Police, 155, 165, 202, 230
Politeness, 124
Ponies, 115, 124, 137–8, 154–5
Portuguese, 40, 62–4, 95
Portuguese consul, 144
Pottery, 125–6
Poyntz, Maj. W.H., 69, 71
Praya, 89, 113, 165, 183
Priests, 73–4
'Prince of Wales', 233
Printing, 64
Prison, 66–8
Prison camp, 237
Prisoner(s), 37, 66–8, 70–1, 102, 165
Prisoners of war, 235
Punishment, 18
Punka(s), 158, 183

Quaker, 24
Queen's Road, 157

Race-course, 114, 154
Race(s), 114–5, 138, 172, 192
Railway, 173, 239
Rain, 88, 161, 183–4
Rat(s), 31, 38, 55, 116–7, 150
Ready, Oliver, 167, 170
Ready, Sybil, 185, 188
Red devils, 73
Redwood, B.C., 232, 233
Relative(s), 92, 100–1, 129–30, 151, 238
Republican movement, 198
'Repulse', 233
Restaurant(s), 208, 218, 239
Revolution, 196
Revolver, 79, 125, 127, 186
Rice fields, 140
Rickshaws or Rickshas (see also Jinrikisha), 164, 229
Robbers (see also Thieves), 69, 78
Robbery, 103, 201
Rogue(s), 18–9, 41, 238
Rouge, 121
Rubies, 181
Russian advisers, 198
Russians, 226–7

Sailor(s), 20–1, 61, 67, 163, 226, 230
St. Andrew's Night Ball, 172, 194
Salt-water girls, 219
Sampan(s), 113, 219, 220, 222–4
Samshu, 69, 71
San Paulo church, 40, 164
School, 34–5
Schoolmaster, 36
Scriptures, 34

Searchlight(s), 190, 231
Seaweed, 108
Sedan chairs (see also Chairs), 41, 70, 118
See, C.S., 218, 220
Selby, Thomas G., 81, 86
Servant(s), 48, 87, 92, 150, 158, 162, 167
Seton, Grace Thompson, 195, 196
Shameen or Shamien, 143, 196, 197, 199, 215–6, 219–20
Shopkeeper(s), 199, 201
Shopping, 41
Shop(s), 119, 156, 163, 201, 208
Shuttlecock, 79, 179
Sightseeing, 157
Sikhs, 155, 181–2
Simpson, Rev. A.B., 145, 147
Slave trade, 69
Slavery, 96
Slaves, 77
Smith, F. Dumont, 174, 176
Smith, Rev. George, 44, 45
Smugglers, 28
Snipe, 140–1
Society, 65, 119, 197
Soldier(s), 54, 151, 196, 230
Songs, 79, 220
Spies, 50, 236
Squeeze or Squeezing, 27, 167
Steamer or Steamboat, 97, 163
Stephens, 194
Stevens, Thomas, 131, 133
Storks, 92, 93
Storm(s), 89, 149
Stubbs, Sir Reginald, 192
Student(s), 198, 206, 212, 221
Sun Yat-sen, 198–9, 210, 212
Superstition, 127
Surrender, 235
Swiss gentleman, 49
Sword(s), 70, 99, 182, 203

Tail, 18, 69
Tailor(s), 157, 170
Taipo, 233
Tamar, 194
Tax, 169
Tea, 47, 73
Temple(s), 118, 146, 221
Theatre, 205, 207
Thermometer, 81, 171, 182
Thieves (see also Robbers), 18, 80, 100, 169, 181
Thomas, Charles Richard, 226, 227
Thomson, J., 87, 89
Thomson, John Stuart, 181, 184
Tiffin, 141, 158
Tipperary, 230
Torture, 103–4

Tourists, 201, 222
Train, 173, 214
Tram or Tramway (*see also* Funicular), 171, 192
Trees, 146
Typhoon, 88

Viceroy, 159, 161-2
Victoria, 46
Village(s), 84-6, 145-6, 238-9
Villain(s), 21, 205
Volunteers, 151, 189

Waiters, 156
Waitresses, 218
Waln, Nora, 197, 199
Wanchai, 233

War, 189-90, 228-30, 232
Watch(es), 25, 50, 110, 111
Watchman, 93, 168-9
Water-buffalo, 141
Water-clock, 111
Water-front, 219
Weather, 79, 88, 148, 149
Wells, Carveth, 228, 231
Weppner, Margaretha, 92, 93
Werner, E.T.C., 143, 144
Whampoa, 28, 75, 78
White negress, 64
Wine, 57, 122, 216, 239

Young, Walter H., 139, 142
Younghusband, Capt. G.J., 154, 156
Yunnanese, 199
Yvan, Dr., 62, 64

256